FINANCIAL TIMES
MANAGEMENT

Knowledge   Skills   Understanding

Financial Times Management is a new business created to deliver the knowledge, skills and understanding that will enable students, managers and organisations to achieve their ambitions, whatever their needs, wherever they are.

Financial Times Pitman Publishing, part of Financial Times Management, is the leading publisher of books for practitioners and students in business and finance, bringing cutting-edge thinking and best practice to a global market.

To find out more about Financial Times Management and Financial Times Pitman Publishing, visit our website at:

www.ftmanagement.com

D0263913

F R A M E W O R K S

Each book in the Frameworks series is a
comprehensive and concise introduction to
the subject. The books are well structured
and provide a step-by-step guide to essential
principles. They develop a basic framework
of understanding to underpin further study
of core business, financial and legal subjects
in the higher education curriculum.

FRAMEWORKS

Services Marketing

Helen Woodruffe

Department of Business and Management
University of Salford

FINANCIAL TIMES
PITMAN PUBLISHING

LONDON · HONG KONG · JOHANNESBURG
MELBOURNE · SINGAPORE · WASHINGTON DC

FINANCIAL TIMES MANAGEMENT
128 Long Acre, London WC2E 9AN
Tel: +44 (0)171 447 2000
Fax: +44 (0)171 240 5771
Website: www.ftmanagement.com

A Division of Financial Times Professional Limited

First published in Great Britain 1995

ISBN 0 273 63421 6

British Library Cataloguing in Publication Data
A CIP catalogue record for this book can be obtained from the British Library.

10 9 8 7 6 5 4 3 2 1

Printed and bound in Great Britain by Bell and Bain Ltd, Glasgow

The Publishers' policy is to use paper manufactured from sustainable forests.

CONTENTS

v

8. Internal marketing 85

The marketing concept and internal marketing · Definitions · The role of internal marketing · Components of internal marketing programmes · Management approaches · Internal marketing planning · Developing internal marketing programmes · Implementing the plan

9. Relationship marketing 95

Building relationships · Relationship marketing management · Quality and relationship marketing · Customer retention

10. Service quality 104

Quality defined · Developing service quality · Quality standards · Benchmarking · Implementing quality service · Monitoring service quality

Part Three
THE SERVICES MARKETING MIX

11. Packaging the service product 123

Service attributes · The life cycle concept · New service development · Positioning the service

12. Pricing the service 138

Key pricing concepts · Pricing issues for services · Organisational objectives and pricing policy · A framework for pricing decisions

13. Promotion and communications in services marketing 149

Internal/external communications · The communications process · The promotional message · The promotional mix · Media choice and selection · Managing the promotional effort · Monitoring and evaluation

14. Services distribution planning 166

Accessibility and availability · Location · Direct distribution · Channel functions · Channel selection

15. People – the fifth 'P' 177

The role of the employee in services marketing · Staff selection and recruitment · Training and development · Human resource management issues

16. Process and physical evidence 187

Corporate image · Corporate identity · Customer perceptions and physical evidence · Process · Technological developments · Atmospherics

Part Four
SPECIAL ASPECTS OF SERVICES MARKETING

PREFACE

This book could not have been completed without the support and encouragement of family, friends and colleagues. I should like especially to thank the following people for sharing their expertise and knowledge in specialist areas and for their valuable insights and help:

Susan Foreman, Henley Management College
Jeff Clements, Salford City Council
Peter Ruddock, University of Central Lancashire
Vincent Saxon, Manchester Metropolitan University
Jon Venner, formerly University of Salford

Additional thanks and appreciation to John Cushion at Financial Times Pitman Publishing and my husband, Steve.

Part One

THE DEVELOPMENT OF SERVICES MARKETING

1

MARKETING –
AN INTRODUCTION

INTRODUCTION

Prior to the time of the Industrial Revolution, virtually all trade and exchange processes involved some personal contact between suppliers and their customers. This meant that individual producers could cater to the needs of their customers, and most trade was very local in nature. The increase in overseas trading and the advent of the industrial revolution heralded the start of new types of trading practice, and the introduction of some of the processes which are part of marketing today.

Initially, producers and manufacturers were concerned mainly with logistical issues – transporting and selling goods to widespread markets, often located far away from the point of production. The focus here was on production, with consumption and consumers being seen as the end result of a production and distribution chain. For as long as demand outstripped supply, which was generally the case as western countries started to go through periods of dramatic growth in economic activity and technological change, producers could all exist profitably simply by producing more efficiently and cutting costs. Little attention was given to the role of the consumer in exchange processes.

In the early twentieth century the realisation that marketing was, in itself, an important part of the business process led to the founding of the American Marketing Association and the development of the earliest aspects of marketing theory and practice. It was much later, however, that the need for a *marketing orientation* was recognised, with a clear focus on the needs of the consumer. This chapter charts the progress of key developments in marketing from these early stages to the present, providing the basis for understanding marketing within a services context.

1. DEVELOPMENTS IN MARKETING THEORY

The greatly increased production of goods which arose out of mechanisation following the industrial revolution was matched by increased levels of demand in the mass market. The problem for producers lay in getting their products to

3

the market. Manufacturers were investing heavily in premises and machinery in pursuit of better and cheaper production. They did not want to be involved in the distribution of the product. A distribution trade grew up to serve every industry.

First Generation Marketing Wholesalers opened warehouses in major cities and bought products in bulk from the manufacturers. They stored the products and organised their distribution to retailers and other smaller organisations throughout markets. This was the development of channels of distribution, still crucial to successful marketing today, and is recognised as *first generation marketing*. At this stage the main concern was getting the product to market – selling all that was produced.

Second Generation Marketing It was only during the second half of the twentieth century that the focus began to shift towards the notion that producers should look at what consumers actually wanted – produce what can be sold to the market, rather than try to sell what is produced. This was the start of *second generation marketing*. The early stages of the second generation saw the development of the idea that firms should take on a marketing orientation – marketing should become the integrated focus of their business policy. Firms should seek to satisfy their profit needs by identifying and satisfying consumer needs.

New ideas in the 1960s also pressed the need for a broader orientation with a focus on consumer needs and criticised firms which were still too product-orientated. By defining their business in terms of their products, firms could constrict their own growth and development – even survival – as consumer needs and technologies were changing rapidly. The essential task for firms was to analyse their business from the consumer's perspective – to look at their market offerings in terms of the needs satisfied, rather than the products offered. Thus the Hollywood film industry, for example, needed to focus on its business as 'entertainment' rather than 'making movies' if it was to enjoy continued profitability and success in the face of increasing competition from television.

Third Generation Marketing From the mid-1960s onwards, marketing thought grew and matured. There was increasing awareness of the role that marketing played, not only in business but through its influence and impact on consumers and society as a whole. Marketing began to be seen as something which was not only relevant to commercial organisations, actively seeking profits at the end of the day. Marketing could be equally important for organisations and services which were not necessarily traditional, profit-led businesses. Schools, health programmes, charities and other types of not-for-profit organisation could benefit from a marketing orientation. Even political parties could employ marketing programmes to win voters. Marketing was viewed as being applicable across a very broad spectrum of commercial and social activity.

From this realisation came the emergence of *third generation marketing*. This hinged on the idea of a broader application of marketing within society, across all types of organisation, and for greater benefit to society. Society's needs should be considered in line with those of consumers, and profits should not be sought at an unacceptable cost to society. This has led to a call for firms to engage in ethical marketing practices and, increasingly, to adopt environmentally sound, 'green' policies.

In moving towards the development of a body of marketing theory, much has been drawn from other academic disciplines. This is especially true of the behavioural sciences, economics and management science. A debate exists as to how much actual marketing theory has been established to date. What is generally accepted, however, is that marketing is evolving as a discipline with a wide base of knowledge, concepts and techniques and areas of theory which may ultimately come together to provide an integrated base of marketing theory.

One of the main reasons for this is the entrance into the marketing arena of a vast number of academics from other disciplines. Social psychologists, economists and statisticians, for example, have all entered the field, together with practising marketers from a whole range of specialisms such as advertising, distribution and product management. Marketing is, in itself, a complex subject covering a very wide area, rich in its diversity. This book looks at the development of marketing in relation to services and offers the reader insights from the extensive range of concepts and techniques available.

2. THE MARKETING ENVIRONMENT

All organisations operate within the marketing environment. This consists of the micro-environment which relates to the organisation itself – its own internal environment – and the external or macro-environment which will affect all organisations to a lesser or greater degree. Environmental analysis is vital for marketing success as organisations must be able to understand (and predict where possible) those factors which may impact upon their marketing strategies.

Environmental analysis plays a key role in strategic planning, both at a corporate and functional level. Essentially, the key steps involved are as follows:

- *Identify influences (positive and negative).*
- *Control those which can be controlled.*
- *Use those which can contribute to competitive advantage.*
- *Overcome, or defend against, potentially damaging influences.*

The **micro-environment** is the internal environment of the organisation. Its influence, therefore, will be specific to a particular organisation. The factors to be analysed in the internal environment will include the following:

a. The company itself – management structure, strong points, distinctive competences, failings, finances
b. Customers
c. Suppliers
d. Channel members
e. Competitors
f. Other publics which may include:

Government or political bodies
Pressure groups
Financial institutions
Shareholders
Influencer markets

In effect, any person or organisation which can influence the company's marketing activities – and marketing success – in any way should be included here. This list is not absolutely comprehensive as individual organisations may need to consider special influences. Remember that the 'company' may in fact be a not-for-profit organisation such as a charity or a public sector organisation, so might need to take into account the influence of boards of trustees, for example, or local council committees.

The **macro-environment** is the wider, external environment in which all firms operate. The organisation should study the macro-environmental factors relevant to their business or operational activities – in other words, in their competitive domain. The types of influences likely to have an impact on present and future activities can be broken down into several main areas:

Political/legal factors
Economic factors
Socio-cultural factors
Technological factors

These factors are studied in more detail in relation to services marketing in Chapter 6.

These analyses, when completed in detail, will form the basis of the SWOT analysis, used in the planning process. SWOT (strengths, weaknesses, opportunities and threats) represents a way of categorising the environmental analysis in a way which can help organisations in determining appropriate strategic action. The internal factors can be divided up into those which are strengths and those which are weaknesses, while the external factors can be similarly categorised as either opportunities or threats.

Sometimes this is not quite so simple as it sounds. For example, the single European market may represent a substantial opportunity for many organisations. Equally, it can also be a threat, due to the possible increased competition from other member countries. Similarly, the innovative entrepreneurship of the head of the organisation might be its outstanding strength, whilst also being a weakness if too much of the organisation's success rested on that one individual as they could go elsewhere, or become unable to work for some reason.

However, organisations should undertake the analysis regularly to help them decide on future courses of action. Organisations should:

Build on their strengths
Attempt to *overcome* weaknesses
Exploit opportunities
Defend against threats.

3. MARKETING ORGANISATIONS

What is meant by a marketing organisation? A marketing organisation has marketing as its key focus. It is organised around marketing and is customer-led or market-led. It anticipates and responds to the needs of the market in designing its current and future strategy. The idea of a marketing orientated organisation can be made clearer by comparing it with other organisational philosophies which have been identified.

Firms which are **production orientated** focus on production as the key to success. In their view, the market will always seek products which are both cheaper and widely available. The organisation's main task, therefore, is continually to improve and refine production efficiency, thereby producing greater numbers of goods at lower prices. This approach does hold some credibility, especially in situations where demand is relatively high, and could increase with lower prices. This is the case in areas such as home electronics where colour televisions and CD players, for example, have become far more popular as supply increased and prices fell. In the extreme, however, it ignores the customer viewpoint and will not succeed once markets have become saturated.

Some companies are **product orientated**, believing that consumers will seek products which are innovative or technologically superior in the marketplace. They constantly strive to develop new products which stand out. This is a high risk approach with significant chances of failure, as seen by the number of 'flops' in the market, such as Sinclair's electric C5 personal transportation vehicle. This approach can work successfully but needs to take into account consumer tastes and wants. Without doing this, firms can fall into the trap of becoming too narrowly constrained, by viewing their business in terms of 'products' rather than in terms of customer need satisfactions. Both a production and a product orientation could equally apply to service providers, where there is too much attention focused on the service and the service provision, rather than on the customers.

A **selling orientation** is where the focus of the firm's attention is on the 'hard sell'; heavy promotion, advertising and sales tactics to get rid of whatever is produced. This technique is evident today, particularly in the area of unsought goods – goods which do not fulfil specific consumer needs, but which are heavily promoted, frequently with deferred payment terms and pressurised sales tactics. A good example of this approach is in the selling of timeshare holidays which usually employs all the tactics outlined above – and often leads to unhappy consumers who claim they were pressurised or misled into signing a sales agreement. This approach can be lucrative in the short-term, but is unlikely to succeed in the long-term.

An organisation which is **marketing orientated**, as indicated previously, aims to achieve its organisational objectives by anticipating and satisfying the needs and wants of its consumers. Long-term customer satisfaction is a key goal, and the organisation is committed to attracting and retaining customers. The business is defined in terms of need satisfaction rather than specific service or product areas, and as those needs change, this should be reflected in the organisation's activities. Additionally, organisations may adhere to a **societal marketing**

orientation, where attention is given to the long-term good of society, as well as consumers. This is becoming more and more evident in today's environmentally conscious marketplace.

4. MARKETING TODAY

The previous sections have outlined the developments within marketing which have led to what we know as marketing today. Arguably, however, it is external factors in the political, social and business world which have shaped the role and development of marketing. Some of the types of influences which have an impact on the development of marketing are as follows:

Political/legal
Changes in government policy towards business enterprise.
The growth of global trade and the impact of trade barriers and currency agreements, for example.
Privatisation (of major importance in the UK).
De-regulation of advertising for the professions.
Legislation on environmental issues.
Consumerism, and the power of consumer pressure groups.

Economic
World economic trends.
Levels of consumer affluence, spending power.
The imposition or relaxation of price controls.
Inflation levels.
Attitudes to, and increases in, consumer borrowing.
The importance of the service economy.
The opening of the single European market.

Socio-cultural
Increased numbers of women in the workplace.
Cross-cultural issues in international marketing.
Increased leisure time, and the widescale pursuit of leisure interests.
Higher levels of education, and increased participation.
Growth in consumer travel and tourism.

Technological
The impact of technology on business processes; the use of scanning systems (EPOS) in retailing and the use of automatic cash dispensers (ATMs) in banking, for example.
Technological developments in consumer products.
Telecommunications impacts on business and society through developments such as telesales, telemarketing, teleworking.
Awareness and use of technology in the home.

The above lists are examples of the factors which have impacted on the development of marketing today. New modes of marketing have come about because of social and technological changes, such as the dramatic growth of direct marketing which can be very finely tuned to customer wants through the use of sophisticated databases. Teleshopping via dedicated satellite TV channels is another new concept. Marketing education is increasing, and the recognition of marketing as a profession is growing, underpinned by the award of Chartered status to the Institute of Marketing, for example. The role and influence of marketing in almost every sphere of society today should not be underestimated. The final section of this chapter looks at one key development which perhaps typifies the way in which marketing responds to changes in society – green marketing.

5. GREEN MARKETING

The advent of so-called 'green', or environmentally conscious, marketing is almost wholly due to pressure from consumers. Although some organisations, particularly in manufacturing, may have started to clean up their act because of legislation against pollution, for example, it is consumers who have made the greatest impact through their demand for greener products. Retailers and fast-moving consumer goods producers were, not surprisingly, the first to respond to these demands. Continued pressure, however, has meant that firms throughout the supply chain have also had to develop green marketing practices.

Perhaps the most obvious developments have taken place in the household goods area. Supermarkets now stock a whole range of 'environmentally friendly' products ranging from pump action sprays for anything from hairspray to air fresheners, toilet tissue made from recycled paper, detergents and washing powders without harmful chemicals and recyclable packaging for many items. Service providers have also entered this race to satisfy the new green consumer by a number of tactics. Fast food restaurants have promoted recycled and recyclable packaging; hotels ask their clients not to waste energy, urging them to switch unnecessary lights off, and to indicate whether towels need to be laundered or may be used again; road transport providers ensure that vehicle emissions are monitored as part of regular maintenance.

Although it can be more difficult to envisage appropriate green marketing strategies within a service organisation, as opposed to retailing or manufacturing, there are steps firms can take to ensure that their operations, at least, are environmentally friendly. A green audit can be undertaken which should cover several aspects, including:

Site audits
A full picture is drawn up of an organisation's operations site. How energy-efficient is it? How is waste managed? Can waste be recycled?

Activity audits

These involve a study of activities undertaken, especially activities which may impact on many areas of business, such as storage and distribution.

Compliance audits

Undertaken to ensure that companies meet legal requirements in all areas from pollution to packaging and labelling.

These aspects seem most relevant to services marketing, although there are many more ways in which organisations can undertake an environmental audit, some appropriate to a particular industry or sector.

Looked at in this light, it is fairly easy to see how many service organisations can develop business strategies which are based on green thinking, and which may impact on marketing programmes. A busy hospital, for example, undertaking activity and site audits may find many ways of becoming more energy-efficient and of reducing waste. If this were achieved, it could feature in publicity and other material presented to patients and the public, enhancing the hospital's image and potentially saving money for re-investment into the service.

Banks and insurance offices can encourage the introduction of the paper-free office through the use of electronic mail and telecommunications, and organise collection of waste paper for recycling where appropriate. They can undertake ethical investment, investing their clients' funds only in businesses which are themselves run on environmentally sound lines. Leisure providers in the public sector can focus on conservation and nature in parks, for example, and promote projects to protect the environment in green belt areas and land reclamation schemes.

However it is undertaken, it is clear that green marketing is here to stay, and environmental performance may become an important measure of an organisation's success and standing in the future. Service organisations need to think 'green' in all areas of activity – especially in services marketing.

6. SUMMARY

Modern marketing really started around the beginning of the twentieth century. The post-war era has seen a massive growth in consumption and the pace of technological development has been increasing rapidly. Marketing tools and techniques have been developed to enable marketing organisations to exploit opportunities and respond to market needs. Other concepts include the product concept, the production concept and the selling concept.

The development of the marketing concept which puts customer needs and wants at the forefront of modern thinking underpins the devlopment of marketing theory. Important issues include the use of marketing environment monitoring and SWOT analysis in long range planning; societal marketing and green marketing.

The marketing environment is made up of two components:

The micro-environment or internal environment
The macro-environment or external environment

Environmental analysis involves monitoring of all influences within these two environmental areas and assessing their impact or potential impact on the organisation's activities. The internal influences can be categorised into 'strengths' and 'weaknesses', the external factors into 'opportunities' and 'threats' – this SWOT analysis is an important part of the planning process.

It is now recognised that marketing applies not only to commercial business enterprises but has an important role to play in all types of organisation. Modern marketing can be used to increase the effectiveness of not-for-profit organisations, charities and public seor organisations as well as firms in the business sector.

Progress test 1

1. Why did the idea of marketing only really emerge from the time of the Industrial Revolution?

2. Distinguish between the terms first-, second- and third-generation marketing.

3. How is environmental analysis carried out? Outline the main factors for consideration in;
   (*a*) the internal or micro-environment?
   (*b*) the external or macro-environment?

4. How is information from the environmental analysis categorised from the organisational point of view?

5. Describe some of the key factors which have shaped the role and development of marketing.

6. What are some of the areas to be studied in a so-called 'green' audit?

7. How can service organisations develop 'green' marketing programmes?

8. Marketing focuses needs satisfied rather than products. How should the following types of organisations define their business, according to this understanding of marketing: an airline, a restaurant, a museum?

Discussion

1. Compare and contrast a production orientation, a product orientation, a selling orientation and a marketing orientation using examples of organisations which, in your view, fall into the various categories.

2. Do you buy 'green' or environmentally friendly products? What motivates you to do so? If not, why not? Do the organisations which supply such goods adhere to the societal marketing concept?

2

IS SERVICES MARKETING DIFFERENT?

INTRODUCTION

In a book written specifically about services marketing, it may seem a contradiction in terms to ask whether services marketing is different from the development, in theory and in practice, of the marketing of physical goods. In marketing literature there is a great deal of discussion about the nature of services marketing, and the unique characteristics of services which present a different set of challenges for marketing managers in the service sector.

This book explores the special nature of services marketing, and the development of specific strategies and concepts for success.

There can be little argument, however, that despite the differences between the marketing of physical products and services marketing, the underlying concepts and management decisions are much the same:

- Marketing-driven organisations, whether in the manufacturing or service sectors, must have an intimate knowledge of the market in order to identify unfulfilled market needs and provide a marketing offering which will meet those needs, thereby satisfying both the customer, and the organisation's objectives.
- Market research, marketing planning, and the development of a set of marketing mix tools are equally important in services marketing and the marketing of physical goods.

In this chapter, the development of services marketing will be reviewed, and the special characteristics of services considered. The marketing mix, in particular, will be explored from a services marketing viewpoint and marketing management tasks will be defined. Many of the ideas which are covered in more depth in later sections of the book are introduced here, to provide a foundation for the reader's understanding of services marketing.

1. MARKETING DEFINED

There are many definitions of marketing laid down but the basic marketing concept is concerned with:

> *identifying and satisfying the needs and wants of consumers by providing a market offering to fulfil those needs and wants through exchange processes, profitably.*

Some important points must be emphasised here:

- Consumers of goods or services may be individuals or organisations, or other groups; for example voters supporting a political candidate.
- The term 'market offering' is used deliberately as this can mean a physical good, or a service, or a combination of the two, or it can be extended to cover other entities to which the marketing concept may be applied; for example political figures and ideas, 'pop' music and charitable causes.
- The idea that an organisation will seek to fulfil consumer needs profitably is not restricted to financially profitable goals as not all organisations aim to make profits as such; for example non-profit making concerns such as medical and educational institutions, or groups such as the Scouts organisation, may adopt marketing principles, but their end objective may be counted in ways other than cash profit.

  Organisations involved in marketing are not necessarily corporations or commercial firms.

The above definition and explanation of some of the ideas associated with marketing gives some idea of the scope of marketing overall. Services marketing embraces the marketing concept, and yet the nature of services marketing is complex, and service organisations may fall into various categories:

- **Service organisations may be profit orientated or non-profit (sometimes called 'not-for-profit') concerns.**
- **They may provide personal services to individual consumers, or business services, or both.**

The key issue is that organisations who want to be close to the market and close to their customers – in other words, marketing-driven – must adopt the marketing concept. A marketing-driven organisation will first of all communicate with its market(s); in contrast, a non-marketing organisation will provide what it believes will sell, not what the market wants.

2. THE MARKETING MIX

In order to be able to satisfy the needs and wants of the market, in a way which suits the organisation's objectives, the organisation needs to design a market offering and present it to the market for consumption. The way in which this is achieved is by means of a set of marketing tools – the marketing mix.

There are any number of tools available to the marketer in designing, distributing, communicating and ultimately selling the offering to the selected target market(s), but these are generally classified under four main headings – the four P's of the marketing mix:

PRODUCT
PRICE
PROMOTION
PLACE

The elements of the marketing mix are equally applicable to services marketing as to the marketing of physical, or tangible, goods, as can be seen if they are explained further:

Product

The 'product' element of the marketing mix refers to how the offering is put together – typically this will include aspects relating to:

Quality
Styling
Colour
Design
Brand name
Packaging
Sizes
Guarantees and other features

Whilst it is relatively easy to see that colour and size range, for example, are more appropriate to the development of tangible goods, there is a good deal of overlap. Services are provided to certain quality standards, they are frequently offered with guarantees and many service organisations have developed high levels of brand-name awareness (Hertz, McDonalds, Holiday Inns, for example). While it may not be appropriate to offer a range of sizes, many services are offered with a range of levels of service cover. The AA motoring association offers different levels of cover, and insurance policies operating in a similar way are good examples of ranges of service offerings developed to meet the varying needs of consumers. The service product is explored in more depth in Chapter 11.

Price

'Price', in marketing mix terms, covers all aspects of pricing:

Discount pricing
Extended credit
List price
Payment period

In services marketing, pricing may present a more complex task to the marketer due to the highly intangible nature of services as opposed to physical goods.

However, services marketers do exercise all their options in developing pricing policies to suit market needs. Airlines and hotels, for example, offer a range of services at different price levels to attract the maximum number of potential users.

Consumers are not so readily able to interpret value-for-money with services as they are for tangible goods as the intangibility of services makes it hard for consumers to determine quality, for example. The price which can be charged, therefore, must take this into account, but service providers can actually win flexibility on pricing due to this. A prestige brand image can allow premium pricing policies so that charges at a top London restaurant or an internationally famous hairdressing establishment will bear little relation to the actual cost of providing the service. Chapter 12 looks at the pricing element of the mix.

Promotion

'Promotion' refers to all the ways in which the product or service – the market offering – can be promoted to the target market, and the communication methods available to marketers. These fall into four main areas:

Advertising
Personal selling
Sales promotion
Public relations

Without promotion of some kind there can be no effective marketing at all. The market must have an awareness of, and possibly some kind of understanding of, what is being offered in their purchase decision making. Excellent services are of no use at all if potential consumers know nothing about them.

Each of the categories of promotional activity – the promotional 'mix' – shown above, has now become familiar in many areas of services marketing. Virtually all services use at least one such form of promotion, but the way the promotional mix is utilised depends on certain aspects of the service offering.

Services which are highly standardised, and offered to large market segments employ mass advertising techniques:

Banks and other financial services, travel and tour operators are examples of service organisations which use extensive media advertising both nationally and internationally in some cases.

Services which offer a greater degree of customisation, particularly on a personal level, may be promoted using more selective means. Word-of-mouth, or personal recommendation is considered very effective, and many service providers encourage this. Personal selling can play a critical role in high involvement purchases, and this is true for services as well as products. Low-key advertising methods, and endorsement through carefully planned public relations exercises may be used. Professional services have long been subject to very strict regulations on advertising, and even though there has been some relaxation in the UK, there is still relatively little advertising of such services:

Cosmetic surgery and other health care services are advertised to a certain extent in the UK, and more so in the USA, but the idea of personal recommendation and word-of-mouth is still seen as very important. The same is true for other services such as legal or professional services.

Many services rely on a combination of the different elements of the promotional mix:

Financial services are frequently advertised on a wide scale, with personal selling also playing an important role.

Sales promotion techniques, especially those of the limited period discount type, or price reductions for frequent users are used by many service providers from health clubs and local authority leisure services to airlines and tour operators.

Weightwatchers UK, a major slimming organisation, uses a combination of media advertising, sales promotion and word-of-mouth to attract new members but its annual competition to find the 'Weightwatcher of the year' which attracts widespread media coverage may achieve the greatest amount of market awareness of their services.

Purchase incentives are offered by many financial services providers; banks offer 'free gifts' to attract student account holders, for example, and insurance companies offer incentives such as weekend breaks, once a policy is in place.

The promotional mix is covered in Chapter 13.

Place

'Place', or distribution, is often perceived as being of far less importance in services marketing than it is in the marketing of physical goods and services. At first glance, the following list of components which make up the 'place' element of the marketing mix may appear to support this idea:

Channels/Coverage
Geographical location
Stockholding/inventory
Transport

Most of these components of distribution would appear to hold far greater relevance to the marketing of tangible goods, than to services marketing. This is not true, however, and it is worth considering each of these aspects in turn:

Channels/coverage It may seem that channels are of little importance in services marketing since one of the unique characteristics of services marketing, in the traditional view, is that the service provider is also the service seller. Many service providers do have direct channels of distribution, for example:

Retail banks on the high street.
Dentists operating from their own dental clinics.

An increasing number of services, however, do have channels of distributions, for example:

Insurance may be sold directly, or through a broker.

Tour operators mainly sell through travel agents.

Freight carriers frequently arrange their business through agents or freight forwarders.

Hotel and theatre booking agencies act as wholesalers for accommodation and tickets.

Decisions about channel quality, types of channel and coverage are therefore crucial.

Geographical location For many of the reasons indicated above, whether operating through channels of distribution or directly, location is of critical importance. Retail service location requires careful location decisions to attract customers:

Banks, estate agents and dry cleaners all need to be located conveniently for their customers, while hotels and country clubs may have to look at quite different criteria in selecting a desirable location.

Stockholding/inventory It is frequently argued that because services are perishable in that they are simultaneously provided and consumed, no stockholding is required. However, that is only one aspect of the service – in many services marketing situations there is a need for stocks or equipment to make the service possible:

Avis must carry stocks of cars, serviced and ready to hire, while McDonalds must carefully monitor inventories of burger products and packaging.

Hotels must have suitable furnishings, and supplies of linen, for example.

Transport Although many services are not transported in the traditional sense, transport is still an important aspect of services marketing. In tourism, it may be necessary to transport the customers to the holiday destination, and the quality of legal or accounting services, for example, may depend on the timeliness with which documents can be delivered to and from the service providers, their customers and other agencies such as the courts and the Inland Revenue. Distribution planning in the services sector is covered in Chapter 14.

3. SPECIAL CHARACTERISTICS OF SERVICES

Services are said to have four key characteristics which impact on marketing programmes. These are:

Intangibility
Inseparability
Heterogeneity/variability
Perishability (simultaneous production/consumption)

It is helpful to consider each of these characteristics briefly:

Intangibility

Services are said to be intangible – they cannot be seen or tasted, for example. This can cause lack of confidence on the part of the consumer. As was apparent earlier, in considering pricing and services marketing, it is often difficult for the consumer to measure service value and quality. To overcome this, consumers tend to look for evidence of quality and other attributes, for example in the decor and surroundings of the beauty salon, or from the qualifications and professional standing of the consultant.

Inseparability

Services are produced and consumed at the same time, unlike goods which may be manufactured, then stored for later distribution. This means that the service provider becomes an integral part of the service itself. The waitress in the restaurant, or the cashier in the bank, is an inseparable part of the service offering. The client also participates to some extent in the service, and can affect the outcome of the service. People can be part of the service itself, and this can be an advantage for services marketers.

Heterogeneity/variability

Because a service is produced and consumed simultaneously, and because individual people make up part of the service offering, it can be argued that a service is always unique; it only exists once, and is never exactly repeated. This can give rise to concern about service quality and uniformity issues. Personnel training and careful monitoring of customer satisfaction and feedback can help to maintain high standards.

Perishability

Services are perishable; they cannot be stored. Therefore an empty seat on a plane, for example, is a lost opportunity forever. Restaurants are now charging for reservations which are not kept, charges may be made for missed appointments at the dental clinic. Perishability does not pose too much of a problem when demand for a service is steady, but in times of unusually high or low demand service organisations can have severe difficulties.

The above characteristics are generally referred to in many texts as being what makes services marketing so different. However, this assumption should be queried on a number of grounds. Like all sweeping generalisations, generalisations concerning services marketing do not always represent the full picture. Consider the question of tangibility. In the main, services can be broken down into three main classifications:

Rented goods services
Consumer-owned goods services
Non-goods services

Some of these categories involve goods which are physical, and which contribute in some way to the service offering. This gives rise to questions about the degree to which services can be classed as intangible.

Another way of classifying services is to consider the distinction between equipment-based services and people-based services. Examples of equipment-based services would include:

Vending machines
Car and tool hire
Airlines

People-based services would include:

Nursery infant care
Architects
Legal services

Yet another distinction can be made between consumer services, which are offered on a personal basis, and business-to-business or industrial services. Some service providers may operate in both these market sectors:

Franchised child care services may offer local services to parents, and operate in-company schemes.
Hotels may cater for the tourist and the business or conference market.
Private health care programmes generally offer personal and corporate rates.

On the other hand, some services such as industry-specific consultancy services or marine salvage operate in quite closely defined market sectors.

4. THE NATURE OF THE SERVICE PRODUCT

Whichever means of classifying services is used, and whether or not there is agreement that the unique characteristics of services really represent unique distinctions, ultimately both physical goods and services provide benefits and satisfactions – both goods and services are 'products' or offerings. Consider the following breakdown of service offerings:

Utilities: gas, power, water
Transport and communications
Recreation and leisure
Insurance, banking and finance
Business, professional and scientific

For most of these categories it is easy to think of 'products' associated with them; insurance policies, heating and light, package holidays and so on. This has implications for services marketing management.

As in traditional marketing concerned with tangible products, the services marketing manager needs to look closely at marketing strategy, including such aspects as:

- A Unique Selling Proposition (USP) – something which marks out the service offering from its competition.
- Positioning, and differentiation of the service offering.
- The notion of the product concept, and the augmented product, which can be applied to services.
- New service development – service organisations need to be more and more innovative in today's competitive marketplace, and in the face of heightened consumer sophistication.

All of these management issues are common to both services marketing and the marketing of tangible goods. The management tools and practices designed to help marketing managers are reviewed throughout this book. Some other critical areas of services marketing management are highlighted in the following section.

5. SERVICES MARKETING MANAGEMENT

There are a number of areas of marketing management which do have special significance for services marketing. It is worth commenting on some of those aspects at this stage, as they are important to developing an awareness of problems and key issues in services marketing.

Productivity and quality

In striving to gain and maintain competitive advantage, both productivity and quality are of key importance. However, the nature of services implies that it is difficult to avoid a trade-off situation, when improvements in service productivity can lead to sacrifices in the level of quality. This is most sensitive in services marketing where people are the service deliverers. If a bank cashier or travel agent needs to process customers more quickly to improve productivity, how can organisations ensure that there is no resulting drop in quality?

Service quality is measured on two levels:

- *Technical quality* – the overall efficiency with which a bank handles its customer accounts in terms of prompt statements, rates of interest offered and so on.
- *Functional quality* – the way the service is actually delivered; this includes personal courtesy, the service environment in terms of comfort and decor, the customer's own role (are there long queues, are pens and forms provided to make the actual transaction simpler?).

The importance which is attached to functional and technical quality depends on the type of service, and the benefit sought by the consumer. A customer visiting McDonalds is seeking a quick bite and fast service delivery – exactly opposite, in fact, to the benefits sought by a diner in another restaurant situation, where a leisurely meal and unobtrusive service might be desired. High involvement purchases, which are typically expensive and infrequent, will also be evaluated by a different set of criteria in the customer's mind to low involvement, inexpensive purchases. In this way, both the functional and technical quality provided by a mortgage broker or a long distance travel specialist may have to meet far more exacting standards than that of a taxi service or a foreign exchange bureau, for example. Service quality is the subject of Chapter 10.

Consumers evaluate service in two ways:

Experience
Credence

Experience is used in service situations where consumers can measure service value in terms of their own experience and expectations. This may be the case in evaluating personal services such as hairdressing or gardening. In cases where the individual has little or no experience of the service offered, and has no personal knowledge in the area, they will make evaluations based on credence.

This can be virtually translated into an assessment of the service provider's credibility. Thus, someone seeking cosmetic surgery or hypnotherapy for the first time will check the qualifications and credentials of practitioners, or a home computer enthusiast will take their computer to an authorised or accredited dealer for repairs. Consumer behaviour, and the buying decision processes, must therefore be comprehensively researched and understood by the service providers in order to manage productivity and quality levels.

Marketing strategy

In developing marketing strategy there are essentially two tasks:

The selection of target markets
The formulation of an appropriate marketing mix to serve those target markets.

However, before the marketing manager can consider target markets, the starting point must be a marketing audit. As this term suggests, this is an audit of the organisation's marketing activities, with particular focus on the analysis of opportunities available to the organisation. The management task can really be seen to fall into four main areas:

Marketing research
Marketing planning
Implementation
Control

The market can generally be divided into the consumer sector and organisational users. Within each of these sectors there are likely to be a number of segments which need to be researched and evaluated before decisions can be made about selecting target segments. When attractive segments have been identified, the services marketing manager must develop an appropriate marketing mix for each segment selected, with each of the elements of the mix being finely tuned to best meet the needs of individual segments.

The role of people in the services marketing situation, and, in particular, the idea of inseparability and the interactive nature of service provision, have been emphasised continuously. Internal marketing is the name given to the concept which embraces commitment to employees, and this has a very important role to play in services marketing.

Internal marketing means treating the internal customers – the employees – with the same care and attention to detail as the external customers. Thus, internal marketing programmes incorporate staff development, training, communication and a total quality approach. Internal marketing relates to the importance of people in services marketing. It is explored in more depth in Chapter 8. Other important aspects which have been emphasised are the degree of intangibility of the service offering, and the significance of functional as well as technical quality.

These aspects are especially relevant to services marketing, so this has led to the development of some additional elements which extend the services marketing mix from four P's to seven P's. These additional elements are:

- **PEOPLE**, where the emphasis is developing the role that people play in service delivery (Chapter 15).
- **PHYSICAL EVIDENCE**, which includes facilitating goods (for example, cars or tools for hire), and surroundings, decor and comfort (Chapter 16).
- **PROCESS**, which is concerned with the functional aspects such as service delivery, queuing systems, timeliness and quality of delivery (Chapter 16)

These additional elements of the services marketing mix, outlined briefly here, are explored in more depth throughout this book, as is the whole sphere of services marketing.

6. SUMMARY

The marketing concept is equally applicable to organisations in the service sector and to manufacturers of physical goods. Understanding and identifying the needs and wants of the market underlies successful marketing for service organisations and other types. The market offering must provide benefits and satisfactions to consumers, whether it is a physical good or a service.

Services have special characteristics which can affect marketing activities. Services are:

Intangible
Inseparable
Heterogeneous
Perishable

The marketing mix is a means of classifying tools available to the marketer in designing, distributing, communicating and ultimately selling the offering to target markets. The marketing mix was originally developed around four main elements:

Product, Price, Promotion, Place

However, the special nature of services marketing has led to the addition of three further categories of marketing tool:

People, Process, Physical evidence

Marketing management tasks are largely similar within services marketing and the marketing of physical goods. There are four key areas:

Marketing Research, Marketing Planning, Implementation and Control

Additionally, *internal marketing* has special relevance for the services sector.

Progress test 2

1. Schedule the different groups into which a service organisation may fall.

2. Give reasons why a successful service organisation must adopt marketing principles when dealing with its customers.

3. Outline the overlap in the 'product' element of the marketing mix between physical goods and services.

4. Explain how service organisations can maximise consumption through their pricing policy.

5. Devise a promotional strategy for
   (a) A major high street bank.
   (b) A mobile hairdresser.

6. Why is the 'place' element of the marketing mix to be treated with equal consideration as the other features?

7. Briefly describe the special characteristics of services – namely intangibility, inseparability, heterogeneity, perishability.

8. What is the basic theory behind 'internal marketing'?

Discussion

1. Consider the number (and range) of services you utilise in an average day (or week); evaluate how important these services are to you.

2. What makes a service good or bad? Recall some specific examples when you have been either satisfied or dissatisfied with the quality of service.

3

THE SCOPE AND RANGE OF SERVICES MARKETING

INTRODUCTION

Throughout the second half of the twentieth century service industries have emerged and entered considerable growth in most western nations. Service industries represent a very substantial proportion of both domestic and international trade, and are the major employers in the UK, the USA and other countries.

There are a number of key factors which have contributed to the development of service industries. New technologies and more complex products have led to an increase in demand for after-sales service, and long-term maintenance and support services. Consumers enjoy more affluent lifestyles in today's society than they did fifty years ago, and they also have considerably more free time.

This factor has led to growth in the demand for leisure services and luxury services such as holidays. Increased consumer sophistication, coupled with greater spending power, has led to increases in financial services, personal telecommunications and in-home services such as satellite television.

Post-war economic growth and stability has seen the establishment of a greater number of public sector services. As well as essential services such as health and education, public-funded services cover a far greater range of facilities for leisure, culture and the arts, for example, than ever before.

In addition to commercial and public sector service providers, there has also been a considerable increase in not-for-profit service organisations and charities. Many of these organisations are large, even multi-national concerns, operating in competitive environments and controlling vast financial budgets.

All these different types of service providers are recognising the importance of marketing within today's competitive environment. The growth of service industries and the service economy has been accompanied by new developments in services marketing theory and practice. The last two decades have seen a considerable increase in the amount of academic literature based on services marketing, and it is a rapidly developing specialism among academics and practitioners alike.

1. THE SERVICE ECONOMY

Many westernised countries now have what is termed a service economy. More than half the workforce is employed in service industries. The growth in the service economy has been accompanied by a number of important factors influencing the overall economic picture:

- The diminishing importance within the balance of trade of primary industries (agriculture, forestry and fishing).
- A similar impact on the importance of secondary industries (construction and manufacturing).
- Accompanying social trends affecting the structure of the workforce; many workers in service industries are employed on a part-time basis, and the majority of these are women.

Services are tertiary industries, traditionally industries which supported the primary and secondary industries by providing distribution and finance, for example. The growth in the service sector, however, is reflected in the far wider range of services now available.

Services are divided between consumer services, business-to-business services and industrial services. These fall between the public and private sectors. Many services offered span more than one of these categories:

- Travel services are generally offered to all sectors of the market, although specific market segments are evident, such as the tourism market and business travellers.
- Contract cleaners may service both industrial premises such as factories and other service businesses in offices and retail service outlets.
- Public sector services such as refuse disposal may offer private, commercially-based contracts for industry as well as providing a municipal service.
- A motor service garage may repair company-owned and commercial vehicles as well as providing a service for the private motorist.
- Banks traditionally provide corporate and consumer financial services.

These differences in classification and the complexity of the service market cause difficulties when analysing the true picture of the service economy. Government statistics and economic indicators illustrate the importance overall of the service economy, but it is not easy to evaluate individual sectors of service activity.

There are a number of reasons for the growth of the service economy, and these can be categorised into three main areas:

New services to meet new needs
Social trends
Demographic trends

New services to meet new needs Developments in technology have led to a demand for software services, data processing services and increased maintenance and support. Training for new technology has mushroomed, together with re-training for redundant craftsmen from traditional industries. There has also been an increase in demand for consultancy services, and specialist services are more frequently bought in by companies.

The globalisation of world markets has brought increased demand for travel and international distribution services. Labour-saving devices in the home, and the decline of manual labour in working life, have led to a demand for fitness and recreational services.

Social trends As more women join the workforce, nurseries and childcare services have grown. Increased leisure time coupled with more affluence has led to a greater demand for consumer travel, recreation and leisure services. The demand for education is increasing, especially in the higher education sector and in vocational and part-time courses.

Demographic trends A greater life expectancy has led to an increase in the demand for nursing homes and medical care. Smaller family size coupled with increasing income levels has led to increased demand for consumer services of all types including banking, investment and insurance services together with leisure services.

The 'grey' market of middle-aged consumers is increasing rapidly, and these consumers are more affluent than ever before. The range of services designed for this market segment is increasing.

The growth of the service economy is reflected in the widening of the range of services sought. As consumer sophistication continues to increase, the range of services offered will continue to grow.

2. SERVICE PROVIDERS AND MANUFACTURERS' SERVICES

Services marketing literature has traditionally tended to focus on 'pure' services:

> tourism, leisure, financial services, hotel and catering, education, cultural and medical services, for example.

Services have, in many cases, been treated quite separately from other industries, and have been attributed with 'unique' characteristics to justify such treatment. Service produced by manufacturing firms has not been considered service production. However, manufacturing and service are becoming increasingly entwined and marketers need to move away from traditional service sector industry to look at managing services overall, or the service element.

This thinking has led to a new focus which is recognised as becoming increasingly important: services from non-service providers. This involves the service element in manufacturing and production. The role of ancillary services traditionally provided by manufacturers such as training, technical support and warranties is becoming a critical differentiator in competitive advantage.

The service element of the augmented product – the characteristics which help distinguish a product from its competitors – is now a key factor in long-term success. Rapid developments in technology which mean that firms can no longer sustain a leading edge position in the marketplace by technological superiority alone has led to the development of service as a marketing tool for competitive advantage. The impact on profitability can be two-fold: profitability can increase not only through superior competitive positioning, but many service divisions now represent profit centres in their own right.

Another important area which is receiving increasing attention from marketers is the not-for-profit service sector. Not-for-profit organisations engage in a broad sphere of activity ranging from cultural, educational and political interests to social and leisure activities. The size of these organisations ranges from very small, local concerns to large, multi-national operations. Chapter 17 looks at not-for-profit organisations in more depth.

3. CLASSIFICATION OF SERVICES

As has already been suggested, there are a number of ways of classifying service activity, and there is inevitably some degree of overlap between the methods available. This section outlines some of the methods of classification commonly used.

End-user

Services can be classified into the following categories:

- *Consumer:* leisure, hairdressing, personal finance, package holidays.
- *Business to business:* advertising agencies, printing, accountancy, consultancy.
- *Industrial:* plant maintenance and repair, workwear and hygiene, installation, project management.

Service tangibility

The degree of tangibility of a service can be used to classify services:

- *Highly tangible:* car rental, vending machines, telecommunications.
- *Service linked to tangible goods:* domestic appliance repair, car service.
- *Highly intangible:* psychotherapy, consultancy, legal services.

People-based services

Services can be broken down into labour-intensive (people-based) and equipment-based services. This can also be represented by the degree of contact:

- *People-based services – high contact:* education, dental care, restaurants, medical services.
- *Equipment-based – low contact* automatic car wash, launderette, vending machine, cinema.

Expertise

The expertise and skills of the service provider can be broken down into the following categories:

- *Professional:* medical services, legal services, accountancy, tutoring.
- *Non-professional:* babysitting, caretaking, casual labour.

Profit orientation

The overall business orientation is a recognised means of classification:

- *Not-for-profit:* The Scouts Association, charities, public sector leisure facilities.
- *Commercial:* banks, airlines, tour operators, hotel and catering services.

4. THE DEVELOPMENT OF SERVICES MARKETING

Firms which produce and manufacture physical goods were involved in marketing long before service providers embraced marketing and developed specific marketing activities. Many of the developments in services marketing are fairly recent. There are a number of factors affecting developments within services marketing:

Organisation size and structure
Regulatory bodies
Growth in service industries
Characteristics of services
Customer/employee interaction
Service quality
Specific service sectors

Organisation size and structure

Many service providers are typically small and specialised – plumbers, lawyers and accountants are representative of the traditional service provider. In the past, they catered exclusively for the existing local demand. Marketing specialists were not employed due to the size of the operations, which may have been sole trader or partnership based, and due to limited competition, especially on a local scale.

Regulatory bodies

Regulatory bodies have also restricted the activities of many service providers. Restrictions still exist today on the amount and type of advertising which can be undertaken by certain professional services, particularly in the medical and legal fields (although these have been relaxed in the UK and the USA). Public sector services and charities are also frequently constrained in their 'business' activities by various forms of legislation and regulations.

Growth in service industries

However, growth in major services industries such as banking, hotel and catering and tourism services has been accompanied by new developments in marketing. Services marketing ideas and techniques have grown alongside the growth of the service economy. Marketing has contributed to the growth and success of service industries in a number of ways. The design of the service product, or offering, has shifted from a product-based focus to a customer focus – the organisation provides what the market needs, not what the organisation thinks the market wants.

Characteristics of services

The characteristics of services – intangibility, inseparability, heterogeneity and perishability – mean that there are new considerations facing services marketers. These differences led to the development of the expanded marketing mix to focus on issues perceived by customers to be important in services marketing.

Customer/employee interaction

The customer/employee interaction takes on a far more significant role in services marketing than in the marketing of physical goods. Consequently, services marketing attaches more emphasis to training and better communications. Relatively new concepts have emerged to support services marketing such as internal marketing and relationship marketing. These are now finding increasing acceptance in mainstream marketing and are being applied to areas outside service.

Service quality

Services marketing also places a clear focus on service quality and programmes for implementing service quality. The development of a clearer understanding of perceived service quality and the customer's perception of quality based on the total service experience has addressed specific quality issues in services marketing.

Specific service sectors

Specific areas of services marketing have attracted interest, especially not-for-profit organisations and professional services. Marketers in these organisations are faced with ethical considerations and other constraints. Certain public sector services are similarly constrained. The adoption of marketing by these organisations, and the growth or marketing expertise in the area, is leading to a greater marketing orientation.

5. TECHNOLOGICAL DEVELOPMENTS IN SERVICES MARKETING

Perhaps the biggest impact of new technology in services marketing is the move away from traditionally people-based service to a higher degree of automation. Automated teller machines – the banks' hole-in-the-wall cash dispensers – are a familiar sight on high streets everywhere. Automatic car washes, computerised self-serve ticket reservation machines, even remote banking services where all transactions are done by telephone are all gaining wide acceptance amongst consumers. Even one-to-one training programmes can now be delivered via interactive video technology.

Technological advances in home equipment has led to a demand for new services. The widespread ownership of VCRs (video cassette recorders) has led to flourishing video film rental businesses. Cable TV network and satellite TV receivers are growing in popularity, opening up new areas of business for installation contractors. Today's motor cars, with 'on board computers', need greater technical expertise for maintenance, which, in turn, leads to greater demand for training.

Technological developments have also had an impact on the services marketing management task. Information technology, electronic funds transfer and the use of databases have revolutionised services marketing management. In fact, most marketing-linked technological developments have a role to play in services marketing management. Many new technological developments have been developed specifically around services as discussed previously, such as cash dispensers. Many restaurants and fast food outlets use computerised till systems, where the order is keyed in to the till, or even a hand-held key pad, and relayed directly to the kitchen while the bill is being produced.

It is not only consumer services which have been revolutionised by new technology. Industrial services are also utilising new technology. Remote diagnostics using the telephone modem facility allow computer service technicians to carry out software adjustments and upgrades from base, even if the customer is located overseas. Libraries and universities can utilise computer databases from anywhere in the world via computer modem links.

In general, it can be seen that new technology increases the demand for services overall. This creates opportunities for marketers in service organisations.

6. INTERNATIONAL SERVICES MARKETING

The UK economy depends on invisible exports for a substantial proportion of revenue. Invisible exports have traditionally included shipping, insurance and investment but now cover a far wider range of services. Service organisations are not only involved in the business of exporting, but are increasingly becoming international. Advertising agencies are an example of a service industry becoming internationalised in response to changes in the world market situation.

London is still one of the major bases for financial services including commodities brokerage and insurance. City financial services and expertise are invisible exports when the customer is from outside the UK.

Exporting is considered to be a higher risk venture for service organisations than for firms producing physical products. The main reason for this is that services tend to be far more people based. Production and consumption are inseparable, and the service provider must, therefore, establish a base in the target export market, with trained service personnel. It is not possible to export a batch of the 'product' to be sold through distributors or agents as it is with physical goods. This means that the level of initial investment, even for a very small overseas operation, is relatively high.

Market entry methods closely mirror those for international marketing of goods. Direct export is possible, as when a firm of consulting engineers sends a member of staff to another country to carry out contract design work. Joint ventures may be undertaken, with the service provider forming a partnership with an organisation in the target country to develop business. Franchising is also undertaken, as evidenced by the worldwide growth of McDonalds fast food restaurants. McDonalds use a combination of franchising and setting up wholly-owned subsidiaries on various locations. Agents who act as employees of the service provider can be appointed in export markets. 'Color Me Beautiful', a personal image consultancy service, has consultants in many countries.

One of the main difficulties associated with international services marketing is the question of cultural differences. Cultural differences take on far greater significance in the high-contact service encounter situation. Service delivery may have to be adapted, and perceived service quality criteria examined from the perspective of the target customers in different markets. The internationalisation of services is explored in Chapter 23.

7. FUTURE TRENDS

The earlier sections of this chapter outlined some of the major factors which contributed to the growth of the service economy. The future will depend on the same factors, to a large degree. There are some new factors, however, which may have an impact.

Public transport, particularly bus networks, have declined steadily with the increase in ownership of private motor cars. However, new trends towards environmentalism, and concern over pollution and traffic in urban centres, have led to calls for better public transport services and a potential ban on private cars in some zones. The city of Manchester has taken a step forward by going back in history. A new tram service which operates on a city centre street network, and also on the railway network to surrounding commuter destinations, was opened in 1994.

Many tertiary industries rely heavily on the state of the economy and the manufacturing sector for their business. If manufacturing industry is performing well, then services such as finance, computing, corporate hospitality and consultancy services will parallel that performance. Future economic trends are a key indicator to the future of this service sector.

Environmentalism is having a growing influence on business activities, and this can impact on the service sector in the future. As well as the transport issue mentioned earlier, new services in the fields of recycling waste, pollution management and conservation are growing. Alternative forms of power are being sought, which could lead ultimately to the development of new services. Concern over the pollution caused by disposable babies' nappies has already created a new service; companies will deliver freshly laundered towelling nappies direct to the home, and take away the soiled nappies on a regular schedule.

There are a number of limitations on the growth of service organisations such as their typically small size, and greater reliability of manufactured goods. Market size can be another limitation, especially in a declining population situation. The UK has already shut down schools and colleges due to the declining birth rate since the so-called 'baby boom' of the 1950s and 1960s.

The future of services and their role within the economy looks likely to continue to gain in strength. Whatever factors contribute to the growth or constraints on the future of the service economy, marketers will continue to see services marketing as a critically important area, and new developments will appear.

With the more recent emphasis on services from non-service providers, there is likely to be more integration of marketing thinking and activity between the purely service-based area and manufacturers' services.

8. SUMMARY

The service sector has emerged as the fastest growing sector of the economy throughout the developed world. This growth has been accompanied by a corresponding decrease in the importance within the balance of trade of primary industries such as agriculture and fishing and secondary industries such as manufacturing. The growth of service industries and the service economy has stimulated interest in services marketing theory and practice. A further development is the internationalisation of services.

The range of services provided is growing throughout the public and private sector. Many traditional public sector services such as education, healthcare, waste disposal and leisure are now operated along commercial lines and are held accountable for expenditure and revenues, client (public) satisfaction and service quality. These organisations and others such as charities and voluntary bodies, as well as professional service providers, are starting to develop a marketing orientation and use marketing tools and programmes to survive in an increasingly competitive marketplace.

Changes in lifestyle have led to increased demand for leisure services and foreign travel, for example, while developments in technology have led to increased demand for hi-tech services such as telecommunications and

computing. New technologies have also revolutionised service provision processes through the use of automation and computerised systems, for example.
Services may be classified in various ways:

1. *End-user type*	Consumer
	Business to business
	Industrial
2. *Degree of*	Highly tangible
tangibility	Services linked to tangible goods
	Highly intangible
3. *People-based*	High contact
4. *Equipment-based*	Low contact
5. *Expertise*	Professional
	Non-professional

There is every sign that the service economy will continue to grow in size and importance and this will be reflected in future developments in services marketing.

Progress test 3

1. Name the key factors which have contributed to the growth in importance of the service economy.

2. This growth in the service economy has been accompanied by a reduction in importance within the balance of trade of which industries?

3. Give an example of each of the following:
   (a) a consumer service
   (b) a business-to-business service
   (c) an industrial service.

4. What types of new services have been developed to meet new needs?

5. Which social and demographic trends have led to the development of new services?

6. Define high-contact and low-contact people-based services, using examples to illustrate your answer.

7. What kinds of services are highly intangible?

8. In international services marketing, there are several market entry methods which are also used in the marketing of physical goods. Suggest three such methods.

9. What is one of the main difficulties associated with international services marketing?

Discussion

1. In what ways have technological developments altered or affected services which you use? Have these changes always been for the better?

2. Consider how your lifestyle is different from that of your parents (and even your grandparents) when they were your age and compare the services you use with those available then.

Part Two

ORGANISATION FOR SERVICES MARKETING

4

THE ROLE OF MARKETING IN THE SERVICE ORGANISATION

INTRODUCTION

Marketing is not only concerned with the development and implementation of successful programmes and strategies. For marketing to be successful, there needs to be a marketing orientation throughout the organisation which fosters the marketing concept and demonstrates a marketing approach to all internal and external activities. Marketing can be described by means of all the practical aspects within a marketing programme: product development and management, advertising, promotion, strategic planning, market analysis and segmentation, for example. A marketing orientation goes beyond this, however. It is based around a philosophy which places the customer first, and it recognises that every action taken by the organisation or its employees ultimately impacts on that customer relationship.

The inseparable nature of services means that the importance of the roles played by the service provider and the customer is often far greater than in the marketing of physical goods. Every interaction between the organisation and its customers can affect the quality of the service and the benefits provided. The majority of these interactions may take place between customers and members of staff who do not work within marketing – that is to say who do not work in the marketing department, or in jobs which are associated with marketing such as sales or public relations. If a true marketing orientation is to be achieved, therefore, all members of the organisation need to know and understand what marketing really means, and how it can shape their approach to their own responsibilities.

This chapter looks at the ways in which marketing can be integrated throughout the organisation across functional boundaries and considers specifically the role of marketing within the service organisation.

1. FUNCTIONS OF MARKETING

There are essentially two ways of looking at the functions of marketing. One way is to set down the tasks which are involved in the marketing process and to identify them individually. Another way is to examine why marketing is needed and what its aims are. The second method underpins a marketing orientation more fully. Simply describing the tasks which are undertaken by marketing management and personnel is not enough to establish the nature of a marketing orientation within the organisation.

Marketing is not something to be done just by the marketing department. The marketing department may set down the requirements for successful marketing and operate at a practical level to ensure these are carried out, by organising marketing research and creating promotional campaigns, for example. The real task of 'doing' marketing, however – delivering benefits to meet customers' present and future needs – is part of everyone's job.

The tasks involved in marketing include the following:

- *Setting marketing objectives*
- *Developing and implementing strategic marketing plans*
- *Market and environmental analysis*
- *Conducting marketing research*
- *Designing the appropriate marketing mix(es)*
    the service product itself
    pricing policy
    promotion and advertising
    distribution systems (making the service accessible)
    people – customer service and marketing training
    delivery processes
    designing the service environment (physical evidence)
- *Marketing input in sales management*
- *New service development*
- *Market segmentation, targeting and positioning*
- *Internal communications (internal marketing)*
- *Integration with other departmental management*
- *Establishing marketing information systems*

The aims of marketing are as follows:

- **To understand and anticipate customer needs**
- **To provide benefits and satisfactions to meet those needs**
- **To ensure consistent quality and customer satisfaction**
- **To retain existing customers and attract new ones**
- **To achieve organisational objectives**

In comparing the functional tasks of the marketing department with the overall aims of marketing, it is easy to see why the whole organisation is involved in marketing. The marketing department may design, say, the marketing mix, but other personnel are involved in actually delivering the service – benefit satisfactions – to the customer. These personnel may have front line contact with the customer (the waitress who serves the meal in a restaurant, or the airline steward, for example) or may be in the background (the kitchen staff or mechanical technicians in an airline).

It could be said that the marketing department's task is to develop the theory

– the ideas and plans – while the practice involves the whole organisation. Everybody within a service organisation can influence service delivery and customer satisfaction in some way. Marketing effectiveness, therefore, is down to the way each individual carries out his or her part of the marketing function.

2. MARKETING AND CUSTOMER ORIENTATION

A customer orientation places the customer at the centre of the organisation's activities. Being close to the customer is at the heart of the marketing concept. All personnel need to be aware of the way in which they can contribute to customer satisfaction, even when they do not have personal direct contact. Internal marketing can play a key role here. Positive feedback from customers can be relayed to everyone in the organisation through internal bulletins. Similarly, any quality problems or customer complaints should also be discussed at all levels to see if systems or processes within the organisation can be improved.

Within service organisations, customer contact takes a number of forms. There are different types of interaction which go in to make up the service encounter. The main types of interaction are as follows:

Direct interaction between the service provider (or their frontline personnel) and the customer
This is where the customer formally receives the service offering, or part of it, from the service provider. The customer may be served in a restaurant, or visit a bank or go to the hairdresser. Usually this is a two-way interaction, as the customer participates in the exchange process with the service provider. The restaurant customer may conform to certain dress codes, and make a reservation in advance. The bank customer will possibly wait in a queue and will need to state what service they actually require, bringing with them the appropriate documentation and perhaps going to a separate department in the bank for, say, foreign currency. The customer visiting a hairdresser will usually act as specifier, instructing the hairdresser as to the style and cut required, and will probably have pre-booked the appointment and turned up at the right time.

Interaction between the customer and the service provider's agents or representatives
Frequently in services marketing it is an agent or broker who actually delivers the service to the customer. A holiday maker may have contact with airline personnel, travel agents and hotel staff before they actually meet someone from the actual tour operator. Many customers of insurance companies place their trust in a broker who acts on behalf of the insurance company. In these circumstances it is more difficult for the service provider to have control over the quality of delivery in the service encounter, but this is where careful channel selection, and training for channel members, play a key part.

Interaction between customers and other customers

In some services, especially in the hospitality industry, this interaction between customers themselves makes up part of the service. Atmosphere, or ambience, in a restaurant is an obvious example. Clubs of any kind, such as health clubs and golf clubs, together with organisations such as those in the voluntary and charity sectors, rely on participation and interaction between the members to create the overall service offering.

Interaction between customers and service facilities

This involves the customer's interaction with the environment, facilities and automated systems offered by the service provider. Customers sometimes create their own service, as when they use automatic cash dispensers or vending machines. A self service restaurant is another example where the facilities and displays enable the customer to participate in the service. The environment provided will also influence customer participation in the service. In a training seminar, for example, the level of participation of the customers themselves can be influenced by simple things such as seating arrangements.

These examples serve to illustrate some of the ways in which customers interact with the service providers and partly create the service themselves. All these different types of interaction need to be considered when looking at how the organisation can become more customer orientated. It may be useful to address the following questions when looking at customer orientation, and how it might be improved:

- Who has responsibility for interaction with the consumer at which stages of the process?
- How can these interactions be managed?
- What do employees perceive as their role vis-a-vis the role of the customer on the service exchange process?
- Is each employee, agent or representative clear about their own individual contribution to customer satisfaction?
- Are frontline employees empowered to make decisions 'on the spot' which can improve customer satisfaction, or overcome difficulties?
- Do employees understand the organisation's mission and objectives?

3. INTER-FUNCTIONAL RELATIONSHIPS

Traditionally, responsibility for business functions within organisations has been assigned to separate departmental managers, for example:

Personnel
Production and Operations
Finance and Accounting
Marketing

In manufacturing organisations, production and consumption of the goods usually occurs separately, with production often taking place far away from the actual consumer market. In this situation the marketing department plays a specific role; it is the link at the company/market interface, and it provides the mechanisms for serving the target markets with the goods required. It does all this through the specialist activities traditionally associated with marketing, such as marketing research, advertising and promotion and marketing planning. It is not necessary, or even likely in many cases, that production staff will have contact with the consumers of the goods produced.

In service organisations production and consumption are often inextricably linked. Each branch of a service provider will engage in production of the service at the customer point of contact. As has been stressed previously, each member of personnel will influence, to a lesser or greater degree, the actual consumption of the service and the resulting level of quality and satisfaction. For this reason, service organisations need to embrace a far more flexible, integrated management structure.

This does not mean that there is no need for a specialist marketing function; the marketing organisation requires the full support of marketing in the following areas:

Analysis and selection of target markets
Segmentation
Design of suitable marketing mix(es) to serve markets
Promotional campaigns

In fact, all the activities needed to carry out effective marketing identified earlier. The difference is that these activities must be carried out by the formal marketing department but in conjunction with the other departments within an integrated framework.

There are three main management functions in service organisations which together help to create and deliver service satisfactions to consumers. These are:

Operations management
Human resources management
Marketing management

Operations management

Operations management plays a major role in most service organisations as it oversees all the activities which go together to make up the service offering. This is not just in terms of developing procedures and practices which enable the organisation to provide services to its chosen markets but also in terms of managing all the people, including frontline personnel, who make up a labour-intensive service organisation.

Human resources management

Human resources management plays a key role which underpins the success of the operations task in selecting, training and motivating the right kind of person-nel for the organisation. The nature and importance of the human resources management task is explored in more depth in Chapter 15. It is clearly a strategic management function within a service organisation where customer perceptions of service quality and ultimately the competitive position of the organisation and its success depend increasingly on the commitment and skill of its employees. Few service organisations operate without considerable interaction between customers and employees at various stages in the service delivery process.

Marketing management

Marketing management, therefore, is not only concerned with undertaking the specific marketing responsibilities and initiatives highlighted earlier, it also needs to facilitate the integration of marketing with the other functional areas identified. Marketing must play a key role in the service organisation, not only as a set of plans, programmes and activities, but as a facilitator in their execution. It is through marketing that an organisation can develop a true customer orientation in all its business undertakings.

The integrative role of marketing

This overview of the interaction between operations, human resources and marketing management should also be considered in relation to other specialist departments within the organisation. Finance and accounting for example may be primarily concerned with controlling costs and their viewpoint may conflict with other areas if introducing a higher standard of service is likely to incur higher costs, for example. Technical departments may be concerned with the practicality of introducing new systems or processes which involve more complex computing systems or machinery. This underlines the role that marketing should play in bringing together management from all relevant functional areas to design and coordinate effective marketing solutions.

There are a number of ways in which marketing can undertake a proactive, facilitating role within the organisation, and aid integration between management functions. All organisations will differ in their actual management structure and the nature of this marketing role. Suggested approaches include the following:

- Including managers from other areas in marketing planning.
- Reducing inter-functional conflict through broader training for managers from all areas.
- Taking operations and human resources considerations on board in designing new services and service delivery processes.
- Internal marketing programmes (discussed in Chapter 8).
- A clear mission, with which all employees and management can identify.

Whilst there is a clear need for formal marketing activities and marketing management, this does not need to be sectioned off in a totally separate department. In fact, in services marketing, this should be avoided as far as possible as this can lead to a gap between the operations function and marketing which will not help in fostering a strong marketing orientation. Essentially, service organisations need to develop organisational structures which involve traditional, specialised marketing activities taking place interactively with operations and human resources within a customer-orientated environment. Marketing activities should be coordinated and implemented throughout all functional areas of the organisation in an integrated manner.

4. MARKETING BY NON-MARKETERS

Much of this chapter has focused on the need for personnel throughout the organisation to be 'switched on' to marketing. Within service organisations the wide range of marketing activities carried out by personnel at all levels ranges from specialised marketing activity, such as marketing research, to what could be termed actual marketing activity, such as delivering the service to the customer and monitoring customer satisfaction.

For this reason, it is emphasised that although there exists a need for a formal marketing department, the marketing function as such should not be confined within it. It could be argued that most personnel involved in marketing activities – i.e. who are responsible for carrying out marketing plans and programmes – will not be marketing specialists. They may be professional specialists such as architects, lawyers and computer programmers or they may be front-line specialists, skilled in customer care.

Organisations need to train all service personnel to undertake this important task. This need not mean specialist marketing qualifications for everybody in the organisation, but it does mean that the aims of marketing should be understood by all personnel if a true marketing orientation is to be achieved. Going back to what was said almost at the start of this chapter, everyone in the organisation needs to understand the aims of marketing:

- To understand and anticipate customer needs
- To provide benefits and satisfactions to meet those needs
- To ensure consistent quality and customer satisfaction
- To retain existing customers and attract new ones
- To achieve organisational objectives

This can, in itself, be a task which can be undertaken jointly by marketing, operations and human resources management. Operations managers can look at how the aims of marketing impact on operational procedures and issues. Human resources management can select and recruit employees who display flexibility and the capacity for commitment to a customer orientation. Marketing managers can ensure that everyone in the organisation is aware of new marketing programmes and initiatives through internal marketing and good communications.

Non-marketers will ultimately hold the key to successful implementation of marketing strategy. Their knowledge needs and skills training should address this fact. The marketing department cannot operate successfully in isolation; it is only through integration with organisational activities at all stages in the service delivery process that marketing implementation can successfully take place. In the highly competitive service environment, customers will respond most favourably to the organisation which demonstrates the highest levels of customer consciousness and the organisation with the highest levels of marketing orientation will respond most positively to the changing market.

5. SUMMARY

A marketing orientation can only be achieved in an organisation if it is underpinned by both management and employee commitment to a marketing philosophy. Marketing should not be seen as a separate functional area – done only by the marketing department – it should be integrated with other management and functional areas throughout the organisation. *Internal marketing* and *relationship marketing* are concepts which depend heavily on a marketing orientation and an integrated approach. Marketing management is a complex area encompassing the management of specific marketing activities and negotiation/interaction with other managers and employees at all levels to develop a marketing orientation and implement internal marketing, management of change and other initiatives.

Specific marketing functions include:

Setting marketing objectives
Developing and implementing strategic marketing plans
Market and environmental analysis
Conducting marketing research
Designing the appropriate marketing mix(es)
Marketing input in sales management
New service development
Market segmentation, targeting and positioning
Internal communications (internal marketing)
Integration with other departmental management
Establishing marketing information systems

The aims of marketing are as follows:

To understand and anticipate customer needs
To provide benefits and satisfactions to meet those needs
To ensure consistent quality and customer satisfaction
To retain existing customers and attract new ones
To achieve organisational objectives

Marketing activities are frequently carried out by non-marketers and many front-line personnel at all levels are in a position to influence customer satisfaction through their participation in the service exchange. These people can have a direct impact on customer relations and potential sales. Again, marketing must be influential throughout the organisation and marketing training and awareness seen as important for every employee.

Progress test 4

1. What is meant by the term 'marketing orientation'?

2. List at least six examples of the tasks involved in marketing.

3. What are the four main types of interaction which make up the service encounter?

4. Discuss the role of each of the following management functions in helping to create and deliver service satisfactions:

   Operations Management
   Human Resources Management
   Marketing Management

5. What are the aims of marketing? Who needs to understand them?

6. Why are non-marketing staff important in marketing implementation?

7. In what ways are production and consumption inextricably linked in service organisations?

Discussion

1. Design a presentation to introduce non-marketing staff to the role and purpose of marketing. What would your presentation cover?

2. "Marketing is far too important to be left to the marketing department." Discuss this statement and analyse why organisations need marketing.

5

UNDERSTANDING THE MARKET

INTRODUCTION

At the core of the marketing concept is the need for organisations to be able to understand and anticipate their customers' needs and wants. This close knowledge of customers can only be found through marketing research, in its various forms. At the simplest level, organisations should endeavour to keep track of its existing customers; who they are, where they come from, their buying patterns and so on. New organisations, or organisations seeking to enter new markets, will need to establish information about the market; its size and structure, current and future demand and the major competitors.

There are many tools which can be used in marketing research to enable service providers to get closer to their customers and to understand the markets in which they seek to operate. The main approaches and methods will be looked at in this chapter. Marketing information may come from both internal and external sources. Many valuable sources of information are frequently to be found within organisations. Information, however, will not provide an effective solution to marketing management problems unless it is timely, accurate and available. Systematic handling of information within organisations can ensure that this is the case.

Marketing information systems can be implemented within organisations to ensure that information is handled systematically. The marketing information system brings together information from many sources, both internal and external, and can be a valuable decision making tool for managers. It formalises information-gathering processes and brings together information and intelligence from employees, the organisation's own records and external and new sources of data. The requirements for successful marketing information systems are also explored in this chapter.

1. MARKETING RESEARCH APPLICATIONS FOR SERVICES MARKETING

Marketing research is used in all kinds of marketing situations. A basic definition of marketing research can be set down as:

A systematic approach to identifying information needs, collecting and analysing information to meet those needs utilising the most appropriate methods.

Although there are an infinite number of reasons for using marketing research, and a wide variety of research methods, it can be described as having two fundamental aims:

- *To minimise risk (when plans are being made)*
- *To monitor performance (after implementation)*

The research process and the methods of conducting research are the same for service providers and manufacturers and retailers of physical products. Examples of service industries using marketing research are widespread, as the following examples show:

The management of Eurostar, Britain's new high-speed London-Paris channel tunnel train service, conducted extensive research to establish what customers expected from the service and which customers to target. Research will be ongoing, with user profiling and satisfaction monitoring playing a key part. Other special techniques, such as the use of 'mystery shoppers', will also figure in future research, to ensure quality standards are met.

First Direct, the Midland Bank's telephone banking offshoot, undertook research into the brand, its image and what values it should represent to its target market, prior to its launch and as ongoing research.

The Co-operative Bank used research to monitor the soundness of its strategy when it ventured to re-position its image not through innovative new services but by reinforcing its ethical stance. It established that its unwritten policies of ethical trading and investment were core principles that customers valued, and designed new advertising programmes to reflect this. Subsequent research was undertaken among new customers who responded to the advertising which reinforced the strategy; in many cases the bank's ethical positioning was given as the main reason for opening an account.

As can be seen, the reasons for using marketing research vary as information needs vary from organisation to organisation. In most cases, however, the marketing research process will be similar.

2. THE MARKETING RESEARCH PROCESS

The marketing research process can be broken down into the following stages:

Problem definition/establishment of research objectives
Secondary data examination (internal and external)
Collection of primary data
Data analysis
Recommendations
Implementation of findings

Before discussing each of these stages in more detail, there are some points worth noting regarding the different types of research (and data produced) and the associated terminology:

Primary or secondary data   Secondary data is data already published in some form.

Primary data is new data collected first hand in response to a particular problem or information need.

Qualitative or quantitative data   Data may be qualitative or quantitative.

Qualitative data explores ideas, feelings and attitudes. It is concerned with answering questions such as "why do they buy?" Qualitative research may be undertaken to provide the basis for designing quantitative research.

Quantitative research is concerned with how much and how many. Typically it involves larger scale research than qualitative research. Statistical methods are used to analyse results.

In house or buy in   Marketing research may be undertaken by the organisation itself, or bought in as a specialist service from outside. Alternatively, parts of the research, such as the fieldwork, may be done by outside specialists and the rest carried out in house.

Customised or 'off the peg'   Specialist marketing research organisations generally offer two types of research.

Customised research is designed and carried out in response to the needs of a particular organisation (or possibly more than one) which commissions the research.

'Off the peg' research is designed by the research organisation to cover areas likely to be useful for businesses in particular sectors, then offered as a fairly standard package to any interested organisations.

Population or sample   The population or universe is the entire group which is to be studied. It may be the whole population of a country or region but may also be a specific population relating to the business area, e.g. all rail users or all existing customers of an organisation, or relating to a particular market segment, e.g. all higher education students in the UK, or all employed males under fifty.

The sample is taken from the population to represent it as a whole. There are various methods of selecting samples, selected usually depending on the degree of accuracy required.

At each stage in the research process, it is likely that decisions will have to be made about each of the aspects described above. Careful research design and selection of the most relevant types of information and sources underpins useful, cost-effective marketing research programmes. The following discussion of the stages in the research process will not always mirror exactly how service organisations design and conduct marketing research, but aims to illustrate good practice and draw attention to important issues.

Problem definition/establishment of research objectives

Defining the research problem or information need is sometimes a relatively simple task or may be highly complex. The issue needs to be set out quite clearly for the research objectives to be established. Examples of the problems faced by marketing managers might be as follows:

What is the potential market for this new service?
Why are sales of a particular service declining?
How successful is our latest advertising campaign?
How do our customers rate us against our main competitors?

When the problem has been identified clear research objectives should be drawn up. These should be quantifiable in some way and lay down the parameters of the research task; one of the main reasons for research not being carried out in the most cost-effective manner is because the brief is too broad.

Secondary data examination (internal and external)

Examination of all relevant sources of secondary data must be undertaken before deciding to collect primary data for two reasons:

- *Duplication:* The information may already be available, so primary research may not be necessary
- *Cost:* The cost of generating primary data is very high, so any possibility of acquiring data from already published sources should not be ruled out.

It is usual to start by looking at internal sources of secondary data as these are likely to be most readily accessible. Internal sources of data include:

Company accounts
Sales reports
Customer database and prospect files
Previously conducted marketing research reports
Competitor information held by the organisation
Trade journals and other publications subscribed to

People are also very important sources of internal information. A great deal of market intelligence is often stored in the minds of sales personnel, for example.

The marketing information system should be a means of ensuring that all information is fed back into the system, via sales report forms and other means to ensure it is readily available. Internal sources of data will probably not solve the information problem, but should be examined thoroughly to establish how much relevant information there is before looking to outside sources.

External sources of data range from free or very cheap information to expensive research reports and publications. Sources of secondary data include the following types:

Government statistics There is a vast array of government-produced data available in the UK covering economic, business and social trends. The official census is a prime example of the sort of research published.

Market information produced by specialist organisations Organisations such as Mintel and Key Note produce and sell regular reports of a general nature covering different consumer and business-to-business market sectors. They provide an overview of the latest trends in the market and its size and structure, for example, and cover topics such as 'breakfast cereals', 'alcoholic drinks', 'printed circuits' and 'tourism in the UK'.

They also produce panel data and audits. These are examples of 'off the peg' research which is designed to be of interest to many organisations, so is general in nature, but is specially designed and collected so is more detailed than other secondary sources. Panels of consumers are monitored over periods and their buying and consumption of certain types of goods (e.g. personal products or consumer durables) recorded and analysed, with the results being made available for sale. Audits are similar but are generally based on retail sales records such as supermarkets, for example, which are then broken down, product by product.

Information on companies Specialist organisations compile data about organisations in the form of directories, financial guides and clippings services. Examples of these include Dunn and Bradstreet (financial data), Kompass (trade directories) and McCarthy Information (clippings). Again, these can be bought or subscribed to on a regular basis.

Information about advertising and media Specialised information for advertisers is available from many sources; BRAD (British Rates and Data) lists all advertising media and their costs, the *Advertisers Annual*, with detailed comparison of advertising agencies and Benn's *Media Directory* which also covers advertising media and services.

Other secondary sources Trade publications publish their own surveys from time to time, as do other organisations and scientific or academic bodies. Information about these sources is likely to be found in the trade press, or made available by professional bodies to their members.

Collection of primary data

When secondary sources of data have been exhaustively searched, any remaining information needs will need to be met through the generation of primary data. The primary data collection needs to be carefully planned and the following questions addressed:

- What data is needed? Qualitative or quantitative?
- Is it exploratory in nature or does it need to be conclusive?
- How will it be generated? What techniques are to be used?
- Who will collect/analyse the data? Internal personnel or specialist research company?
- Who is to be studied? (population or sample?)
- When is the data required by?
- How much will the study cost? Are the costs of undertaking the study justifiable in terms of the costs associated with the potential risk of going ahead without this research?

The main methods of gathering primary data appropriate for services marketing are as follows:

Survey: personal; postal; telephone
Observation: human; mechanical
Experimentation

Often, more than one type of approach is needed in order to satisfy the data requirements. For example, personal in-depth interviews may be used in the preliminary stages to identify the key themes or issues which need to be addressed in a large-scale postal survey, for example. A combination of experimentation and observation could be used. The following outlines the approaches to the various methods.

Survey The survey is one of the most commonly used methods in marketing research. It is especially useful where large-scale studies are to be carried out, and may be used to obtain both qualitative and quantitative data. There are various tools for collecting survey data:

Interview – may be unstructured or structured.
Questionnaire – may be 'closed' or 'open'.

Interviews
Interviews may be conducted in person or by telephone. Structured interviews will generally involve the use of a questionnaire so that specific items of information are gathered, addressing set topics.

Unstructured interviews or depth discussions may also be done in person or by telephone. Often they are done with a group of respondents (a focus group) and the interviewer's role is really that of facilitator – to allow the discussion to flow in an unstructured free way, but remaining close to the topic under investigation. Unstructured interviews are often useful when the organisation really does not know what sort of information it is looking for. Focus groups using unstructured interview methods are exploratory in nature and may be used in a number of situations to generate qualitative data:

Concept testing In concept testing, to introduce a new product or service concept to potential customers to obtain their ideas and reaction.
Preliminary research As a preliminary stage in designing a large-scale survey –

the participants' views are noted and form the basis of the questionnaire. For example, a university was about to upgrade its teaching accommodation and wanted to solicit input from all teaching staff. To establish what were the most important features and facilities from the staff point of view, focus group discussions were held. From these discussions, detailed lists of equipment and other priorities were drawn up for inclusion in the questionnaire, which was then circulated to all staff. The same approach can be used by all types of service organisations, initially discussing the ideas with a number of customers or members, then using the results to formulate a wider survey.

Attitude research In attitude research, where the underlying feelings and attitudes are the focus of attention. Sometimes facilitators may be psychologists with ability to draw participants and encourage them to open up. Depth interviews, on a one-to-one basis may also be used for this purpose. They can be done by telephone, but will usually be done in person as they can take a long time and depend on a relaxed, confidential atmosphere.

Questionnaires There are two main types of questionnaires:

Open questionnaires
Closed questionnaires

Open questionnaires 'Open' questionnaires can also be used to elicit qualitative data. These are questionnaires where the questions do not have fixed answers but space is left for respondents to write their own ideas. They are difficult to administer for two reasons:

Low response rates
Difficult and time-consuming analysis

They suffer from a very low response rate due to the time and effort involved on the part of the respondent in completing the questionnaire. They are also extremely difficult to analyse as it can be horrendously difficult, not to say time-consuming, to attempt to categorise the responses.

One or two open questions are often used alongside closed questions, however, to attract some comment and ideas, often at the end. This might be along the lines of "please use the space below to give any comments or suggestions you may have as to how our service can be improved. . . ."

Closed questionnaires 'Closed' questionnaires are those where the questions are closed, i.e. they offer set responses, usually in the form of alternative choices to be ticked off or indicated in some way. This is the most widely used form of questionnaire and it can be administered in person, by telephone or by mail. It is suitable for very wide scale surveys. The researchers (or field workers) seen with clipboards in the street or going from house to house are usually carrying out questionnaire-type surveys. Advances in technology mean that responses can be input directly into a computer, either at the interviewer's desk, if conducting telephone surveys, or by means of a hand-held scanner by a field worker.

Administering the questionnaire Whichever method is used, the questionnaire will be designed so that information can be easily analysed and collated. The design of the questionnaire will also have to take into account the way in which it is to be administered. Mail questionnaires, to be completed by the respondent themselves, must be clear and easy to follow. Telephone surveys and street interviews will need to be fairly short. Interviews to be conducted in the respondent's home or place of work can be much lengthier and more detailed, provided the respondent is willing to spend the time.

Questionnaires can even be administered by electronic mail, if all the respondents use the same electronic mail (e-mail) network. A university information technology service wished to survey all its users, who all had e-mail addresses. A questionnaire was transmitted via the network and responses sent straight back. As new developments in communications technology continue to spread, both in the business and domestic environment, this type of direct contact with respondents may increase, thus enabling new survey methods to be introduced.

Observation Observation techniques may be used in a number of ways to show how people behave in particular circumstances. Retail traffic studies, for example, are set up to observe the flow of customers around the establishment. They may be carried out by human observers in the store, or, as is more likely, by analysing video recordings from cameras placed at strategic points. They can be used to monitor which displays attract customers' attention, which route customers take through the sales floor and so on, and are helpful in planning store layout and siting special displays for maximum sales impact. Similar techniques are useful in service retail outlets such as banks and restaurants.

Observation may be useful in situations where a questionnaire might be inappropriate such as monitoring very young children's responses to toys or cats' tastes in petfood. Watching how people serve themselves in self-service restaurants, or how they use vending machines, can be helpful in improving the design or efficiency.

Observation can be carried out by humans (e.g. the mystery shopper, who observes the quality of the service) or by mechanical means, such as video. Other types of observation by mechanical means have been developed to monitor human reactions to various stimuli. The attraction of images used in advertisements, for example, can be measured by showing the images to potential customers and using technological methods to measure the amount by which their pupils dilate. Observation tends to be a very objective method of carrying out research but it has limitations in that it may show how people do things but not why they are motivated to act in that way.

Experimentation Experimentation takes various forms and can be a useful tool for predicting purchase behaviour. It is based on traditional scientific experimentation methods where an experiment is conducted to test something against other factors. In clinical testing a group of patients may try a new drug while another group – the control group – is given standard treatment without the new drug. The results of the experiment can be found by comparing the results of the two groups. In marketing, experimentation is frequently used to test new products, such as food items, where respondents take part in taste tests. Other applications are equally appropriate for services marketing, however. A new promotion can be tested by launching it in one region then comparing the results against another region where standard promotional activities have been taking place. Measuring the difference in sales can indicate how successful the new campaign has been, and its potential for more widespread use.

In test markets, experimentation can be used where a new product or service is tested with a particular marketing mix in a market area and a slightly different marketing mix in another area. The results of the tests can be examined and adjustments made before going on to a wider test or a full launch. When a new cleaning product was launched, in the test in one area the product was priced just two pence lower than in the other test region. Sales of the lower priced product were fifty per cent higher than sales levels at the higher price. This was extremely helpful in determining the correct marketing mix, prior to national launch.

Once the primary data has been *collected* the data must be *analysed*.

Data analysis

Good research design is the key to facilitating data analysis. Many techniques are used and developments in computer technology have meant that it is now far easier to handle great volumes of data than ever before. Statistical techniques may be used to analyse quantitative data. The analysis may be undertaken by the organisation itself or by outside specialists such as marketing research firms or statisticians. Qualitative data may need very subtle analysis. Recorded discussions from focus groups or depth interviews may be analysed by psychologists, for example. Explanation of actual methods of statistical analysis is beyond the scope of this chapter but it is important to appreciate that the analysis stage is as important as generating the data – 'raw' data, however much of it there is, will not help marketing managers to make decisions.

Recommendations and implementation of findings

It may be possible to draw conclusions from the results of the research and even to establish sound forecasts and predictions. It is up to the expertise of marketing management, however, to use the information effectively. To do this, it is necessary to go back to the research objectives. The following questions must be addressed:

- What was the specific purpose of this research?
- Are the results sufficient to meet our information needs?
- Can the problem be solved?
- Is more research required?
- Can plans be made with confidence? (risk reduction)
- Are existing plans on course and meeting targets? (monitoring)

When these questions have been answered implementation of the research findings can take place. The research does not stop there, however. Marketing research should be ongoing in many ways and when specific research projects end, continuous monitoring programmes start. A feedback loop needs to be built in to the process to meet the new information needs which will arise out of the implementation of current findings.

3. GATHERING AND STORING MARKETING INFORMATION

There are many ways of gathering marketing information, as the preceding section illustrates. Organisations need to identify what their ongoing information needs are and how they can be met. Typically marketing management will need information on the following:

Level of sales
Sales trends
Market size
Market growth rates
Pricing trends
Competitor activity
Promotion effectiveness
Profitability by service division/product line
Advertising effectiveness
Technological developments in the field

The range of information needed is unlimited and will depend on the organisation's activities. It may be used in all kind of situations, including the following:

Market measurement and analysis
Medium to long term forecasting
Identification and profiling of target segments
Factors influencing performance and success
Calculating market share
Assessing customer satisfaction levels

The sources of such information will be varied and come from both within the organisation and from external sources. Essentially information must be:

timely   accurate   accessible   available

Information must satisfy all these requirements if the marketing manager is to remain well informed, be in a position to manage proactively and make sound forecasts and decisions. The sources of information may vary, as suggested. Company reports, accounting records and customer databases are useful records as are customer complaint records and sales figures. External data may be obtained by subscribing to specialist journals and market reports, for example, and competitor activity might be monitored by members of the marketing department.

The amount and type of data required will be as variable as the possible range of sources of such data. Organisations need to ensure that it is handled systematically in order to ensure that it is continuously updated and available. This is where the marketing information system comes in.

4. THE MARKETING INFORMATION SYSTEM

The marketing information system (MkIS) can be defined as follows:

A marketing information system is designed to meet the information needs of marketing management for effective decision making by developing procedures for people and computer systems which ensure such information is available at the right time and in the right format.

This definition highlights the key aspects of the MkIS – it must take place within the organisation, involving all those people and departments which will ultimately have something to contribute to marketing decisions and outcomes. The MkIS cannot exist within a vacuum; as with marketing itself, its success is dependent on the input of all parts of the organisation – a managerial process which works towards corporate objectives. It should also incorporate information from outside the organisation, when the information will affect, or help, the organisation in its quest to satisfy these objectives.

The MkIS is made up of a number of components which feed in together to build up a bank of information which should be continuously updated. These components will cover the various sources of information needed. They can be broken down as follows:

Internal information As discussed in earlier sections, the internal information will come from reports and records within the company. It is essentially information about the organisation itself. Financial records, production reports and customer records will all be contained in this part of the system, or should be accessible to it. Existing customer databases should be contained within this system. Sometimes various functional or departmental reports are produced and handled as separate items within the various divisions of the organisation – the task of this component of the MkIS is to set down procedures and methods whereby such information can be assimilated to provide a cohesive overall picture.

External information External information is all the information concerning the macro-environment and particularly the competitive environment. Much of it will be obtained from outside sources such as trade journals, market research reports bought from specialist organisations and other sources of information about the industry sector. Sometimes this information can be generated internally; indeed, much of this sort of market intelligence is obtained through sales staff and other front-line personnel who have contact with customers and other suppliers. The role of the MkIS in this area is to ensure that specific mechanisms and procedures are put in place to harness all such information and feed it into the system.

Marketing research   All marketing research carried out by an organisation, for whatever purpose, contributes to its information needs and should be looked at in relation to the other information about the organisation and its markets. For this reason, it is important that all new and ongoing research also feeds into the MkIS for it to be available quickly and effectively.

Other components or aspects of the system   Frequently organisations are literally swamped with information of the kind described above and although the MkIS might be working reasonably well, it can be difficult for managers to extract specific information variables required for decision making. To counteract this, and largely due to the introduction of powerful computer systems on a widespread basis, new systems have been developed to manage data more effectively. Often based on sophisticated computer modelling techniques these systems can use data to prepare projections and forecasts, and help managers' decision making by producing "what if?" scenarios (e.g. What is the likely impact on sales of a ten per cent price reduction? What is likely to happen to our market share if competitor A enters this market sector?).

Marketing decision support systems   These systems are generally called marketing decision support systems (MDSS) and can be bought as computing packages or custom designed. They are traditionally large and very expensive and therefore mainly suited to larger organisations although new personal computer technology has meant that smaller, cheaper systems are now available on a more widespread basis.

To enable the MkIS to operate correctly, the information entered into it must itself be:

> **timely**
> **accurate**
> **cost effective**
> **easy to analyse**
> **easy to assimilate**

This can be achieved by ensuring that there is a standardised reporting system within the organisation, which is properly understood and implemented by management and personnel in all areas. A properly coordinated system can yield the following benefits:

- A fast response to changes or problems within the marketing environment.
- Increased accuracy (in forecasting, targeting etc.).
- More timely and effective reports.
- Integration of marketing into the organisation.
- Prevention of information being suppressed by individuals within the organisation.

Computerisation has had a massive impact on the volume and type of data stored by organisations. It has also revolutionised marketing information systems.

However it should be remembered that it is not the volume of information processed, nor the speed by which the computer can process it which counts; it is the utilisation of information and the processes which ensure it is fed into the MkIS which are key factors for success.

Computerisation has also led to the development of analytical systems of higher levels of sophistication than ever before, and dependency on such systems has increased dramatically. However, the system will only be as good as the manager who feeds information into it, and interprets decision-model processes and results. The MDSS cannot act on its own initiative, nor provide a substitute for real management thinking processes.

The basic design of the MkIS which allows for smooth interchanges of information within the organisation coupled with responsive and responsible interaction between functional managers and all staff is more important than expenditure on advanced computer systems. A tightly run formal system which has marketing as its focus, but which involves the whole organisation, is critical.

5. SUMMARY

Successful marketing is dependent on knowing the consumer and understanding the market. This is equally true for commercial organisations and not-for-profit organisations who need to know and understand their users, donors, sponsors or voters.

Marketing research is used in all kinds of marketing situations and has two main purposes:

To minimise risk when plans are being made
To monitor performance (after implementation)

The marketing research process can be broken down into a number of stages:

Problem definition/establishment of research objectives
Secondary data examination (internal and external)
Collection of primary data
Data analysis
Recommendations
Implementation of findings

Once information has been gathered and analysed, marketing management need to ensure that it can be accessed and utilised for marketing decision making. Information should always be:

timely
accurate
accessible
available

A Marketing Information System can be designed to store and continually update all the marketing information needed. Such a system will incorporate a number of components including marketing intelligence and internal reporting systems as well as marketing research.

Progress test 5

1. What is at the core of the marketing concept?

2. What are the two main aims or purposes of marketing research?

3. Outline the stages in the marketing research process.

4. Internal sources of data should be fairly easily accessible. Why is this so, and what are they likely to include?

5. Distinguish between the following types of data:
   (a) primary and secondary data
   (b) qualitative and quantitative data

6. Describe the four main ways of generating primary data.

7. When might it be particularly useful to use focus groups in marketing research?

8. Why are open questions sometimes used on questionnaires? What makes them different from closed questions?

9. In what research situations might observation be most appropriate?

10. What sorts of information are marketing managers likely to need?

Discussion

1. Prepare a discussion document for a management meeting to say why an organisation should have a marketing information system and how it should be set up and run.

2. Is secondary data by its very nature second rate, compared with primary, first-hand data? Discuss the value of secondary data in the marketing research process and suggest possible disadvantages associated with its use.

6

SERVICES MARKETING MANAGEMENT

INTRODUCTION

Marketing management is concerned with the process by which organisations prepare and implement programmes for marketing success in line with the marketing concept. It is based on the underlying need to understand the market and to develop programmes designed to satisfy market needs, thereby achieving organisational goals. Specific management tasks include analysis, planning, implementation and control of marketing programmes.

In general terms, the marketing management process is the same in the marketing of services and tangible products. Certainly the scope of marketing management is very broad. In this chapter, the aim is to present an overview of marketing management and to explore the key tasks identified previously – situation analysis, marketing planning, implementation and control – in the light of services marketing issues.

Marketing management should not be looked at in isolation; however, it is important to recognise its relationship to long-term corporate strategic planning. Strategic planning and the marketing management process are very closely linked. The following framework outlines this relationship and demonstrates the stages in the management process.

1. CORPORATE MISSION AND OBJECTIVES

Without a clear understanding of the organisation's mission and objectives, marketing activities cannot be coordinated and implemented successfully. The mission should provide a clear vision for future directional focus. It should identify the organisation's desired role within its industry and markets. A simple example of a mission statement is as follows:

> To be leaders in global communications by providing the highest possible service to our customers and by striving to be at the forefront of technological development always.

A mission statement should define the organisation's competitive domain, the nature of the business, commitment to employess and the needs and wants of target markets. It should also reflect the vision and values of top management and offer a long-term perspective. Realistically, most organisational mission statements are far longer than the example shown and will typically start with a brief statement, followed by additional paragraphs which break down in greater detail the areas mentioned. It should not be too long for all employees must grasp and understand it easily and it should be readily communicable, internally and externally.

The organisation's objectives should be clearly defined. Objectives should be achievable and measurable. It is not sufficient to hold that a company's long-term objective is 'growth', for example. Growth should be defined in a quantifiable manner. A leisure centre might define growth in terms of number and quality of facilities available, and throughput of users for instance, perhaps based on increasing annual targets, as well as looking at financial targets. A quantified objective can define a specific organisational goal in the following way:

Leisure Centre

Organisational Objective
Increase profits to 15% before taxes.

This can help marketing managers develop clearly identifiable goals for their area. The first step is to consider *how* to increase profits to 15% before taxes. This step involves situation analysis (what is the current situation, what future opportunities are available?). The marketing manager will then set marketing objectives accordingly. These could include:

Increase major facilities revenue by 20%
Increase revenue from other services from current 5% of turnover to 15% of turnover.

Other managerial divisions will also play a role in organisation strategic planning. In manufacturing companies the production managers and research and development managers will set their own objectives, along with financial management. In the example shown using a leisure centre, the human resources manager may also identify goals based on the organisational objectives. Such a goal may be to:

Increase staff productivity by 10%.

How strategies are designed and implemented to achieve these objectives will be discussed later in the chapter. The key issue, however, is the importance of a central strategic focus. This ensures that all divisions of the company will be working as a coordinated and integrated whole towards the long-term goals of the organisation.

Once objectives have been determined, a company performance analysis must be undertaken to establish how near (or far) the company will be to achieving its objectives based on its current efforts. Smaller organisations will take a company-wide perspective, but larger organisations may be sub-divided into *Strategic Business Units*.

Strategic business units are separately identifiable businesses within the organisation. They may operate in different markets, and have their own management hierarchy and mission statements. A large insurance company may have strategic business units in the fields of pensions, life insurance and motor insurance, for example.

The organisation must assess its overall performance and the performance of individual strategic business units in order to make decisions on future strategy. Most organisations look for some form of long-term growth, and current activities may not provide that growth. Organisations will then select strategic options to help them achieve their objectives.

2. STRATEGIC GROWTH OPTIONS

There are three ways of achieving strategic growth. These are:

Integrative growth
Diversification growth
Intensive growth

Integrative growth

The organisation can achieve integrative growth by expanding its market activities by buying suppliers or channel members (*vertical integration*) or buying out its competitors (*horizontal integration*).

Diversification growth

This type of growth occurs where the organisation diversifies its activities by buying other firms not necessarily in related fields.

These two forms of growth strategies involve external growth – they do not rely on the existing organisation to provide growth in itself. The third growth strategy available, which does depend on internally-generated growth is intensive growth.

Intensive growth

This can be achieved via three main strategic routes:

Market penetration
Market development
Product development

Market penetration Market penetration aims to increase market share within an organisation's existing markets. It can be achieved by selling more services to existing customers, attracting completely new customers, or persuading competitors' customers to switch to the organisation's own range of services. A leisure centre may do this by encouraging visitors to use additional facilities or to use the centre more often. Promotional tactics may be reduced prices for use of the solarium after a swim, or discounted tickets for frequent users. A bank might mailshot all current account holders to inform them about other services such as credit cards or pensions. Advertising and other communications methods may be used in both cases to attract new customers.

Market development Market development can be undertaken when an organisation identifies new markets, or new market segments, to which it can offer its existing services. Hotels may offer business and conference facilities as well as tourist accommodation. A car hire company may decide to offer fleet leasing services to companies as well as individual cars for hire.

Product development Product development can be successful when an organisation identifies new offerings for its present customers. Package tour operators may start to offer winter holidays or long-haul exotic holidays. Banks continually update their service product portfolio to meet the changing needs and wants of their customers.

After the strategic planning for the whole organisation and individual strategic business units has been completed, management will focus on functional or divisional planning. Planning for each function must still be firmly in line with the organisation (or strategic business unit) mission and goals.

3. STRATEGIC MARKETING PLANNING

Only when there is a clear understanding of the organisation's mission and corporate objectives can marketing managers address the question of how to achieve results that will lead to success in organisational terms. The first step in strategic marketing planning is to analyse the position of the organisation, and in particular its marketing activities. Whilst the future situation is of paramount concern in forward planning, analysis of the past and current situation can be the most helpful indicator in forecasting the future situation.

The situation analysis can be divided into two main areas:

Internal, or Micro-environmental analysis
External, or Macro-environmental analysis

In both cases, the key task is to identify those influences which can affect future marketing activity. The internal analysis relates to those factors which are specific to an individual organisation, as discussed in Chapter 1. These should be identified and analysed in terms of STRENGTHS and WEAKNESSES – in other words, those aspects which can help or constrain future plans. A situation analysis should also review in detail an organisation's present marketing mix.

The external analysis studies environmental factors which affect all companies or organisations operating in any distinct industry or market. These should be defined in terms of OPPORTUNITIES and THREATS for future plans.

These analyses should have been carried out at a corporate level, and a SWOT (strengths, weaknesses, opportunities and threats) analysis developed as a starting point for corporate strategic planning. Marketing management follows the same pattern of analysis, concentrating specifically on the marketing department and marketing activities. Many factors will affect the organisation overall, not just its marketing activities. Some, however, may have a much more identifiable impact on marketing and related plans and activities.

The factors which must be assessed and analysed fall in to a number of major groupings, as follows:

External environment

There are four main types of influence which need to be looked at here:

Political/Legal
Economic
Socio-cultural
Technological

It is useful to consider each of these separately.

Political/Legal In analysing the political environment, the marketing manager must focus on all aspects of the political environment which can impact on marketing activity in the market/s in which the organisation operates (or hopes to operate). In extreme situations there may be political unrest or instability which could have an adverse effect on all business activity. Certainly this influence has had a major impact on multi-national banking services and tourism and travel in recent years.

On a more local level, factors such as the Government's attitude to business activity can impact on future plans. So, too, can government-led initiatives such as campaigns for health awareness or nature conservation, for example.

Legislation can impact on many services marketing activities. Regulations restrict advertising in many professional service areas, although there has been some relaxation in recent years. Business activity can be controlled by legislation such as the Financial Services Act. The Monopolies and Mergers Commission pays close attention to the dealings of larger companies, especially in banking and related fields. Gaming and lotteries are subject to strict controls; entertainments providers are governed by various Licensing Acts.

Economic The economic environment can impact on almost every type of marketing activity within the services sector. Obvious key indicators such as levels of income and discretionary income are important in determining market attractiveness and potential. In recessionary times this is crucial as service organisations tend to be very badly hit. Research has shown, for example, that in periods of recession, firms cut back on budgets for training and advertising. This has a strong negative effect on business-to-business services.

Consumer spending is also constrained in periods of recession and high unemployment, so spending on luxuries – trips to the cinema, meals out and holidays, for example – tends to be curtailed. Charitable service organisations can be doubly affected by a recession – the demand for their services can increase, while subscriptions and donations may be falling.

National factors such as levels of inflation and unemployment should be looked at together with world economic trends. Current and past trends need to be closely monitored and future trends assessed, in the light of the likely impact on marketing activity.

Socio-cultural Social and cultural trends are major influences on services marketing activity. This is especially true in consumer services, as so much of the service economy is linked to leisure and pleasure. Trends in leisure vary dramatically between cultures, and are also closely linked to social trends. The social trend of leading a more healthy lifestyle has led to significant increases in sports centres and fitness clubs, and health services such as screening.

Cultural aspects impact greatly on any consumer market. Attitudes to alcohol or gambling, for example, from a religious or cultural perspective denote clear constraints for certain services marketing activities in certain regions. However, more subtle influences can be difficult to define. Lifestyle is one such example.

Lifestyle relates not only to the way in which people live their lives, but also the lifestyle to which they aspire. Today's mass media publicises different lifestyles to everybody, often portraying a very glamorous and affluent lifestyle which people wish to emulate. The success of 'Hello!' magazine which specialises in photo-tableaux of the lives of the rich and famous illustrates consumer pre-occupation with the lifestyle concept.

Consumers from all social strata are prepared to pay to enjoy the high life, and are becoming increasingly sophisticated in their tastes. Some services have status value – personal communications services (mobile phones, faxes), satellite television, even personal fitness trainers have both a utility and a status value in the eyes of the consumer. Travel abroad has become so commonplace that the task for many tour operators is to offer increasingly exotic and remote locations to satisfy their customers' needs for something 'different'.

Other aspects of lifestyle vary between countries and even between regions within the UK. The wine and beer markets, for example, show major regional distinctions, and this is coupled with a tendency to choose differing types of social leisure. Wine bars are more popular in London and the South-East, for example, Brass Bands and Working Mens' Clubs in the North.

Social trends affect many business sectors. Traditionally, weekly waged employees who were paid in cash did not have bank accounts, and turned to building societies for savings and mortgage services. This pattern is changing slightly in recent years as fewer people are paid in cash, and the business activities of banks and building societies now have far greater overlap. Marketing managers in service industries need to monitor and assess these influences.

Technological The last two or three decades have seen revolutionary changes in technology, and the speed of change is increasing. Technology impacts on markets as an enabling factor. Many services have arisen directly from advances in technology – computerised market research services, for example, video services (for promotion, training or consumer purposes), even computer dating.

Advances in technology have also affected the way in which marketing activities can be carried out. The very high incidence of domestic telephones now in the UK means that telesales techniques can be used for consumer, as well as business, services. Telecommunications technology has led to services such as those mentioned earlier – mobile communications and satellite TV, for example. The AA motoring association is launching a new emergency in-car phone service based around current telecommunications technology. Computerised telephone answering networks, for example, can improve the quality of service delivery.

Level of technological awareness is an important factor, too. In countries or regions where there is extensive use of technology; adoption of new services or products linked to technological skills is likely to be far quicker. These factors should all be explored by marketing managers in service and other sectors.

Once the situation analysis has been completed, the next stage in the management strategic planning process is to determine *marketing objectives*. Organisational strategies and goals can be translated into marketing (and other functional) objectives. An overall organisational objective of increasing profitability can mean reduced marketing costs in some areas.

Marketing management are now faced with the task of *selecting target markets*. Markets should be continuously monitored and trends assessed, so some information should be readily available. For new organisations, however, or when new markets are to be developed this information will need to be gathered and fully evaluated.

All of this decision-making depends on information to enable managers to make informed judgements when planning. This information gathering and processing is another part of the marketing manager's task. *Marketing research* is essential, and *marketing information systems* should be up to date.

The final stage in the planning process prior to implementation will be the design of an appropriately tailored marketing mix to serve each of the selected target market segments. In services marketing, this means consideration of each of the seven P's:

PRODUCT
PRICE
PROMOTION
PLACE
PEOPLE
PROCESS
PHYSICAL EVIDENCE.

Each of these elements need to be fine-tuned, as far as possible, to the needs of different market segments.

4. SUMMARY

Marketing management refers to the process by which organisations prepare and implement plans and programmes in line with the marketing concept. Marketing plays a key role in relation to long-term strategic planning. Marketing activities cannot be implemented and co-ordinated successfully without a clear understanding of an organisation's mission and objectives. In order to achieve its objectives, an organisation can consider strategic growth options:

Integrative growth	Horizontal integration
	Vertical integration
Intensive growth	Market penetration
	Market development
	Product development

Diversification growth

A key part of the strategic planning process is the analysis of the internal and external marketing environment – the SWOT analysis. Key influences which should be monitored include:

Political/Legal
Economic
Socio-cultural
Technological

Other key marketing management tasks include the selection of target markets using marketing research information and the design of appropriate marketing mixes for the selected markets.

Progress test 6

1. Why should a service organisation's objectives be defined and measurable?

2. How do larger organisations split their operation to ease company performance analysis?

3. Suggest how a fast-food restaurant chain can achieve growth through:
   (a) Market penetration
   (b) Market development
   (c) Product development.

4. What are the two major groupings which result from an internal analysis?

5. In what ways does the service sector particularly suffer in times of economic recession?

6. To what extent are socio-cultural factors important in consumer services marketing?

7. Explain how 'lifestyle' influences can be used in advertising:
   (a) A new type of bank account aimed at executives.
   (b) Inter-city rail travel.

8. Outline the effect of technological advancement in service industries.

9. Briefly describe the three stages which follow the situational analysis, and lead to the implementation of the plan.

Discussion

1. Compare and contrast the characteristics of a successfully managed service organisation with those of a badly run one.

2. "Research and Information are the keys to effective management decision-making." Consider this comment with particular reference to the service sector.

7

MARKETING PLANNING FOR SERVICES

INTRODUCTION

Whilst there appears to be general agreement amongst both marketing academics and practitioners that marketing planning is critical to the long-term success of the organisation, research has consistently revealed that the vast majority of organisations do not have established systems in place for marketing planning and programme implementation. This seems to be due to a number of causes; perhaps the most likely being management weakness in the area of planning coupled with a lack of line management support and inadequate organisation structures.

Sometimes marketing planning is carried out, but on a piecemeal short-term basis. Managers undertake an annual planning exercise for marketing but constrain their activities to reactive programmes which are economically viable in response to market changes. An in-depth look at the organisation's marketing policies, strategies and structures is what may actually be required in order to do planning properly, rather than create purely short-term measures. This is equally true for both service organisations and companies in other sectors, and is of increasing importance in non-traditional marketing organisations such as charities and public bodies.

The preceding chapter discussed strategic planning and the marketing management process, from the corporate mission and environmental analysis through objectives setting and marketing management tasks. This chapter builds on this with a practical review of marketing planning and the various stages involved in implementing and monitoring successful programmes. The marketing audit is also covered in some detail as a practical management tool for evaluating marketing practice within the organisation as a precursor to actual planning activity. This can be particularly helpful for organisations new to marketing, such as those in the public and not-for-profit sectors.

1. THE MARKETING AUDIT

Rather like financial audits, the marketing audit should be carried out periodically to check on current practice and evaluate systems and procedures. A marketing audit can be defined as follows:

A marketing audit is an independent, comprehensive evaluation of the organisation's marketing environment, objectives, strategies and activities, carried out systematically in order to pinpoint difficulties, problems and opportunities and make recommendations for improved performance.

Many marketing textbooks explore the marketing audit in some depth, and definitions and descriptions of the audit process may vary. The following considerations and practical guidelines are useful, however, for service organisations generally. The marketing audit has the following distinctive characteristics:

Breadth of focus   The marketing audit is broad in nature, reflecting the broad role of marketing within the organisation.
Objectivity   It should be conducted by someone who is independent of the organisation under scrutiny, for reasons of objectivity.
Systematic   It should be carried out systematically in an ordered and precise way.
Regular   The audit needs to be undertaken periodically, not carried out urgently in response to a crisis or sudden downturn in the company's fortunes.

The audit is generally performed in three stages: the scope and approach are agreed, the analysis is carried out and the resulting information reported back to management. The analysis stage is likely to be the most time-consuming as there will be a great deal of information to be gathered and scrutinised, and this can only be carried out effectively with the co-operation of all involved parties. The information should be presented in stages as the audit takes place, so the preliminary findings and issues emerging can be given prompt attention. As the report is finally completed, it is important that the organisation has decided on a plan of action for following up the findings and handling any problems or weaknesses uncovered.

The marketing audit usually consists of several audits in fact, centred around the following main components:

Marketing environment
Marketing strategy
Marketing organisation
Marketing systems
Marketing productivity
Marketing function

Some or all of these components may be investigated within the marketing audit (together with additional components relevant to a particular organisation or its activities) but the starting point is usually to examine the external environment and the changes taking place within it. The audit then gradually narrows its focus from the general aspects of the organisation's marketing activity to the more specific, until, finally, specific problem areas or difficulties can be probed more closely if required. It is useful to understand the components identified above, and the main questions which should be addressed in the audit.

The marketing environment

The marketing environment is made up of two parts: the macro-environment (or external environment) and the micro- (internal) environment. The macro-environment represents all the outside influences which will impact on an organisation's marketing or business activity. It includes economic and political factors and socio-cultural trends, for example. The external environmental influences will affect all organisations within a sector to a greater or lesser degree. The internal environment relates to a particular organisation and its publics. A more detailed description of the marketing environment can be found in Chapter 6.

Marketing strategy

The environmental analysis can be used as a basis for SWOT (strengths, weaknesses, opportunities and threats) analysis. The audit can now focus on the corporate mission and objectives and consider the organisation's marketing objectives in the light of existing opportunities and strengths, and possible problem areas. The current marketing strategy should be examined to ensure that it represents the most appropriate course of action for the successful achievement of organisational goals. The strategy should fulfil the organisation's marketing objectives in a way which makes optimum use of resources while taking account of strengths and weaknesses. It should also be assessed for its suitability with regard to opportunities and threats facing the company.

Marketing organisation

The role of marketing in the service organisation is a critical one, and the way in which companies organise themselves for marketing can be crucial for success, as discussed in Chapter 4. Integration between management functions, internal communications and established links between different functional areas should all be looked at within the marketing organisation audit. Training and human resources issues should also be considered as a particularly important issue for labour-intensive service industries where people play a key role in all aspects of marketing.

Marketing systems

This examines the systems used by marketing management to gather information, design plans and programmes, implement plans and monitor their effectiveness. Processes and procedures set down for marketing activity of all kinds need to be included. The focus here is on the actual modes of implementation and monitoring rather than the marketing strategy itself. New product or service development processes, budgeting and reporting procedures, marketing research and marketing information systems are all examples of the areas to be investigated by the auditors at this stage.

Marketing productivity

A complete marketing audit will include a comprehensive examination of financial information to determine levels of profitability and costs. Marketing programmes need to be cost-effective and measures should be established as far as possible to identify how marketing costs break down and which expenditure brings the highest returns. This is not always possible with some marketing activities where the results can be quite intangible (advertising designed to boost the organisation's image, for example) and it is not easy to say what the real impact on sales and profit is. Efforts should be made, however, to ensure that marketing costs analysis is undertaken accurately and routinely within marketing programmes.

The marketing function

In this stage of the audit, attention is turned to specific functional areas of marketing. Advertising programmes, for example, may be set up in a very loosely controlled way, or there may be weaknesses within the sales force which need investigation. The audit may have revealed potential problems in one or more functional areas within marketing and a decision can be made whether to undertake functional audits and, if so, how many areas to audit in this way.

Marketing effectiveness

The marketing audit can perform more than one function. Its key aim is to analyse the organisation's overall marketing effectiveness. It can also have an educational role, creating greater awareness of what constitutes effective marketing among managers throughout the organisation. In the service sector, many organisations are becoming more marketing driven, especially in the not-for-profit and public sectors, for example. In organisations where there has previously been no formal marketing activity a marketing audit can be used to highlight what activity should be undertaken and to what extent a marketing orientation exists. The following checklist gives suggestions for formulating approaches to the audit:

Macro-environmental issues:

- Is government activity likely to affect the organisation through new legislation, tax regulations?
- What legal requirements is the service subject to?
- What effects are inflation/recession/interest rates/trends in consumer spending likely to have on the organisation's activities?
- Are demographic trends likely to affect served markets?

- Are consumer pressure groups influential in this sector?
- What is the position regarding international activity?

Micro-environmental issues:

- Market analysis – size, structure, growth, market share, segmentation, positioning.
- Competitor analysis – who are the main competitors? How do they operate?
- Who is the customer? How do they buy? What are their needs and wants? What benefits do they rate most highly?
- How are channels selected and managed?
- SWOT analysis.
- How does the organisation structure affect marketing?
- Who are the key stakeholders in the organisation?

Marketing strategy issues:

- How do the marketing objectives measure up to the organisations strengths, weaknesses and competitive environment?
- Are corporate and marketing objectives clearly understood?
- Is the strategy sound and well supported with adequate marketing resources and expertise?
- Are marketing efforts being channelled in the right directions for optimum success?
- Is there a formalised planning system?
- What control systems exist for monitoring once plans have been implemented?

Marketing organisation issues:

- Does marketing management have the required expertise and knowledge? Do they receive full support from marketing staff and at corporate management level? To what extent does marketing play an integrative role with other departments?
- Are intra- and inter-departmental communications effective?
- Is further training/investment in personnel needed to achieve marketing objectives?

Marketing systems issues:

- Is there a marketing information system? Is it effective, accurate and up to date?
- Are there formal reporting procedures set down?
- What other formal and informal control systems exist?
- How is new service development carried out?

Marketing productivity issues:

- Are marketing costs regularly monitored and analysed against performance?
- Is profitability analysed and measured in terms of markets, segments, service types and channel?
- Are any marketing activities unnecessary?

Marketing function issues:

- How effective are service design and delivery systems?
- What controls exist to monitor marketing mix activities?
- Are marketing functions (e.g promotional programmes) carried out efficiently and with optimal use of resources?

The marketing audit forms a basis for the marketing planning process. Marketing plans focus on specific, detailed marketing strategies and programmes, designed to help the organisation achieve its marketing objectives within its chosen markets. The marketing plan coordinates and manages the marketing effort.

2. THE MARKETING PLANNING PROCESS

Marketing planning is one stage in the marketing management process. Marketing management is responsible for:

Analysing marketing opportunities.
Marketing research and selection of target markets.
Designing marketing strategies.
Designing and implementing detailed marketing plans.
Effective monitoring and control.

(Aspects of services marketing management are discussed in more detail in Chapter 6.)

Marketing planning is a sub-set of corporate strategic planning. At the corporate level, organisational objectives and strategies are established. These are then translated into functional objectives and strategies. Marketing is only one of these functions; finance and accounting, production and other functional areas will engage in planning to meet their own objectives. The marketing planning process actually goes beyond designing effective marketing plans and programmes; it encompasses decisions and procedures necessary for effective plans to be drawn up and for their successful execution. It addresses the questions:

"Where are we now?" (analysis stage),
"Where do we want to be?" (planning stage),
"How do we get there?" (implementation stage)
"How successful are we?" (monitoring stage)

The stages in the marketing planning process can be viewed as follows:

Analysis stage

Current marketing situation analysis:

the marketing audit
the environmental analysis
SWOT analysis

This stage covers the relevant background information necessary for plans to be formulated and decisions to be made. It includes detailed analyses of the current market situation, the organisation's existing products/services situation, the competitive situation and the SWOT analysis. The outcome of the current situation analysis and the SWOT analysis in particular provides a foundation for the next stage in the process.

Planning stage

Defining the requirements of the plan:

objectives setting
strategic outline

At this stage, marketing managers are fully aware of the factors in the organisation's current situation which will influence its marketing activity so will look at corporate objectives in the light of this information to develop marketing objectives and evaluate strategic alternatives. Marketing objectives should meet certain criteria:

- They should be stated clearly and unambiguously.
- They should be measurable (by sales volume, or percentage increase over the last three years, for example).
- They should be consistent with the organisation's objectives and resources.
- They should be set down in order of priority.

Strategy is based on the idea of a game plan, as in chess, or in military strategy. Thus, marketing strategy sets down the game plan by which the objectives are to be achieved. Each objective should be viewed very closely and strategic alternatives drawn up. For example, a desired increase in sales revenue from a particular service could be achieved in a number of different ways; by greater market penetration, for example, or by enhancing the service offering and charging a higher price.

Strategic options should be carefully evaluated for each objective and the best possible course(s) of action selected in each case. The next step is therefore to establish plans of action for each selected strategy.

Implementation stage

Putting plans into operation:

designing action programmes

assigning responsibility for their execution
costing the programmes

This stage is concerned with the operationalisation of marketing strategy. The strategy defines the broad areas of marketing activity which must be undertaken to enable the organisation to meet its marketing objectives. These must be translated into programmes of action to be carried out by the various functions within marketing. At the implementation stage, the key questions to be addressed are:

"What needs to be done?" (defining appropriate action)
"When will it be done?" (scheduling and timing)
"Who will do it?" (designating clear areas of responsibility)
"How much will it cost?" (budget planning)

The marketing plan will focus on the various marketing mix activities which make up the organisation's service offering within its chosen market(s):

The service package – features, benefits
Pricing policy
Promotional programmes
Distribution – making the service accessible
People aspects of successful service delivery
Process design
Physical evidence

Each element of the marketing mix activities proposed must be carefully costed and analysed for optimal use of organisational resources and to ensure the most suitable approaches are used so that marketing objectives can be met. Measurable targets should be built into the plan to allow for effective monitoring programmes. Clear areas of responsibility for carrying out designated tasks must be set down and understood by all concerned for successful implementation.

Monitoring stage

Controlling the plan:

establishing required performance targets
monitoring performance against targets
designing corrective courses of action where required
contingency planning

The last stage in the marketing planning process sets in place control techniques for monitoring the plan's performance. Usually this entails a systematic review of all aspects of the plan against targets set, usually on a monthly or quarterly basis. The review must be carried out regularly to ensure prompt attention and action in areas when the results lag behind targets set. Managers and others responsible for implementation of all elements of the action programme should be involved in the monitoring process. Control mechanisms should be in place based on the components identified above:

Establishing required performance targets Targets are derived from the marketing objectives set down in response to corporate objectives. They should:

- Indicate clearly required levels of individual performance.
- Allocate responsibility for individual achievement to the appropriate persons.
- Delineate clearly between areas of individual responsibility for which individuals have control and uncontrollable factors which should be excluded from that individual's required targets.
- Be prioritised and ensure they are feasible and compatible.
- Have some built-in flexibility in order to respond proactively to changes in the organisation's environment.

Monitoring performance against targets Measures for evaluating performance against targets need to be established. Individual targets for all functional areas within marketing should have appropriate criteria set down for performance to be measured against, and this should be clearly communicated to the individuals concerned at the time the targets are set. In some areas, performance against targets will be relatively easy to assess, while at other times the reasons for failure to meet targets may not be immediately obvious. The main criteria for determining the level of success against targets will be based on:

- Market analysis: market share, market penetration.
- Financial analysis: sales volume, profitability, contribution.
- Functional effectiveness: specific measures of advertising effectiveness, results of promotional campaigns, productivity of sales or marketing personnel.
- Customer satisfaction: complaints monitoring, satisfaction surveys.
- Efficiency measures: improved processes, response speed.

Adequate levels of performance against all targets is necessary for the longer-term implementation of successful marketing programmes. Vastly increased sales volume, for example, will not represent success if the number of complaints increases dramatically and customers are not retained.

Designing corrective courses of action where required The purpose of an effective monitoring system is to identify areas of shortfall between actual performance and targets quickly and deal with problem areas promptly. If advertising is not achieving the required results, then perhaps the budget needs to be increased, or the effort may be best diverted into another activity such as sales promotion. Fine-tuning of all elements of the marketing plan is the key task here, and it is dependent on an accurate and timely monitoring system.

Contingency planning This is designed to focus management thinking on alternative courses of action which can be taken when unexpected situations arise which make the designated action programme, or parts of it, unworkable. Contingency plans should be drawn up as part of the overall plan, and reviewed as part of the monitoring process. They should be designed into the monitoring programme so that they can be implemented readily if required.

The marketing planning process coordinates and directs the organisation's marketing effort. It contributes to the overall organisational objectives by setting down action programmes to meet agreed marketing objectives. Its successful implementation depends on careful analysis and evaluation of strategic alternatives; development of programmes which will operationalise the strategy and meet objectives; accurate monitoring and implementation of corrective action or contingency plans where appropriate. Successful marketing planning and implementation also depends on the organisation itself, its structure and marketing orientation and the performance of individuals within it.

3. ROLES AND RESPONSIBILITIES

Effective implementation of marketing programmes requires co-ordinating the efforts of all employees. Their co-operation is essential in realising strategies designed to increase productivity and customer service to gain and maintain competitive advantage. The marketing planning process provides the necessary structure and direction for marketing activities to bring about desired changes and results but the key task for managers is finding means to ensure plans are effectively carried out. This can be achieved through the following:

Internal marketing
Motivation and leadership
Effective communications
Co-ordination of the marketing task

Internal marketing

This is a means of involving staff at all levels in effective marketing programmes by enabling them to understand more clearly their role within the marketing process. Internal marketing can be defined as follows:

> *Treating with equal importance the needs of the internal market – the employees – and the external market through proactive programmes and planning to bring about desired organisational objectives by delivering both employee and customer satisfactions.*

Internal marketing programmes consist of training and staff development, effective internal communications and integration schemes, designed to enhance knowledge and understanding of the overall marketing orientation within the organisation. Internal marketing is the focus of the next chapter. Briefly, the aims of internal marketing are to ensure that all personnel:

- are committed to the goal of guaranteeing the best possible treatment of customers
- are themselves motivated

- see themselves participating actively in achieving the organisation's goals.

Motivation and leadership

Internal marketing can play a key role in motivating employees throughout the organisation and is especially important in motivating marketing personnel whose task it is to implement marketing plans. Motivational programmes can be developed by management and geared towards the ultimate attainment of corporate goals, but must focus on the needs of the employees. Such programmes may incorporate tangible rewards schemes:

- Performance-related pay
- Staff incentive schemes

However, employee commitment and job satisfaction is also closely linked to their understanding of their own role in the organisation, and the recognition of their individual contribution. The role of management in motivating employees is crucial.

Marketing management have a dual role within the organisation:

- to develop strategic marketing plans and action programmes to mobilise marketing personnel and resources within the organisation to meet organisational objectives by serving customer needs and wants most effectively
- to help instill a marketing and customer orientation amongst all management and employees.

Marketing managers must have close links with top management, therefore, to ensure that marketing receives full support and the resources necessary for successful implementation of marketing programmes. They should also communicate closely with marketing and other personnel to help them to get the job done and they should lead by example. Human resources management should work with marketing managers to help in motivating staff, and integration with other functional areas of management is important. This clearly underlines again the central, integrative role of marketing.

Effective communications

Good communications can also play a key role in ensuring that plans are implemented effectively and motivating personnel.

- Marketing managers need to communicate with top management to ensure that plans and programmes always match organisational objectives accurately.
- They need to communicate with marketing and other staff to ensure that activities and responsibilities are clearly understood and operationalised effectively.

Internal marketing programmes incorporate communications as their main component and other management tools such as the marketing information system are useful. Communications should be established as a two-way process, so that a dialogue is achieved between:

Marketing managers and marketing personnel

The marketing function and other functions and staff throughout the organisation

Marketing management and corporate-level top management.

Systematic reporting procedures and a structured flow of information both upwards and downwards within the organisation all contribute to effective communications.

Co-ordination of the marketing task

The marketing function involves many different specialisms and task areas, which must be managed as a cohesive whole for effective implementation. Management tasks include:

- Scheduling and synchronising individual activities
- Designing reporting and control procedures for all separate task areas
- Liaison with other functional management
- Integration with other internal functions
- Integration and co-ordination with external players; advertising agencies and other suppliers, marketing channels and agents.

Internal marketing and effective communications programmes will help in the task of co-ordinating the marketing effort. Each individual both within the organisation and outside it who has an input into the marketing process needs to understand precisely their own role and responsibilities. Pulling together the marketing effort underpins successful implementation of the marketing programme.

4. SUMMARY

The *marketing audit* represents the first stage in the marketing planning process. The audit is used to review and evaluate the current position of the organisation's marketing activities and to analyse the organisation's overall effectiveness. The marketing audit, once completed, forms a base for marketing plans to be designed and implemented.

Marketing planning is essentially a process comprised of four main stages:

Analysis stage
Planning stage
Implementation stage
Monitoring stage

Monitoring is critical to the successful implementation of any plan and control mechanisms should be built into the plan to ensure prompt attention and action if the plan lags behind targets set. Effective control can be established using the following key steps:

Establishing required performance targets
Monitoring performance against targets
Designing corrective courses of action where required
Contingency planning

In order for marketing plans to be successfully executed, however, the efforts of all employees need to be co-ordinated. Effective implementation can be aided by:

Internal marketing
Motivation and leadership
Effective communications
Co-ordination of the marketing task

The marketing planning process provides structure and direction for marketing activities and should be undertaken as a medium to long-term commitment not, as is frequently the case, on a peicemeal short-term basis. A systematic and thorough approach to marketing analysis, planning, implementation and monitoring is critical to the successful achievement of organisational objectives.

Progress test 7

1. Explain what is meant by the 'marketing audit' and outline its role in the marketing planning process.

2. Give up to six examples of the main components which make up the marketing audit.

3. Marketing management is responsible for what five specific areas relating to marketing planning?

4. Outline what special criteria marketing objectives should meet.

5. Which key questions should be addressed at the implementation stage?

6. Performance targets are crucially important for controlling the plan. How are they established and monitored?

7. What is meant by 'contingency planning'?

8. It can be said that marketing management has a dual role within the organisation; explain what this means.

9. Give details of some of the key management tasks involved in implementing marketing plans.

Discussion

1. Outline the procedure for carrying out a marketing audit in an organisation you know or your college. Discuss the practical steps involved; think about the questions which you envisage asking and the likely sources of information and co-operation.

2. Consider the suggestions made in section 3 of this chapter for achieving successful implementation (internal marketing; motivation and leadership; effective communication; co-ordination of the marketing task). What ideas could you add to those given? What possible pitfalls do you see?

8

INTERNAL MARKETING

INTRODUCTION

The concept of internal marketing has its origins in conventional marketing theory and the marketing concept itself. It is interesting to note that the internal marketing concept has been developed largely within the context of services marketing, where it has long been recognised that high levels of customer service depend heavily on the personnel who interact with customers.

The employees are in many senses an important part of the service product, as has been stated in previous chapters. They represent the fifth 'P' in the services marketing mix. Internal marketing addresses employees – the internal market within an organisation – whose participation and role is recognised as being critical to levels of service quality and delivery. However, internal marketing is now being seen as more and more essential for *all* organisations in striving for marketing success.

Internal marketing is a means of involving staff at all levels in effective marketing programmes by enabling them to understand their role within the marketing process. Internal marketing programmes consist of training and staff development, effective internal communications and integration schemes, designed to enhance knowledge and understanding of the overall marketing orientation within the organisation.

Whilst the importance of internal marketing is widely recognised, criticism has arisen due to the difficulties in implementing internal marketing, and the lack of planning tools available to managers wishing to do so. This chapter reviews the internal marketing concept but also focuses closely on implementation issues. A framework for implementing internal marketing is proposed and some practical issues are addressed.

1. THE MARKETING CONCEPT AND INTERNAL MARKETING

In order to understand internal marketing it is useful to review the idea of the marketing concept and to examine some of the fundamental ideas put forward.

The marketing concept can be generally defined as a human activity directed at satisfying needs and wants through exchange processes. Other definitions include planning, pricing, promotion and distribution, and also consider issues such as firms serving customer groups more effectively than the competition, for example. Almost all descriptions of the marketing concept, however, focus on the key element of exchange processes, which lead to some form of satisfaction – for the customer, the organisation, even society as a whole.

Internal marketing takes the marketing concept as it is applied to external customers and applies it *internally*. It gives employees the status of internal customers, with the same level of importance as external customers. The underlying theory is that optimum levels of customer satisfaction will be gained when employees themselves are satisfied, and organisations should pay as much attention to their internal marketing programmes as to their external marketing plans and strategies.

2. DEFINITION OF INTERNAL MARKETING

Internal marketing can be defined as follows:

> *Treating with equal importance the needs of the internal market – the employees – and the external market through proactive programmes and planning to bring about desired organisational objectives by delivering both employee and customer satisfactions.*

Internal marketing should also cover issues which are traditionally linked with other areas in organisations, such as human resources management. This is highlighted by training needs which should be thoroughly examined, and the implementation of training programmes designed to enhance:

- Knowledge of the firm's product/service mix.
- Pride in the firm itself, and individual jobs.
- Awareness of opportunities for new service and business development.
- Specific marketing skills.

It is clear, therefore, that internal marketing is concerned with more than treating the employee as a customer; it means that the organisation should constantly endeavour to develop programmes and strategies for enhancing employee satisfaction in much the same way as external marketing plans which are continuously updated and improved to meet external customer demands.

3. THE ROLE OF INTERNAL MARKETING

If it is possible to ensure that the staff of a firm:

- are committed to the goal of guaranteeing the best possible treatment of customers
- are motivated
- see themselves participating actively in achieving the organisation's goals

and if internal marketing is the key to this, then the potential for long-term success is evident.

Customer service is the critical element which internal marketing influences, whatever business or industry the organisation operates in, and customer service is one of the most crucial aspects of an organisation's competitive advantage.

Internal marketing is attracting increasing attention and growing recognition as an implementation tool for adoption by all organisations. The most advanced systems for developing marketing plans and strategies are worthless if the plan fails at the implementation stage. There are a number of areas where internal marketing can play a key role:

Management of change, where internal marketing may be used to place, and gain acceptance of new systems such as the introduction of information technology and new working practices, and other changes.

Building corporate image, where internal marketing's role is to create awareness and appreciation of the company's aims and strengths – as all employees are potential company ambassadors.

Strategic internal marketing which aims at reducing inter-departmental and inter-functional conflict and developing the co-operation and commitment needed to make external marketing strategies work.

4. COMPONENTS OF INTERNAL MARKETING PROGRAMMES

How is internal marketing to be implemented? It is essential to explore what are seen to be the fundamental criteria for a successful internal marketing programme, and to identify the components of programme formulation.

The four most important areas within the organisation's internal environment which are essential to an internal marketing programme can be described as:

Motivation
Co-ordination
Information
Education

This set of ideas clearly interlinks with the perspectives of internal marketing discussed earlier, but what steps can be taken to ensure these areas are rein-forced? To formulate any programme an analysis of the critical components must be undertaken. This may involve information gathering to assess

Employee knowledge
Attitudes
Behaviour.

Once this has been done, management action needs to cover:

Selection
Training

Motivation
Direction.

In this way, managers can help employees to make a more effective contribution to the organisation's marketing objectives, providing overall guidance and support for the internal marketing programme. Communication should reach all employees and include all messages about information and action in order to achieve increased motivation and effectiveness.

5. MANAGEMENT APPROACHES TO SUCCESSFUL INTERNAL MARKETING

It is important that management embrace the underlying philosophy of internal marketing if they are to develop and direct successful programmes. Managers should lead by example, and set high standards of customer relations and job effectiveness by their own good practice, not by simply dictating rules or making unreasonable demands on employees.

It has been stated earlier that internal marketing is closely related to the area of human resource management within the organisation. However, whereas a traditional view of human resource management may be seen as 'getting things done through people', internal marketing moves towards an alternative idea – developing human potential so that organisational goals can be achieved through the satisfaction of individual goals.

Employee commitment and loyalty cannot necessarily be bought on an economic basis alone. Equally important is a clear and visible long-run programme which really does put the customer first, whether in the internal or external marketplace. Consistency on the part of management, both in action and word, in all dealings with internal and external customers is the foundation for marketing success.

6. INTERNAL MARKETING PLANNING

As internal marketing has been developed directly from conventional marketing theory, and the marketing concept, it is argued that internal marketing planning is therefore made simple. There should be no difficulty in taking conventional marketing planning tools and developing internal marketing programmes along the same lines.

Adopting this method would mean that for every marketing mix decision, for example, which the company took for its external marketing strategy, there would be a corresponding internal marketing mix decision. This would, in turn, affect the outcome of the external marketing strategy which may lead to new marketing mix decisions being implemented both internally and externally.

The main criticism of this approach might be that it seems to assume that, for any organisation, the internal and external markets (or customers) will behave in a similar fashion and can therefore be treated in an almost identical manner. But this is not likely to be the case, for the following reasons:

Changing external markets
Internal market characteristics

Changing external markets Many firms operate in more than one market, and these markets can be very different indeed. Even segments within the same market can have individual and distinctive characteristics. This means that most firms will have external marketing plans, which are continuously being monitored and 'fine-tuned' to changing market conditions, whilst the internal market may be changing either more slowly or at greater speed.

Internal market characteristics Organisational behaviour theory and research may suggest that internal markets in firms of similar size and structure, regardless of what product or service they provide, may be more closely aligned in terms of their behaviour and needs, than the internal markets of all firms operating in one particular external marketplace, which may be widely differing in all aspects.

The answer could be to focus on the overall external strategy (sustained growth, total quality, market development, etc.), and then find a way of developing the internal market so that it will provide optimum levels of support and commitment to the success of the strategy. In order to do this well, the internal market should be researched and approached as a special and unique entity, and internal marketing programmes will reflect this without necessarily matching closely the external plans and activities.

7. DEVELOPING INTERNAL MARKETING PROGRAMMES

Internal marketing has an important role to play in the acceptance and subsequent implementation of marketing plans. But what is the process for the implementation of internal marketing? Should service organisations look beyond traditional planning concepts for internal markets?

Recommended internal marketing methods and planning tools to assist managers in their course of action are vitally important, and this whole area has been the focus of a great deal of interest recently, both among academics and practitioners. There is no single methodology to meet all internal marketing needs but it is possible to develop a planning framework of internal marketing at this stage.

A number of key components of internal marketing programme formulation have been discussed. An action plan for implementing internal marketing encompasses the following stages:

Market definition
Market research
Market segmentation
Marketing action

Marketing communication
Marketing orientation

The successful implementation of internal marketing within the organisation hinges on integration, co-ordination and co-operation within the internal market. To achieve this, it is essential to study and fully understand the characteristics of the organisation's internal markets. Accordingly, the action plan starts at that point:

Market definition

The internal market should be clearly defined to ensure that providers and receivers of internal services can identify with the concept of internal customers, whose needs require satisfaction. Each player is participating in, and serving, a clearly defined market. This may be across the whole organisation, or reflect inter- and intra-departmental relationships and activities. The structure of the market is important, with attention being paid to both formal and informal lines of communication and power.

Market research

Information should be continuously collected and analysed at all levels in the organisation. This contributes to the identification of opportunities both internally and externally. It must be both compatible with external research activities and contribute in the same manner to decision-making. The internal market should itself be researched to explore issues which are likely to affect the successful implementation of internal marketing programmes and individual roles and responsibilities. Subjects for research may include:

- Employee attitudes towards the organisation and its mission
- Levels of job satisfaction
- Assessing skill and knowledge needs
- Needs and wants of employees

Market segmentation

This is necessary to ensure most effective, accurate and appropriate targeting of internal marketing efforts. Bases for segmentation may be determined as a result of the market research but may include, for example, level in organisation. The best route for segmenting the internal market may not be by existing department/line management divisions as this can lead to a less unified approach. Internal marketing should be viewed as a means of reducing potential communication problems or friction between different functional areas.

Marketing action

This involves the selection and implementation of appropriate marketing activities to achieve optimum internal marketing success. Better internal communications, teamwork and employee empowerment are some of the aims of internal marketing. Practical initiatives to achieve these aims need to be worked out and assigned to individuals and management teams. Customer care programmes and staff training and development are some of the methods available.

Marketing communication

Accurate and timely spreading of marketing information should be undertaken, both internally and externally. This process should be targeted to encourage participation in achievement of personal and organisational goals. In-house magazines, regular team briefings and encouragement of better two-way communications are the sorts of approaches which are helpful.

Marketing orientation

The overall aim should be to create an internal environment which is flexible and responsive, and which nurtures common values and behaviour which reflect the organisation's goals. The organisation's marketing objectives and mission must be made clear to all emplyees, and clearly defined individual goals set down to enable personnel to see their own contribution to achieving the organistion's objectives.

8. IMPLEMENTING THE PLAN

Implementing internal marketing programmes can be achieved through co-operation between top management within the organisation and functional managers. It requires a flexible approach which will lead to an internal environment which is both committed to organisational goals and responsive to changing organisational needs. The changing needs of employees must also be taken into account.

Marketing management should work with human resources management to develop a plan for action, as they will have the specialised knowledge and insight necessary to operationalise the stages outlined above. It should be emphasised, however, that responsibility for implementing the plan lies with all managers and employees throughout the organisation.

Taking a marketing planning framework, the internal marketing plan can be viewed as follows:

Marketing audit Carry out a marketing audit of the internal market, paying particular attention to the areas highlighted previously.
Marketing analysis Conduct an analysis of the internal market in terms of its strengths, weaknesses, opportunities and threats.
Objectives setting Review the organisation's objectives in the light of internal marketing and develop internal objectives
Strategy development Strategic options relating to the internal market need to be examined. Enhanced customer service may be attainable through better training or greater staff empowerment, for example.

Designing action programmes This can be undertaken by managers to determine the most appropriate courses of action and the likely costs and resources required. PR managers may assist in developing a staff magazine, for example, while human resources management can develop training programmes.

Assigning responsibility for their execution This is the area which needs to be looked at from a company-wide perspective, and action plans should be broken down into their core components for implementation by the most appropriate individuals.

Monitoring and controlling the plan Some measures need to be determined to establish the success levels of internal marketing programmes. These must be established alongside the programme objectives. Some aspects may be incorporated into staff performance evaluation and appraisal schemes, for example, while others may be monitored according to reduced levels of customer complaints or better quality levels.

The planning framework illustrated should represent a dynamic flow process: as situations arise within the internal market place, and changes take place within the internal environment, management will respond and the plan may be fine-tuned as it evolves. The internal environment should foster an atmosphere which is both flexible and responsive; this is most important. Within today's ever-changing external environment it becomes even more so. The Institute of Management in the UK undertook a major research initiative to look at the future for business organisations through the 1990s, and concluded in its published report that:

> "In today's demanding business environment an organisation needs to be responsive and flexible if it is to survive. It must continually adapt to changing situations and requirements."

In order to meet these demands (and this does not only apply to British organisations), a service organisation depends more and more upon its people. If all personnel are:

- actively participating in the firm's overall strategy
- given every opportunity to develop their full potential
- keen to understand and believe in the firm's goals

the chances of success must be high. They will be prepared and equipped to be flexible and responsive. The costs of implementing internal marketing programmes throughout the organisation can be high. This should not prevent internal marketing from being given high priority. The potential costs of failed external marketing strategies are far higher.

9. SUMMARY

Internal marketing is based on the notion of communicating with internal markets as well as external markets – treating employees like customers. It

92

affords recognition to the vital role of people within the service organisation and represents a means of involving staff at all levels in effective marketing through the application of the marketing concept internally.

Internal marketing encompasses a number of elements, all of which help contribute towards enhanced customer service and a greater degree of marketing orientation within the organisation. These elements include:

Training programmes
Internal communications
Motivational programmes

For internal marketing to be successful it requires careful attention and planning. An action plan for implementing internal marketing encompasses the following stages:

Market definition
Market research
Market segmentation
Marketing action
Marketing communication
Marketing orientation

A marketing planning framework can be developed for internal marketing which needs co-operation from top management and employees throughout the organisation; it should not be the sole responsibility of marketing management.

Progress test 8

1. Why did the internal marketing concept originate in the area of services marketing?

2. What is the key element which links the marketing concept with internal marketing?

3. Describe how internal marketing has links with human resources management.

4. What areas are essential to an internal marketing programme?

5. In what ways can the behaviour or attitudes of management influence successful internal marketing programmes?

6. Should internal marketing planning within an organisation be just the same as external marketing planning? Give reasons to support your answer.

7. Successful implementation of internal marketing within the organisation hinges on certain factors. These are?

8. Outline the stages in the internal marketing action plan.

9. Explain the idea behind the planning framework, and what it can help to achieve.

Discussion

1. To what extent are you aware of internal marketing in your organisation, or any organisation that you know of?

2. How would you set up and implement internal marketing within an organisation? Who do you think would be the key decision makers/ influencers?

9

RELATIONSHIP MARKETING

INTRODUCTION

Marketing is continually evolving in response to the changing environment. New strategies, techniques and tools for marketing managers are constantly being developed. This book has demonstrated how many areas which were not traditionally associated with marketing, such as the not-for-profit sector, have increasingly become the focus of marketing attention.

Marketing has also moved away from the original idea of bringing about mutually satisfying benefits or exchanges. Societal marketing, for instance, addresses a wider need – in societal marketing, the exchange should result in benefits to society as well as the organisation and its customers.

Green marketing, following the trend towards environmentalism which is growing through concern for the world's resources, suggests that no marketing decision should be undertaken without regard to the possible long-term effects. Product design, packaging, manufacturing process and distribution decisions are examples of the issues influenced by 'green' thinking.

Consumers have responded to these changes and have become more sophisticated in their demands and expectations. They are prepared to seek out products which are more environmentally friendly, for example, and will think twice before investing money in a bank which invests in countries or industries which are politically and environmentally unsound, in societal terms.

Services marketing is also a growing speciality, and concepts such as internal marketing have been developed within the services sector, but are now widely recognised to be highly relevant to all organisations. Internal marketing calls upon the organisation to have equal regard for its internal customers – the employees – as for its external markets. Internal marketing programmes can enhance employee and customer satisfaction through increased involvement between all members of the organisation in its marketing efforts.

Relationship marketing goes a step further. Organisations are urged to focus not only on their relationship with customers – external and internal – but with other elements within industry and society which can impact on the organisation's long-term success. The emphasis too is not on bringing about exchange processes, but on building relationships. Quality service is the key to customer retention through customer satisfaction. Customers who keep coming back for more is the goal; zero defections rather than zero defects.

1. BUILDING RELATIONSHIPS

The key focus of marketing has always been the market – customer needs and wants. However, there are many other influences on an organisation's marketing activity. In conducting a SWOT (strengths, weaknesses, opportunities and threats) analysis, an organisation must consider these micro-environmental factors. As well as the organisation itself, and its internal and external markets, its publics must be considered. An organisation's publics include:

Suppliers
Intermediaries and other channel members
The government and its agencies
Shareholders
Community groups
Affiliated trade and professional associations
Trade unions
Banks and finance houses
Consumer groups

The aim in relationship marketing is to build and maintain relationships with all the organisation's publics. The list given is not comprehensive, and some publics will obviously have more influence over a particular firm's activities than others. The task is to identify those groups which are the main influencers and to design marketing programmes and strategies which take the influencers into account.

Relationships with channel members

Out of all the influencers discussed above, a particular group merits special attention when it comes to building relationships. This set of publics interact directly with the organisation at the input and output stages. They are co-operators in the business activity. They are all channel members and they represent both the supply side and the distribution side. Some sources focus solely on supplier markets but channel members such as intermediaries and agents in the distribution market can have an equal impact on an organisation.

If fully integrated channels are the most efficient (where a single organisation operates at every channel level), then it is obvious that, where full integration is not possible, relationships must be developed within the channel. Even in services marketing, where channels may not exist to the same degree, this is vital. Package tour operators must have positive relationships with their suppliers (hotels and airlines, for example) and with their distributors (travel agents). Financial organisations must have confidence in brokers who trade in their services. Restaurants, hairdressers, auto-service stations and hotels must be on good terms with their suppliers to be able to operate effectively.

The objective of relationship building with these groups is to develop co-operation and co-ordination between all the parties who can impact on the overall satisfaction of the ultimate consumer. Quality of service delivery is paramount, and suppliers and channel members play a major role in service quality.

Relationships with customers

Relationship marketing is also about building relationships with customers, rather than creating exchange processes. Customer contact should be maintained after the sale has been completed, and the focus is on retaining customers, rather than simply trying to attract new ones.

North West Securities, a financial services company specialising in consumer credit, telephones every one of its credit customers three or four times a year. This telephone contact is used to check that the customer is still satisfied with the service they are receiving, and to update them with details of new services available. A 'freefone' number is given to customers who can use it to call any time, free of charge. They aim to maintain a high customer retention rate.

Car manufacturers and dealers have long recognised the value of this type of after-sales marketing. Existing customers are invited to social events when new models are launched, and are contacted periodically by dealers anxious to maintain a 'front of mind' relationship. Manufacturers actually employ sales and marketing professionals to develop innovative after-sales strategies to increase customer retention.

Insurance companies developed this kind of relationship in the days when the 'Insurance Man' – the representative – used to call on all his customers every week to collect payment. It was not unusual for the Insurance Man to become a family friend, and he was guaranteed all the family's insurance business, from life and savings policies through to pensions and funeral policies. Personal contact is still of critical importance in this market.

Referral markets

Another important influence on an organisation's performance is the level of business (or activity) arising from referrals. This is especially important in services marketing where 'word of mouth' recommendation can be a key factor in the consumer decision process. Frequently, referrals are informal – through family or friends, for example – but often they are more formal, as in industrial markets where specifiers (who may be from outside the client organisation) play a major part in buying decisions. Architects or consultants are often cast in the role of specifier when they advise their client where to source materials and services.

In consumer markets, formal referrals exist in many forms. The first-time buyer in the housing market may well take their estate agent's advice on which mortgage company to approach, and which solicitor to use. Travel agencies recommend which holiday tour operator will meet a customer's requirements. Insurance agents put forward the best policies for their clients.

Most organisations will find that a proportion of their customers come to them via a referral of some kind. For this reason, it is important to direct some marketing activity towards the members of the referral market – the specifiers – wherever possible. This is already done in many formal referral situations, where insurance agents and travel agents receive commission and other incentives to ensure their support. The pharmaceutical industry spends massive amounts on promoting their products to doctors who act as specifiers.

Where referrals are largely informal, however, it can still be possible to use innovative methods to develop this area. Health clubs invite members to introduce their friends for a trial session. If the friend takes out a subscription, the existing member receives some incentive, such as free sunbed sessions. The British Benefit Society (a Friendly Society specialising in savings and loans) offers small cash gifts to members who recruit further members. Existing customers can be the best source of referrals there is, *provided that they are themselves experiencing high levels of satisfaction with the service they have received*. This demonstrates again the potential power of relationship marketing.

Internal markets

Relationship marketing may go further than internal marketing but it still retains a very clear focus on the needs and wants of the internal market. Specially formulated internal marketing programmes to communicate, train and motivate internal market members are very important if the relationship is to be a positive one.

Relationship marketing places the emphasis on building *and maintaining* a good workforce. Service quality depends to a very great extent on people, and developing long-term relationships with internal customers is just as important as building relationships with external ones.

Service organisations, in particular, have to pay special attention to recruitment of quality personnel. Recruiting the individuals of the right calibre is not always easy, especially under the current demographic changes being experienced in the UK (and other areas) today. Recent forecasts show that by the end of the 1990s the demand for graduates will far outstrip the supply.

Evidence also suggests that prospective employees, like consumers, are becoming more sophisticated in their demands. A 1990 survey of marketing, administration and personnel professionals showed that in choosing a firm to work for, a socially responsible image and 'green' policies were the most important factors.

Organisations need therefore to communicate with prospective employees – the employee market. Building relationships with the employee market, especially through long-term positive visibility on the graduate recruitment scene, for example, can help to ensure the future well-being of the organisation.

In summary, relationship marketing is concerned with building long-term relationships rather than bringing about exchange processes. It is customer and market orientated, but it identifies a number of 'markets' which the organisation needs to understand and relate to. The organisation must design and implement strategies and programmes for successful relationship marketing. The markets which need to be addressed are as follows:

Customer – existing and potential
Internal markets
Influencers
Referral markets
Channel markets – supply and distribution
Potential employees

2. RELATIONSHIP MARKETING MANAGEMENT

Relationship marketing strategy development is really no different to marketing strategy generally except that there should be a clear directional focus on relationship building throughout the formulation of strategic plans. A strategic focus is important for any successful marketing organisation, and, as stated earlier, relationship marketing just goes a step further. This section provides an overview of strategic planning in relationship marketing:

Objectives setting
The mission
SWOT analysis
Market analysis and segmentation
Strategy formulation
Developing the relationship marketing mix

The major objective in relationship marketing is quality, because relationships cannot be sustained if there are any problems with quality. This is particularly applicable to services marketing, where delivery of quality service is most important.

The mission

The starting point in strategic planning is the mission statement, and this provides a centralised strategic focus for the organisation. An organisation which is committed to relationship marketing will develop a mission which reflects this through a focus on shared values and people-based goals. Customer and employee loyalty, even specific statements about customer confidence in making recommendations, are some of the key ideas which the mission statement should include in relationship marketing. It is very easy to relate these ideas to services marketing.

Customer service should play a key role in the organisation's mission statement. This can help the mission to become something that is 'owned' by everybody in the organisation because it reflects the role that all employees can play in customer service. The mission statement should be accessible to everyone in the company.

SWOT analysis

The next step in the strategic planning process is the SWOT analysis. This will cover the broad areas of the company's macro- and micro-environments, but will look in greater depth into the six market areas identified previously. An in-depth internal examination of the organisation should be undertaken to assess strengths and weaknesses. The internal market analysis will also contribute to this.

The competitive environment must be thoroughly examined, and the relationship with competitors. This will tend to follow the industry structure, and other major competitive factors such as the degree of rivalry and barriers to entry.

Strategies relating to competitors, while not actually relationship building in the same sense as relationship marketing, should focus on co-operation and avoid devaluing the industry or service market sector. Competitors can work co-operatively to develop markets, and this should be the aim. The objective of this analysis is to identify opportunities and threats.

Market analysis and segmentation

The next state in the strategic process is market analysis and segmentation. In relationship marketing, this should include, as far as possible, analysis of the six market groups identified earlier. These groups might then be segmented so that the organisation can focus on means of tailoring the relationship to the specific needs of different groups. Not all of the market groups will be addressed by formal marketing programmes – some segments may require more informal communication to build and maintain the relationship.

Internal markets should be analysed and segmented as part of this process. There are a number of ways of segmenting internal markets, and these tend to be organisation-specific. Researching the internal market will help in determining the best way to segment it.

Strategy formulation

Once the macro-environmental analysis and internal review have been completed, objective setting is the next step. Management then need to select the strategic options which will provide the greatest chance of successfully achieving the organisation's goals.

Developing the relationship marketing mix

It is in the marketing programme formulation that relationship marketing can be seen to be put into effect. In services marketing, this will focus on the seven P's:

Product
Price
Promotion
Place
People
Process
Physical evidence

The marketing mix must be tailored to each of the six markets previously identified, although the various elements of the mix will be used to a lesser or greater degree in the different cases. The product, or service offering, will be present mainly in the customer market, except when it is also used in or offered to the referral market. The promotional mix is the one most likely to be targeted to each market segment.

Relationship marketing can be used to differentiate the product or service in the perception of the consumer. This enables the organisation to undertake product (or service) positioning. Quality service, in particular, stemming from consistent and supportive relationships can be a very useful tool for positioning.

3. QUALITY AND RELATIONSHIP MARKETING

Throughout this chapter it must be clear that relationship marketing has as its central strategic focus the role of quality. By improving and developing relationships with the six key markets through the design and implementation of formal organisational plans and systems (rather than leaving the relationship aspects to chance) quality becomes integral to the organisation's activities.

In services marketing where the service delivery is the fundamental measure of quality, and where people are the service providers, developing relationships through people helps build quality into the service.

Relationship marketing goes beyond internal marketing in this context, and it also builds on other advancements in quality such as Total Quality Management (TQM). There are a number of ways in which systematic relationship building can help increase service quality levels.

Increased customer contact – it should not only be the job of field service staff to visit customers. Relationship marketing should allow for more customer contact (and on a more regular basis) between the customer and the organisation on many levels. The relationship can be helped enormously be allowing non-frontline staff to mix with their opposite number, for example on the customer organisation staff; customer conferences and focus groups can present an excellent forum for feedback and new ideas.

Enhanced customer service – increased (but not necessarily more expensive) communications with customer groups can enhance customer service. Regular updates, progress reports and newsletters can be amongst the simplest and most effective forms of communication. Acknowledgement of orders and documents, together with brief but courteous notes if the service delivery is to be delayed at all, can help raise perceptions of service. In legal practices, for example, cases can drag on for years, and end up being very expensive so there is an enormous bill to settle at the end. In relationship marketing, the client would be regularly updated on any news (and also if there was no news which can be as important), and the bill could be negotiated and spread over the duration of the case. This would solve two of the major complaints from consumers: that they are 'left in the dark' while waiting for the outcome of their case, and that the final bill is always too high.

4. CUSTOMER RETENTION

As well as quality, the other key aspect of relationship marketing is customer retention. Loyal customers who keep on re-purchasing are extremely valuable.

Compared with the cost of attracting new customers through advertising, sales promotion and other means, any effective method of retaining existing customers who will continue to spend money with the organisation must be important.

A number of tools can assist in the process. An example of this is *database marketing* where customer-buying histories and other information can be listed on a database, and then referenced and cross-referenced in the future to target new products or promotions accurately.

Another important aspect of the task of analysing how to retain customers is to carry out market research amongst customers who have defected. Why did they go to a competitor? Why have they stopped using your service? The answers to these questions can hold vital information for services marketing managers.

Research is important to establish why customers defect, as studies have shown that a large proportion of dissatisfied customers never complain – they simply stop using the service. By the same token, customer complaints handling procedures should be properly carried out to ensure that

- the complaint is rectified and the customer is satisfied
- the necessary action is taken to prevent that problem occurring again.

5. SUMMARY

The relationship can be seen to be the core focus for the organisation seeking to enhance customer service and marketing orientation through relationship marketing. Relationship marketing does embrace marketing concepts which have evolved during the latter half of this century; and it takes them further.

As customer sophistication increases, organisations are having to communicate far more, and more widely than before, especially with regard to environmental or societal issues. Putting this communication into the context of relationship marketing makes sense. The idea behind relationship marketing is to build relationships with the organisation's publics – or, at least, those groups which are the main influencers, for example:

Relationships with channel members
Relationships with customers and potential customers
Referral markets
Internal markets and potential employees
Influencers

Customer retention is a key focus of relationship marketing as well as quality and enhanced customer service. Relationship marketing is especially relevant to services marketing, as noted earlier, and to particular areas within services marketing. Not-for-profit organisations and charities who serve two distinct markets in donors and clients – and who are answerable both to the public and to bodies such as grants boards, trust funds and governing committees with regard to their undertakings – should adopt and develop relationship marketing within their programmes.

Progress test 9

1. What should organisations focus on, according to relationship marketing?

2. List examples of a company's publics.

3. Explain what is meant by the following:
   referral markets
   channel members

4. Why is building and maintaining a good workforce seen as important in relationship marketing?

5. Outline the stages in relationship marketing planning.

6. In what ways can systematic relationship building help increase service quality levels?

7. What is meant by database marketing?

8. How should customer complaints handling procedures be carried out?

Discussion

1. Consider the examples given of ways in which organisations try to build and maintain customer contact after the sale has been completed. Can you think of other examples, based on your experiences as a consumer, or suggest possible approaches an organisation might use?

2. Is 'zero defections' a realistic goal for relationship marketing? What can relationship marketing achieve that is not covered already by other developments in marketing?

10

SERVICE QUALITY

INTRODUCTION

Service quality is of crucial importance to both customers and service providers. Organisations are becoming increasingly aware of the importance of quality in maintaining competitive advantage. Total Quality Management has been a buzzword for business during the last decade, and the whole issue of quality has received massive attention in business and academic circles. Consumers have grown more aware of quality, and consumer 'watchdog' associations have emerged to monitor service quality in many areas.

Consumer complaints about quality in major public service sectors such as telecommunications or travel are widely publicised in the Press. Complaints reported in the early 1990s by the Central Transport Consultative Committee (the official rail users' watchdog committee in the UK) include the following:

- A passenger being overcharged by varying amounts every week for the same journey
- A young boy requiring hospital treatment after being crushed on an overcrowded train
- As many as three out of four trains running late on certain routes and up to thirty trains cancelled each day
- Journeys regularly taking twice as long as the specified duration which force passengers to wait in overcrowded, unclean carriages.

Clearly these problems are service-centred and reflect grave cause for concern. British Rail is not the only organisation which receives a large number of complaints, by any means, but the incidents highlighted above occurred in the period when British Rail launched its much-publicised Passengers' Charter, designed to foster enhanced customer service.

The role of marketing in developing quality service is an important one. The needs and expectations of customers are critical factors in assessing service quality. A marketing and customer orientation throughout the organisation can ensure that service providers get close to their customers, thus ensuring that service delivery meets customer expectations. Perceived service quality is explored in this chapter together with programmes for improving service quality.

1. QUALITY DEFINED

There are many definitions of quality, and in many senses quality is subjective. To many people, quality implies luxury or excellence; a Rolls Royce rather than a Ford; cordon bleu instead of fast food. However, quality can also be measured in terms of fitness for purpose, and a Ford Escort is regarded by many owners as a quality family car, while McDonalds provide a quality fast food service.

In seeking quality service, consumer needs and expectations may differ. An elderly customer in a bank might appreciate a cashier who takes time to chat and who addresses the customer in a familiar way, while a business customer might expect to be spoken to in a professional manner and the transaction to be completed as efficiently and quickly as possible. Yet the functional service required in each instance may be identical, from the same cashier.

In manufacturing, quality is seen as an element which can be gauged precisely and measured in terms of conformance to specification. Quality control was applied at the end of the manufacturing process when units were checked for quality and defective units rejected. This has changed now to the extent that the emphasis is in building quality into the manufacturing process; quality of supplied materials, quality of production processes and quality assurance procedures mean that quality is built-in, rather than poor quality being filtered out at the finished goods stage. This built-in quality is still measured in terms of conformance to what are, largely, internally developed specifications which can themselves be constrained by cost and productivity considerations.

Service quality is not easy to measure in a precise manner. The nature and characteristics of services can have an impact on quality issues:

The **intangibility** of many services means that it can be very difficult for service quality to be measured and assessed.
Inseparability of the service itself from the service provider highlights the role of people in the service transaction, and their influence on quality levels.
The **heterogeneous** nature of service means that a service is never exactly repeated and will always be variable to some extent.
The **perishable** nature of services can lead to customer dissatisfaction if demand cannot be met (if a hotel room or air ticket is not available at the time a customer demands it, for example).

The most relevant approach in defining and measuring service is the user-based approach. The idea that quality is subjective and will be strongly linked to the individual's needs and expectations recognises that consumers have different criteria for judging service quality. This user-based approach equates quality with maximum levels of satisfaction.

In measuring quality in this way, however, a distinction needs to be drawn between quality of service delivery and the service output, or benefit. The customer may be involved in the service production, thus impacting on the quality of the service delivery process. The actual output of the service may be judged by the customer in terms of their expectations of the outcome or benefit.

The customer's overall judgement of service quality can be an evaluation of both the process and the outcome, compared with the customer's own expectations and desired benefits. This leads to an important idea in assessing quality from a services marketing perspective: **perceived service quality**.

Perceived service quality represents the customer's judgement of an organisation's service based on their overall experience of the service encounter. Understanding *how* customers arrive at this judgement – that is to say, how they decide whether or not they are satisfied with a particular service – is very important for services marketing management.

Research has indicated that consumers make these decisions using a number of key criteria to judge the service. These key factors relate to areas covered by the extended services marketing mix: people, process and physical evidence. They can be broadly categorised as follows:

People

- credibility, professionalism, efficiency, courtesy
- approachability, accessibility, good communications,
- identifying and understanding customers needs

Process

- timekeeping, dependability, trusted performance levels
- promptness, efficiency

Physical evidence

- appearance of tangible aspects of the service,
- physical surroundings, smartness

This list illustrates some of the criteria used by customers in judging quality. Understanding the concept of perceived service quality is important for services marketing management. The next section explores this further within the context of developing service quality.

2. DEVELOPING SERVICE QUALITY

The reasons why developing and delivering a quality service is so important can be broken down into three main areas:

- Organisations with a reputation for consistently high quality can sustain an enviable competitive advantage in the service marketplace.
- Quality is 'free' – that is to say getting it right first time costs far less than providing remedies when services fail to meet the customer's required standard.

- Better quality services can attract premium prices. Consumers are prepared to pay a higher price for services that fulfil all their expectation criteria.

Each of the above reasons for putting quality first can have a direct impact on profitability. However, in terms of image and customer or user satisfaction, they are equally applicable to organisations operating in the not-for-profit sector.

Assessing service quality

Determining what makes a quality service is not easy, and differences between service organisations mean that there is no single set of factors which can be classified to produce recognisable standards. Leisure services, financial services, education and medical services will all be judged on vastly different grounds. Services cover such a broad spectrum of activities, ranging from the highly tangible to the highly intangible, that universal regulation of quality standards is impractical.

However, the common element in service quality, whatever the service, is that quality is based on the customer's perception. With this in mind, it is important to note the features which all services share:

Customer participation Customers are frequently active participants in the service process – they co-produce the service.

Intangibility Highly intangible services may be based on philosophical or conceptual elements. This abstract nature of some services makes them difficult for the service provider to describe, and for the customer to evaluate.

The service encounter Services are often comprised of a number of component parts, and it is the sum of these, or the overall experience of the service encounter, which the customer will use to form judgements.

Inseparability Many specialised services are inseparable – the characteristics of the service provider in terms of expert knowledge or skill, for example, are a constituent part of the service quality.

Service is, perhaps most importantly, a process and it is this element which can be investigated and developed to meet specified standards. The Total Quality Management philosophy has for its main focus the interaction between people and systems. People are the critical ingredient in total quality, but in order to operate effectively, people require appropriate frameworks and systems.

3. QUALITY STANDARDS

Quality standards were originally developed within the context of production and manufacturing; the main concern was product quality and conformance. However, the development of systems to ensure performance quality now covers all functions, not just production and operations. Finance, administration and marketing all have an impact on the organisation's performance and customer satisfaction levels. Quality systems designed to reinforce performance in these areas focus on procedures and processes. These must attain certain quantifiable standards in order to gain approval.

There are now both national and international quality performance standards which show that organisations are implementing quality operations. The approved standards are identified as follows:

National: BS (British Standard) 5750
European: EN 29000
International: ISO 9000

BS 5750 was generally the first standard of its kind in the world. The British Standards Institute (BSI) spent many years developing the standard, and numerous steering committees took several years to generate the standards by which service could be measured. BSI literature at the time discusses the problems posed by the task, raising such questions as How do we put quality and its measurements in place for a service organisation? Is quality important to the customer or the vendor?

They suggest that it is important that quality is really that perceived by the customer, despite the fact that service may be said internally to have quality. Quality systems need to be set up in line with the BSI recommendations which, whilst appearing quite complex, can be broken down into more simplified areas. Quality should be functional, not restrictive, and should reflect the overall business (or business-like) activities of the organisation. The most important aspect for success is the commitment of everyone in the organisation, not some specified quality manager. The BSI proposed that quality is a team concept.

Marketing relates closely to this idea. Concepts such as internal marketing and relationship marketing, discussed in other chapters, focus clearly on the commitment and involvement of everyone in the organisation in implementing successful marketing plans and programmes. There is, in fact, a very strong link existing between marketing and Total Quality Management. Both have a customer needs-based philosophy, and many organisational issues are common to both. Marketing can play a significant role in quality.

Setting standards

The true definition of quality will be unique to every organisation as no two organisations will operate identical services marketing. Quality is situation-specific, and the parameters of what constitutes high quality can change over time. Market research needs to be undertaken to pinpoint exactly what makes a quality service experience – perceived service quality.

This market research should be undertaken in both the internal and external markets. This is most important as it can reveal *quality gaps*. Quality gaps occur when a shortfall arises between the customer's expectations and the service actually delivered. Quality gaps can be generated internally, as when managers do not fully understand what customers expect, or when they are not fully committed to tailoring the service to meet these expectations. Shortfalls in service quality can also arise when the performance of service delivery personnel fails to meet expectations.

A further cause of inadequate service quality can be when advertising or other external communications lead customers to expect a higher standard of service than that which is actually delivered. A dry cleaning company offering a two-hour service may create customer dissatisfaction if the time taken is three hours when, in reality, a same-day service may be perfectly acceptable to that particular customer. The service delivery must match the expectations of the customer at that point in time, and in relation to that particular transaction.

The quality audit

A good starting point for internal market research is the *quality audit*. In the same way as a marketing or environmental audit is carried out, the whole company and all the processes which go to make up the service offering must be investigated and analysed. The audit should cover all functions and departments, not merely frontline personnel.

The quality audit provides an assessment of what is currently happening within the organisation; market research should now be used to analyse how near (or far) the organisation is to getting it right – delivering the right service 'fit' through matching the service offering to the customers' expectations.

Internal market research can be carried out through focus groups or discussion sessions. It is probably best if these are held away from the normal working area and are conducted by interviewers or discussants who are not line management personnel. This should engender an atmosphere where participants feel able to discuss quality issues frankly and without inhibition.

A checklist for the types of issues which need to be raised in internal market research includes the following:

Internal service delivery

This recognises the fact that there are many parts which make up a service, and effective service delivery can depend on all of those parts combining together precisely. Besides service delivery personnel there are many other actors within a service organisation who facilitate the service delivery. These employees, in conjunction with front-line personnel, all need to consider the following questions:

- Who is your internal customer? How many internal customers/suppliers do you have?
- What are their needs?
- How does your interaction with internal customers in the organisation impact on the service quality perceived by the ultimate (external) customer?
- What problems exist, and how can you overcome them?
- What do you think the role of marketing should be?
- Do you think that we deliver exactly what we have promised to the customer? If so, how often? If not, why not?

- Do you think that improvements could be made in your area? In other areas? If so, how?
- Do you think that we should measure performance and/or quality? If so, how should this be done, and how often?

Internal service quality

The employees' own perceptions of the organisation's service quality must be examined in order to assess where potential quality gaps may arise. The following questions need to be addressed:

- How do you measure service quality?
- What are your/the organisation's (internal) standards for:
  excellent quality
  satisfactory quality
  poor quality?
- How do you know when you are achieving or failing to meet these standards? What processes for monitoring service quality exist?

Service delivery quality

Frontline personnel who are actually involved with customers in the service delivery process should consider issues relating to their understanding of service quality:

- What do you understand to be the customer's expectations from this service encounter?
- What can you do to ensure that customer expectations are met fully?
- Are you doing anything which has a negative effect on the quality of service delivery? Does anyone else in the organisation?
- Who is your favourite customer, and why?
- How often do you have interaction with a customer?

The results of this type of internal market research can only be utilised effectively if there is accurate information available on the needs and expectations of the external market. Market research to assess and measure customer expectations thoroughly is essential. Research must be designed to address the following issues:

- How do our customers judge the quality of service we provide?
- What is their judgement criteria?
- How do they compare the quality of our service with that of our competitors?
- What are the key differences that make our service quality better (or poorer) than our competitors?
- How, in the customer's view, can the quality of service we provide be improved?

Market research of this nature should be ongoing to reflect changing needs and expectations. As consumer sophistication increases and new services become available in the marketplace the criteria by which customers judge service quality will change. Market research programmes and the development of marketing information systems are covered in more detail in Chapter 5.

Market research techniques for assessing service quality expectations vary, but will depend on getting close to the customer and building an understanding of their perception of service quality. Many restaurants, hotels and other service providers routinely offer their customers the opportunity to give feedback on the service they have received by providing customer satisfaction questionnaires for the customer to complete each time the service is used.

Shops and retailers have customer service counters to deal with complaints, but in situations where the service is highly intangible it can be much more difficult to monitor customer satisfaction levels. High street shoppers will not hesitate to return goods which are unsatisfactory in any way, and customers who have received poor service from domestic trades people, for example, will be inclined to complain until they receive satisfaction. In cases, however, where services are far less tangible and customers are unhappy about the service they have received they may be unwilling to complain for a number of reasons:

Embarrassment – customers may feel embarrassed about complaining for a service which they feel dissatisfied with. Many people do not want to 'make a fuss' if they receive poor service from, say, a hairdresser or restaurant.

Lack of specialist knowledge – customers buying the services of a lawyer, an accountant or a hypnotherapist, for example, may feel that the service they have received is not up to their expectations, but do not feel qualified themselves to take the service practitioner to task.

Level of substitutability – if there are many service providers offering a particular service, then a customer who is not satisfied may find it simpler to change service providers than to complain.

Substitution – swapping service providers when a service is not of satisfactory quality can result from any of the issues outlined above. On the other hand, research has shown that customers who *do* complain and then receive a positive response from the service provider which leads to customer satisfaction will be *more* inclined to use that service provider in the future. If one of the key factors in long-term success is customer retention, then it is vital that customer satisfaction be maintained, and customers are given the opportunity to discuss their service experiences.

Research along the lines discussed will enable the service provider to establish what makes up service quality in their business. Quality gaps – where the employees' understanding of what constitutes quality falls short of customer expectations – can be investigated and training or better communications implemented internally. In summary, the organisation's approach to developing service quality standards and implementing quality practice can be represented by a seven point plan:

- *Internal and external research*
  what do customers really want and value?

- *Listening*
  to what customers and employees feel about performance against these factors
- *Evaluation*
- *Action*
- *Monitoring*
- *Improving and building*
- *Motivating*

4. BENCHMARKING

The organisation which has fully researched quality issues in both its internal and external markets should now be in a position to set quality standards which can be regulated and monitored and which meet customer requirements. In order to do this, standard measures need to be determined. This section looks at how this can be achieved through benchmarking.

The establishment of a baseline figure and a common index is an essential part of measuring performance, both externally and internally. The baseline is the target operating norm of the organisation. This can be termed a benchmark – a standard against which performance can be measured.

This should take into account the standards against which competitors will operate and should reflect optimum quality standards within the competitive environment. This may also mean taking into account the standards set by indirect competitors as well as organisations offering the same services.

This would mean, for example, that airlines would not only gauge their benchmark standards by looking at other airlines' quality standards, but also by considering the services offered by the railways and other alternative forms of travel and comparisons with their service quality.

Studying best practice amongst organisations which are non-competing (either directly or indirectly) can also help in achieving the objective of being the best – outperforming other organisations in the marketplace. Collaboration with non-competing firms based on sharing expertise in areas in which the organisations excel can lead to mutual benefits.

Knowledge and experience regarding best practice can be shared, and this is likely to be more reliable and open than information sought concerning the competitions' best practice. The idea of synergy can operate here as well; management from very different types of organisations, possibly in completely different industries, may be able to find solutions and new ideas from each others' viewpoints which they could not find in their own experience or within their own organisation.

The benchmark standards will be adjusted over time to reflect the achievement of increasingly higher standards through enhanced process quality and in response to new customer expectation levels. An index, which is a common scoring or weighting system which takes into account the different characteristics of the subject for measurement, should also be developed. This will enable service providers to measure performance and quality between different sized branches or based on newness of service activity in a particular market sector, for example.

The actual values assigned to benchmarks will be situation-specific. They will be developed as a result of the research carried out by a particular organisation. The key focus will be the same in any situation, however; the service delivery process and all the activities which go into it will be examined and broken down into component parts for which measurable targets, or benchmarks, can be set.

This may translate quite simply into measures derived from variables which impact on the service encounter. Response time is one factor which impacts on service quality, and which is controllable by the service provider. Examples of standards or benchmarks based on response time variables include the following:

- Time taken to answer telephone enquiries – Automatic Call Distribution systems can ensure that all calls are answered within a certain number of rings, and that calls are then managed efficiently.
- Queuing systems designed to ensure that all customers are served within an 'acceptable' time.
- Response time to assist motorists in difficulty – the National Breakdown organisation guarantees that assistance will arrive within one hour of the problem being reported.

Benchmarks can be created for all the component parts of an organisation's operations. The examples discussed above relate to just one area – response times. Some examples of the areas within an organisation for which benchmarks can be established are as follows:

Sales force: Call-to-order ratios, training, size, customer retention.

Administration: Response times to written/telephone enquiries, quality of materials and literature used, training, expertise on both company and range of services.

Resources: Implementation and management of systems, premises utilisation, staff development.

Finance: Profitability levels, return on investment, costs reduction.

This list is not comprehensive and it will, in practice, be made up of areas identified as being of the greatest importance in enabling the organisation to out-perform others in the marketplace. Specific variables can be defined following analysis of the competitive arena, and the criteria used by customers in their own judgement of service quality. Benchmarking in this way will enable the organisation to build in service quality, and to fine-tune its market offering so that all customer quality standards are met or exceeded.

5. IMPLEMENTING QUALITY SERVICE

Marketing management can play a key role in achieving quality service throughout the organisation. Service quality is contingent on a highly developed customer orientation, and on meeting or exceeding the customer's expectations. It has already been shown that market research must be carried out both internally and externally in order to establish service quality standards – benchmarks – by which the organisation can measure and assess its performance.

Internal marketing has a key role to play, too. Quality in service organisations is largely inseparable from the service delivery, so the key focus in service quality is on people. Quality results from a team effort; a customer-consciousness which permeates through all levels of the organisation, from top management down. Internal marketing is concerned with people in organisations and effective internal marketing programmes address the issues which impact on quality.

Two of the most important components of internal marketing which are critical for any organisation seeking to implement quality service are:

Communication
Training

Perceived service quality, the customer's individual evaluation of their service experience with an organisation, derives from the values associated with both technical and functional service quality, and their relative importance. Technical quality and functional quality levels will depend on the implementation of service quality throughout the organisation. Good communication – both internal and external – and training of staff are critical factors in ensuring that quality performance standards are met.

Communication

Communication internally may need to be improved to ensure that there are no breakdowns in communication between the elements within the organisation which make up a particular service. Communications should be designed to foster co-ordination and integration, enabling employees to be responsive to their internal customers and suppliers.

Internal communications can also be a useful tool in engendering a team spirit and in motivating personnel. This can be very important in the drive for service quality. Management should ensure that every employee knows what the organisation's objectives are, what desired quality goals have been set and what their individual role is in achieving these targets.

Training

Training needs to be undertaken to develop employees' understanding of how they can deliver service quality. This training might include customer care programmes, and specific technical training to develop expertise in advising customers about the services offered. Training for personal development is also important, as motivation and job satisfaction are key elements in the provision and maintenance of quality service.

The links between service quality and marketing

Total Quality Management and marketing have very strong links within the organisation. Both share a customer-directed philosophy, and both focus on teamwork and commitment from all levels of the organisation. Managing service quality as outlined throughout this chapter combines the aims of marketing – meeting customer needs and expectations – with a framework for implementing quality which has similarities with Total Quality Management. Developments in internal marketing and relationship marketing combine to provide an approach which fosters integration and commitment to quality throughout the organisation.

The extent to which the organisation is 'doing it right' should be demonstrated by the findings of the internal and external research carried out. This will be an important factor in planning future programmes. If a quality gap is uncovered, then this will set clear pointers for areas where quality improvement programmes need to be implemented. Other measures of the degree to which quality improvements are needed will arise from the analysis of the competitive arena and from customer satisfaction and retention studies.

Information of this nature can be used in quality programme definition. With the emphasis on the people and process elements of the services marketing mix, frameworks can be developed to ensure quality service implementation. These frameworks should be rigorously defined so that the chance of anything going wrong in the service delivery process is minimised. On the other hand, they should allow for flexibility and scope for the personal approach where appropriate.

This idea brings service quality back to the marketing concept and the marketing mix. By fine-tuning all the elements of the marketing mix to the customer's needs and wants and ensuring that the customer receives the benefits and quality which they are seeking, organisations build in service quality to their marketing programmes. This should include both internal and external marketing programmes.

To summarise, the quality process for service organisations can be outlined as follows:

- Define and understand quality within the organisational context.
- Carry out market research, both internally and externally.
- Research the competitive arena.
- Develop organisational quality standards – Benchmarking.
- Identify where quality standards are being met/exceeded/not met.
- Develop a QUALITY STRATEGY to close quality gaps and build existing quality standards.
- Design programmes for implementation:
  procedures/frameworks
  training
  communications
- Implement service quality programme.
- Monitor and evaluate the programme and fine-tune where necessary.

Implementing the service quality programme is really only a starting point; the programme must then be monitored and evaluated and it should be continuously performance-tested. The use of benchmarks makes this possible. Developing service quality strategies and programmes should be a cyclical process so that standards are updated and changed whenever needed to continue to maintain competitive advantage.

6. MONITORING SERVICE QUALITY

There are a number of techniques which can be employed to monitor service quality. These fall largely into three main categories:

Internal performance analysis
Customer satisfaction analysis
Specialist market research

These areas will be discussed individually in this section; in practice a service organisation would develop monitoring and evaluation schemes based on a combination of these methods.

Internal performance analysis

Internal performance analysis will be undertaken by all organisations to measure the success of their planning, not necessarily relating solely to quality. Quality benchmarks will be used in the internal performance analysis to measure the quality standards being achieved in practice. Steps should be taken very quickly to rectify any shortfall in service quality and internal monitoring should be continuous.

Sales figures, and other internal reporting data which is not directly quality-based, should also be referred to in monitoring service quality. Customer retention levels are a key indicator to quality performance, while other figures can also represent trends which reflect quality issues. Staff at all levels should be involved in the monitoring process and should be encouraged to be proactive in identifying and resolving quality problems. Internal market research should also continue to ensure that no further quality gaps arise, and that staff are satisfied that all areas are working together for optimum service quality,

Customer satisfaction analysis

Organisations can use a number of methods to monitor customer satisfaction. Typically, this involves carrying out some sort of follow-up survey amongst customers who have used a service recently. National Breakdown, a motoring assistance organisation, sends its members a satisfaction questionnaire after every breakdown. The questionnaire invites the customer to comment on the service delivery, and to assess specific features, such as the response time and the action taken. British Telecom telephones new subscribers after they have had a telephone installed to ask how they would rate the service received. Many hotel chains leave guest questionnaires in rooms, or present them at the time of checkout, for guests to comment on service quality.

Focus group discussions and other market research techniques can be utilised to ask customers directly about their satisfaction with service quality. All these methods address the customer about satisfaction levels, but another very important element in quality analysis is monitoring the times when the customer addresses the organisation directly. In particular, it is important to monitor customer complaints.

Customer complaints should be monitored closely to see whether any trends are emerging, and the nature of the complaints. This is critical, especially when the vast majority of customers who have experienced dissatisfaction may not complain, but simply switch to another service provider. The number of complaints received may be much smaller than the total number of dissatisfied customers, and steps must be taken to rectify the problems notified.

Systems should be established therefore to carry out customer satisfaction analysis on a continuous basis. Market research, follow-up questionnaires and courtesy calls should be implemented, and a proper system for handling complaints set in place. A complaints handling system should not only ensure that complaints are dealt with speedily and positively, but also that the information regarding the complaint is fed back through the correct channels within the organisation, so that future decisions and actions can be taken on an informed basis, and any underlying problems ironed out.

Specialist market research

This type of research can involve a number of techniques, but perhaps the most common is the 'mystery shopper' technique. A mystery shopper – a trained market researcher – will visit the branches of the service provider and pose as an ordinary customer. They will assess such aspects as the expertise of the staff, courtesy and response times and will report back their findings. They may also observe the cleanliness of the premises, the overall appearance of the staff and the customer environment. The purpose is to monitor overall standards and impressions of quality, not to single out individual members of staff.

Mystery shoppers are widely used by banks, building societies and other service outlets. Mystery diners have long been the basis of some of the best known restaurant guides, and mystery guests are used to judge hotel standards.

Observation techniques can also be used in assessing quality standards. The layout of waiting rooms and other facilities, in, say, hospitals, can be improved by observing the behaviour of visitors. Signposts and directions can be made clearer if necessary, and vehicle access improved if observation suggests that these cause difficulty for users of the service. All of these considerations contribute to the customer's perceived service quality, and improvements should be made where necessary.

The purpose of monitoring and evaluation in all of these methods is to ensure that plans and programmes are working effectively, and that desired standards are being achieved. There must be systems to feed back the findings of monitoring processes into the service quality programmes so that continual improvement can result. The quest for high quality service delivery never ends; in fact, the quality goalposts keep changing as consumer tastes and developing technology bring about higher standards.

7. SUMMARY

Organisations are becoming increasingly aware of the importance of quality in gaining and maintaining competitive advantage. Service quality can only be measured against the needs and expectations of consumers. The special characteristics of services make it difficult to define quality in traditional ways. A user-based approach can be used which equates quality with the maximum levels of satisfaction; this is the idea of *perceived service quality*.

Because all services are essentially different, it is not possible to develop a single set of standards or criteria against which quality levels can be measured. Specific common features which are likely to impact on service levels in all service organisations include the following:

Customer participation
Intangibility
The service encounter
Inseparability

A starting point for assessing quality within the organisation is by means of a quality audit which examines the whole company and all the processes which together comprise the service offering. Checklists can be raised to address specific issues concerning each of these areas:

Internal service delivery
Internal service quality
Service delivery quality

Benchmarking is an important step in measuring and monitoring service quality. A benchmark is a standard against which performance can be measured. It should take into account the standard at which competitors operate and should reflect optimum quality within the competitive environment. Implementing quality service requires far more than the setting of benchmarks however; a highly developed customer orientation is vital if the organisation is to meet and even exceed customer expectations continually. A detailed process for implementing service quality involves the development of a quality strategy, programmes for implementation and monitoring and evaluation procedures.

Service quality can be monitored through various techniques based around the following:

Internal performance analysis
Customer satisfaction analysis
Specialist market research

Information should be fed back into the quality system and used for continual improvement. The organisation which seeks to outperform its competitors and maintain competitive advantage must focus on service quality for customer retention; zero defections, not just zero defects.

Progress test 10

1. Why does marketing play an important role in developing quality service?

2. Outline some of the ways in which quality can be defined.

3. What sort of criteria do customers use to judge the quality of a service?

4. Give details of the three main areas or reasons why developing and delivering a quality service is so important?

5. Services share certain features which can influence the customer's perception of service quality. List the features and comment on why they are infuential.

6. Explain what is meant by the term 'quality gap'.

7. Which two components of internal marketing are critical for any organisation seeking to implement quality service?

8. What are the main techniques used to monitor service quality?

Discussion

1. Design a framework for carrying out a quality audit within a service organisation – either an organisation you have experience of or one of the following examples. Give details of the types of questions to be addressed by both internal and external research and suggest how benchmarks might be established. Examples:
    (a) A building society;   (b) A college or university.

2. What evidence do you see of organisations implementing quality programmes and continually improving service quality? How do you measure service quality?

Part Three

THE SERVICES
MARKETING MIX

11

PACKAGING THE SERVICE PRODUCT

INTRODUCTION

The term 'product' is widely used to refer to a market offering of any kind. In its broadest sense this may be anything from the physical – a tin of baked beans or a television set – to the abstract – an idea or a moral issue. Generally, however, most products are made up of a combination of physical elements and services. This is true in services marketing, where the service offering can include tangible features, such as food in a restaurant, or be a 'pure' service, intangible in nature.

Packaging usually refers to the actual external packaging of a product and it plays a key part in, for example, fast-moving consumer goods marketing. The packaging, as well as protecting the contents, will perform a vital selling and promotional role, presenting the product and company image to potential customers. Essentially, in this sense, packaging is how the final product is put together and presented to the market.

The same issues are vitally important for services marketing. Designing and developing the ideal service is not the full story; the way the service is 'packaged' and presented to the market is the key issue. Branding the service, developing the right elements within it, adding tangible features – all these are critical tasks for services marketing management.

This chapter looks at packaging the service product in its widest possible sense, and explores these issues together with an overview of product management in services. Ways of classifying services are considered, and an understanding of the service concept is developed. Traditional product management tasks – new service development and positioning – are also reviewed.

1. SERVICE ATTRIBUTES

In attempting to develop an understanding of the service concept, and what actually constitutes a service, it is worth drawing on issues addressed in earlier chapters to focus on the special nature of services, and the service offering:

Special characteristics of services

Services share several distinguishing characteristics, when compared to physical products. These are:

Intangibility
Inseparability
Heterogeneity
Perishability

Each of these will influence decisions in developing and packaging the service product.

Classification of services

There are a number of ways of classifying service activity, and there will always be some degree of overlap between the various methods used. The following are some of the most commonly used classification methods:

End-user Services can be classified into the following categories:

Consumer
Business-to-business
Industrial

Service tangibility The degree of tangibility of a service can be used in classification:

Highly tangible
Service linked to tangible goods
Highly intangible

People-based services Services can be broken down into labour-intensive (people-based) and equipment-based services:

People-based services (high contact)
Equipment-based (low contact)

Expertise The expertise and skills of the service provider can be broken down into the following categories:

Professional
Non-professional

Profit orientation The overall business orientation is a recognised means of classification:

Not-for-profit
Commercial

(A more detailed discussion of the above examples can be found in Chapter 3.)

Having looked at some of the specific aspects relating to the service product, the service concept – what actually constitutes the service product – can be explored.

Need satisfaction

In many ways it is hard to equate the properties of physical goods with those of services. Physical goods have shape and form, they may be sold according to weight, size or colour; they can be tasted or felt. These characteristics are only *features* of physical products, however. Consumers may have preference for certain types of physical characteristics when they are choosing a product, but their underlying motivation for making a purchase is to satisfy a need. They are looking for something which will provide the right kind of *benefits* to satisfy their need.

This is equally true of services. Even in relation to the most intangible service, customers receive benefits to which they attribute value, and a perception of quality.

The idea that customers are looking for benefits rather than features is at the heart of a marketing orientation. Product-led companies (discussed in Chapter 1) focus on adding more and more features to products in order to attract customers. Marketing, however, places the focus firmly on the customers' needs and wants and aims to provide want satisfactions, or benefits.

The service concept

Physical goods and services can be looked at in terms of benefits offered, as well as features and specific attributes associated with those benefits. The notion of the service concept is based in the idea that actual service offerings (or physical products, in fact) can be broken down into a number of levels relating to customer need-satisfactions, benefits and features. Typically, three levels are identified:

The core benefit/service
The expected service
The augmented service

The core benefit/service The core benefit sought relates specifically to the customers' need. The customer may be feeling hungry, or may feel that they don't look their best. The customer might be a business needing help with promotion and advertising, or experiencing financial problems.

- *The core benefit satisfies the need/solves the problem.*

The expected service This relates to customers' expectations of what kind of services are available to satisfy their need. The hungry customer may decide to visit a snack bar or restaurant in order to satisfy their need for food. They will expect a certain level of service to be offered – a range of items on the menu, for example, clean and pleasant surroundings and prompt attention from staff. Someone visiting a hairdresser will have an idea of the range of facilities and treatments which should be available. Similarly, the business customer will expect professional advice, expertise and practical help from an advertising agency or financial consultant.

- *The expected service reflects standards required or expected by customers to satisfy their needs.*

The augmented service Augmenting the service offering, or making it better in some way, is the means by which service providers differentiate their offering in an attempt to influence consumer choice. Extra features, over and above the expected service, can be added to make the service more attractive to prospective consumers. Often innovation is the key. Restaurants may work at creating a special ambience, perhaps through decor and music, or a snack bar may offer customised sandwiches and video games. A hairdressing salon might offer additional beauty therapy, free refreshments and a certain image. Professional service organisations might seek to augment their service offering with a range of specialists, for example, who are expert in specific industry areas, or they may focus on a more caring, personal service for their clients.

- *The augmented service is the way in which service providers fine-tune the marketing mix to differentiate their service and make it stand out from the competition.*

The following table illustrates the service concept further:

Core Service	Expected Service	Augmented Service
Food provision	Clean facilities	Upmarket decor
	Choice available	Exotic menu
	Prompt service	Silver service
	Take away	Free delivery
		Fine wines
		Live music
Hairdressing	Well appointed salon	Luxury salon
	Qualified stylists	Famous stylists
	Range of treatments	Specialist treatments
		Refreshments
		Beauty therapy
		Sunbeds
Business-to-Business	Expert advice	Professional qualifications
	Reliable service	Affiliated to professional body
	Range of services	Specialist areas
		Overseas branches

In marketing mix terms, it is often the special aspects of the service mix which can contribute to the augmented service. The inseparable nature of services, for example, means that service quality is often closely linked to the people element of the mix. Perceptions of service quality often depend also on consumers' judgements about the surroundings in which the service is offered – the physical evidence – and the promptness of the service – the process. The following ideas suggest ways in which marketing mix variables can be adjusted to help differentiation:

Product (service)	Superior quality
	Well known/trusted brand image
	Unusual or additional features
	Extended guarantees
	The 'unique sales proposition'
	Tangibilisation
Price	'Value added'
	Special discounts
	Preferential credit terms
Promotion	Innovative advertising campaigns
	Loyalty promotions, e.g. frequent flyer offers
	Special offers
	Direct mail
	PR, sponsorship
Place	Extensive availability
	More outlets than competitors
	Innovative methods, e.g. telephone banking
	Careful selection of quality channels
People	Highly trained staff
	Better customer care
	Greater efficiency
	Personal attention
	Specialist skills
Process	Advances in technology, e.g. automated queue
	Systems, cash dispensers
	Fast response times
Physical evidence	Comfortable surroundings
	Superior decor
	Qualifications
	Evidence of professional standing – membership of professional bodies
	Strong, recognisable corporate image – staff uniforms, house style
	Supporting literature, documentation
	High quality 'tangibles'

Long-term success and survival, however, means far more than developing a marketing mix for a differentiated service offering. To keep up with changes in consumer trends and new technologies, or to cope with new situations, service organisations need continuously to review and develop their service offering. The range of services offered – the service portfolio – should always be monitored and new services introduced or existing ones withdrawn at the right time.

2. THE LIFE CYCLE CONCEPT

Products and services are often said to have 'life cycles'. This idea is based on an analogy with natural life cycles: birth, growth, maturity and so on. The product life cycle is frequently illustrated as being comprised of four stages:

Launch, or introduction
Growth
Maturity
Decline

The product life cycle is typically represented graphically in terms of sales over time. Plotting the level of sales over a period will result in a life cycle curve which may look like this:

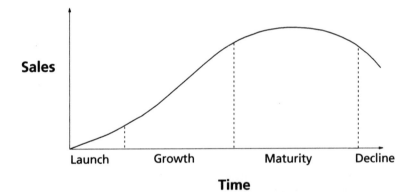

Sales, or even usage rates, of a service can be plotted in the same way as sales of physical products, and monitored over a period. This can be useful in managing the organisation's range of products or services, and in making decisions about promotion, for instance, or withdrawal of a service which has become outdated. The product life cycle concept holds that the different stages of the product life cycle have certain characteristics which are, more or less, common to all products or services.

Understanding and analysing the various stages, therefore, can be helpful in determining the appropriate marketing action.

Introduction

At the introduction stage the product or service is very new. Promotion will be intense and costly, and may need to be boosted if the service fails to meet initial targets. It will be aimed at getting users to try the service, and create interest. Television shopping is an example of a new service recently launched in the UK. This is a high risk stage, because the service will not yet have proved that it will be successful, and the costs of pre-launch development may be very high. Close monitoring is required.

Growth

As uptake of the service starts to grow, revenues will increase and profitability may be even achieved. The longer-term success of the service can be more easily assessed at this stage as market penetration increases. However, if the product appears to be doing well, it is likely at this stage that competitors will bring out rival offerings. This is the case with mobile telephones; when the market reaches near saturation they will have moved from the growth phase into the mature phase. Promotion may again need to be boosted to maintain the speed of growth and will focus on attracting more new users, and repeat purchase. Further investment may be required.

Maturity

As growth slows down, the overall volume of sales may reach a fairly steady plateau, which continues over time. Competition will probably be well established, and promotion efforts reflect the battles between leading brands. Credit cards are an example of a mature service offering. New entrants may still be entering the market, as is the case with building societies offering their own cards. Marketing effort is aimed at keeping the level of sales high, thus ensuring continued profitability.

Decline

At some stage, the popularity of a product or service will begin to die. Levels of sales will fall off, and profitability diminishes. This may be due to a number of reasons, as when services have been superseded by new technologies or when consumer tastes have changed. Facsimile machines have more or less replaced telex communication services, for example, and insurance services sold directly by telephone have started to replace the need for individual brokers on the high street. The main decision for management is whether to continue to produce and sell the product or service if it is still creating profits, or to delete it altogether, perhaps because the organisation has launched newer services to replace it, and deletion would enhance their chances of success, or possibly to cut the risk of it being a drain on resources.

Scope of the life cycle concept

These illustrate the basic ideas behind the life cycle concept, and its use as a management tool. There are many criticisms of the concept, mostly relating to the vast difference in the type of curves that can be seen (fads, for example, may grow sharply, but then drop off altogether, and never become mature). Cinema attendance in the UK all but died off altogether in the 1970s, resulting in the closure of many cinemas, but cinema has been successfully relaunched in a new format with the opening of hugely successful multi-screen cinema complexes.

There can also be ambiguity in what should be measured; industry cycles may differ for specific products, for example. The demand for information has never been higher, but, as mentioned previously, the means of transmitting information has changed, so telex machines have died, and so have telegrams, while fax and telephone usage have increased dramatically. The important thing is to monitor progress of all the organisation's offerings, and to consider stages in the life cycle as part of that analysis, but not to rely on the life cycle concept in isolation as a predictive or prescriptive management tool.

3. NEW SERVICE DEVELOPMENT

Managing the organisation's service portfolio, and developing and positioning new services, are functions critical to the organisation's success. The new product development process, as carried out by manufacturing companies, has been the focus of a significant amount of marketing literature for many years. The main reason for this is that it is both essential for long-term success, and a very costly, high risk process. The costs associated with the development and launch of a completely new product can be phenomenal and if the product fails to meet target sales figures – or, even worse, is a total flop – then the company may not survive.

Unfortunately, the literature is full of classic tales of such misadventure as the Ford Edsel car and the Sinclair C5, and estimates of the failure rate of new products range from fifty per cent to nearer ninety per cent of all new products launched. Even relatively minor developments to new products can be a high risk undertaking, as was the case when Coca-cola launched its new version and quickly had to bring back the old, 'classic' version (although some suggest it was actually a clever tactic to reinforce the brand, which may be true, but would certainly be too risky for any lesser brand to try). Persil washing powder also had to re-introduce its original product after the new 'improved' version was alleged to have caused allergic reactions in some cases.

Although the risks associated with failure may, at first sight, appear less for service providers than manufacturers (no expensive production facility to set up, for example) this is not necessarily the case. The costs of building a world class hotel are substantial, to say the least, and if that hotel remains half empty it is a failure. Even highly intangible new services such as insurance will cost a great deal to launch in terms of staff re-training, production of sales literature and documentation and expensive television advertising campaigns. To ensure the optimum chance of success for a new product or service, therefore, the development process must be systematically organised and monitored.

The **New Service Development Process** is a systematic, staged process which organisations should adopt to screen new service ideas and maximise their chances of success in the market. Typically it comprises the following stages:

Generation of ideas
Screening
Testing the concept
Business analysis/evaluation
Practical development
Market testing
Launch

The idea behind this stages process is that, at each stage, the new service must satisfy all relevant criteria absolutely before it should be allowed to progress to the next stage. Each stage will generally become more costly as the project takes on more substance and becomes more of a drain on company resources. The whole process can be viewed in terms of incremental costs; the investment payback will only start to occur after the product has been launched successfully in the market. *Ideas may be withdrawn at any stage.* These stages will now be explored in more detail:

Generation of Ideas

Idea generation can come from any number of sources, both internal and external to the organisation. The following are suggestions for sources of ideas:

Internal	*External*
Sales staff	Customers
Front-line personnel	Experts in the field
The 'suggestion box'	Market demand analysis
New developments arising	'Gap' analysis
from existing services	

Ideas from any of these sources may end up being completely wasted if no system exists to ensure that any new ideas are looked at properly. Systematic collection and review of ideas can be carried out in a number of ways:

Internal sources of ideas Sales staff reports should allow for any new ideas which might arise from their contacts outside to be fed back into the organisation for review. Similarly, any personnel who obtain ideas from customers or competitors should be able to report such information through the appropriate channels. This kind of formal and informal market intelligence can be extremely valuable. Sadly many organisations fail to monitor it effectively.

A suggestion box should be provided to encourage staff to come up with their own ideas. At a more formal level, sales staff and management might participate periodically in 'brainstorming' sessions to generate new ideas.

The performance of existing services should always be closely monitored within the competitive environment and this may lead to ideas for new versions of services, or incremental developments.

External sources of ideas   As stated, organisations must feed back information from customers in a productive way. This might be in the form of specific ideas, information about competitors or even simple offhanded remarks which can spark off ideas.

Organisations should keep abreast of developments in their field and may consult experts for ideas. They should follow the trade press, watch out for new trends or ideas and attend conferences and seminars related to their area.

Marketing research should be undertaken continuously to identify new areas of growing demand for services which they do not currently offer, to assess whether the area is one they should enter. Gap analysis can also be undertaken, which is research specifically undertaken to establish if there are any new areas of unfulfilled demand not being met by any players in the market.

All of these point to the importance of a well organised *Marketing Information System* within the organisation, to ensure routine information gathering and scrutiny especially in terms of market intelligence and internal and external information. The marketing information system is discussed further in Chapter 5.

Screening

The screening stage should be quite a ruthless filtering process for all new ideas generated. Decisions should be made as to whether ideas should be:

dropped completely,
considered as future possibilities,
allowed to proceed further straightaway.

The criteria for measuring an idea's potential can be based on the following key questions:

- Is the idea compatible with the organisation's overall objectives and mission?
- Does it seem achievable in terms of the organisation's resources?
- How well does it fit with the existing range of services offered? Will it complement the existing range or, in fact, be a competitive offering which may harm the existing market position?
- Does it have the full support of management?
- What is known about current/likely demand for this service?
- How quickly can we develop it for launch? Are there significant time constraints?
- Who are the main competitors in this market? What is their competitive reaction likely to be?

(Again, the marketing information system should be a valuable source of data here.)

It is important at this stage to be aware of possible pitfalls and to be quite ruthless, as costs will be incurred once ideas pass through the screening stage. A common problem is that of a 'pet project', where the idea is very close to someone's – usually a senior manager's – heart, and they push it through regardless of shortcomings in line with the key questions raised above. Such projects can be costly and damaging to the organisation. Sometimes a project may simply be too ambitious, and will place far too much drain on organisational resources, financial and otherwise.

Testing the concept

Ideas which have successfully passed the screening stage need to be tested to establish their potential. What may seem attractive to the board of directors may not be so readily accepted by the buying public. Concept testing is usually done through marketing research. It involves presenting the idea, or concept, to the target market and studying their reaction. In product marketing, this stage may make extensive use of mock-ups, models and artists' impressions to get the idea across to the audience. Testing a new financial service concept, for example, might involve producing brochures and literature to illustrate the idea. More intangible services, however, might be concept tested purely by discussing the actual idea. Typically focus groups might be used, and other small-scale surveys of existing or potential customers.

Business analysis/evaluation

At this stage, ideas which have been selected to be developed further require in-depth exploration and evaluation. The key task is to produce a formal analysis of the idea's market potential in terms of forecasts and costings of all aspects of developing and launching the service. This analysis will focus on the following areas:

Defining the market
Market size and structure
Consumer trends in the market
Levels of demand, current and future
External environmental factors likely to affect performance
Competition
Market share forecasts
Financial forecasts, costings, breakeven analysis, etc.

Practical development

At this stage it is virtually 'all systems go' as preparations are made for developing and launching the service. Service providers might not be faced with the need to set up new manufacturing plants and production facilities as such, but there is likely to be a lot of work to be undertaken at this stage in terms of designing and supplying literature and supporting materials. Supplies of the tangible elements of the new service will have to be sourced, or production established.

A full-scale marketing programme must be developed to encompass all aspects of the mix as necessary:

Advertising and promotional campaigns
Channel selection (if appropriate)
'Packaging' the new service offering
Pricing policy
Staff training (and possibly recruitment)

Additionally, existing processes may need to be adapted to accommodate the new service and new premises may have to be provided, or existing ones upgraded.

Market testing

Although extensive marketing research will have been carried out earlier in the process, and all the signs must be favourable for a product or service idea to have got this far, some sort of market testing can help reduce risk. This may be done artificially, perhaps using panels of consumers who will sample the product or service in their home, for example, or it may be done by testing in the actual market but in a small area, say one town or one television region.

Test markets can help organisations fine-tune the elements of the marketing mix to optimise the chances of success, and can also be a strong indicator of likely performance in the wider market. The main problem with test markets is that competitors will get to know of new ideas being developed, but they would find out pretty quickly at the actual launch in any case, so this risk has to be balanced against the risks of not using a test market. In very sensitive situations, where the risk of competitors copying ideas is high, the best strategy may be to stick to simulated test markets before going to full launch.

There are problems associated with the selection and use of test markets, as well as the threat of competitor reaction. It can be difficult to select a test market which really is representative of the overall market. It is also sometimes hard to gauge over what period the test market should be allowed to run as it is repeat purchase – not trial – which is important to establish an indication of performance.

Sometimes a combination of test market methods will be most suitable, and these may culminate in a 'rolling' launch where the service is tried out in one market, and if successful extended to another market and tested there, and so on.

Launch

The final stage in the development process is the actual launch. It is at this stage that the life cycle is said to commence, and the new service moves from being purely a cost, to bringing in revenue. The launch may be on a roll-out basis, as described above, or it may be done nationally, or even internationally. The launch is critical for future success and should not be regarded as the last stage in the development process, but rather as the first and most important stage in the life of a successful new product or service.

4. POSITIONING THE SERVICE

The idea of positioning relates to the way consumers perceive and evaluate products and services. Specifically, it relates to the way in which consumers rank the features and attributes of a service against those of competing services. Consumers will perceive certain brands as being higher or lower in quality, for example, or of being more or less expensive than other brands. These perceptions stem from a complex set of ideas and beliefs about products or services which make up a consumer's attitude towards them.

The way in which service providers differentiate their offering impacts on its position in the consumer's mind. The aspects of differentiation referred to with regard to the augmented service can all contribute to this. Thus a service provider may be seen as being more caring, or offering more value for money. Promotion often centres on positioning. Examples of this are seen in advertisements for Stella Artois lager – 'reassuringly expensive' – and Midland Bank's 'the listening bank' campaign.

Different attributes of a service reflect different values which can be attached to that service in the consumer's perception. A high price, for example, can reflect an idea of quality or luxury when other features also reflect these values. If other features do not reflect these values, a high price might translate as being not good value for money, or being overpriced in the consumer's view. In developing service positioning, organisations must understand aspects of *consumer behaviour*. Answers to the following questions must be sought:

- What attributes of the service do our consumers rate most highly?
- How do they rank our competitors' performance against ours with regard to these attributes?
- Who makes the decision, and how do they establish criteria for such a decision?

The answers are often highly variable, according to the circumstances and situation of individual consumers at the time. A family might decide to stop for a quick lunch at a fast food restaurant, but choose a restaurant for a celebratory family gathering. The main criteria for selecting the lunch venue might be cost and convenience, whereas these may actually be relatively minor factors in selecting a restaurant for a special family outing. Similarly, when choosing a hire car, price and availability might be the prime attributes considered, whereas when choosing dental care or legal advice, professional reputation and the personality of the provider may be the key attributes.

The key task is to select a positioning strategy which will most closely correspond to the consumer's selection criteria within selected segments, thus maximising the chances of success. An organisation should play to its strengths and not try to create a positioning strategy which is unattainable, or which will not hold credibility. This holds true for commercial service providers as well as not-for-profit or public sector organisations.

A university, for example, may be rated only average academically, but may have close links with industry and an excellent record of graduate employment.

This may be the main selection criteria for a large segment of the student market, and the university can position itself specifically to attract this segment. It would be unwise to try to position itself as a centre of academic excellence if potential students would rate it poorly against its competitors on solely academic attributes.

Positioning is very important for services marketing as it involves careful tailoring of the service offering to the needs of target segments, which underpins marketing success. Additionally, however, positioning enables the organisation to respond to the competitive environment positively, highlighting market opportunities and fulfilling specific market needs better than its competitors.

5. SUMMARY

'Packaging' the service product means more than designing and developing the ideal service but putting it together as a whole, with features such as branding and added tangible elements which will help differentiate it in the marketplace and attract customers.

Services can be classifed in a number of ways, including:

End-user
Service tangibility
People-based service
Expertise
Profit orientation

The service concept is a way of breaking down the service offering into three main levels:

The core benefit/service
The expected service
The augmented service

Analysis of the offering in this way helps service marketers to focus on key issues; customer needs and differentiation, for example.

The life cycle concept is another tool which can be used by marketing management to monitor and analyse performance in terms of the various life cycle stages:

Introduction
Growth
Maturity
Decline

Despite limitations, the life cycle concept can be helpful when used in conjunction with other forms of analysis and forecasting.

New service development is critical if organisations are to ensure their service offerings meet the changing needs and wants of consumers and if they wish to remain competitive. The *new service development process* provides a framework for developing new ideas and innovation with the necessary care required to cut down the associated costs and risk.

Positioning relates to the way in which consumers rank the features and attributes of a service against those of competing services. It is important in services marketing as it involves careful tailoring of the service offering to the needs of selected target segments, which is at the core of marketing success.

Progress test 11

1. Explain each of the following service classifications using examples to illustrate your answer:

   End-user
   Service tangibility
   People-based service
   Expertise
   Profit orientation

2. What is meant by the service concept? What are three levels into which it can be broken down?

3. Give an overview of the life cycle concept.

4. Why is new service/product development a risky business?

5. Outline the stages in the new service development process.

6. Give details of the areas which the business analysis stage will focus on.

7. What is meant by 'positioning'?

8. What questions need to be addressed in order for organisations to develop positioning strategies?

Discussion

1. Consider the examples which are given in this chapter of ways in which marketing mix variables may be adjusted to help differentiation. From your own experiences as a service consumer, analyse the marketing mix of leading service organisations and assess the extent to which they achieve differentiation.

2. Critically evaluate the usefulness of tools such as the service/product concept, the life cycle concept and the new service development process.

12

PRICING THE SERVICE

INTRODUCTION

The price is a key element of the marketing mix; it must be acceptable to target customers and it must reflect the other components of the mix accurately. The price of the service is the value attached to it by the service provider and it must correspond with the customer's perception of value. If the service is priced at too high a level, it will be seen as poor value for money by customers who will not buy it. On the other hand, if the price is too low, the service may be perceived as shoddy or inferior in quality.

Many service providers offer a range of services at various price levels to meet the needs of different target segments who may have different levels of spending power. Airlines offer business class and economy class travel, for example, and theatres offer seats at different prices according to the layout of the theatre, the view accorded by the seats and their relative proximity to the performance. Both airlines and theatres also offer different prices to customers buying the service at certain times, with lower prices being charged in the less busy, 'off-peak' periods.

Many factors influence the price which is ultimately charged. The type of organisation, the structure of the market, the life cycle stage of the service and prices charged by the competition may all have an impact on pricing decisions. Organisational objectives are also part of the pricing equation. If the service provider wants to position itself as offering a value-for-money, family restaurant, for example, the menu prices will be quite different from those of an exclusive gourmet establishment. Sometimes service providers, such as those in the public sector, have constraints imposed over the prices they can charge to customers. This has an impact on other aspects of the marketing mix, as the elements are always linked interdependently. These aspects of pricing the service are explored in this chapter.

1. KEY PRICING CONCEPTS

There are many alternative pricing concepts and techniques available to marketing organisations. As with all aspects of marketing concepts and tools, certain of these have more relevance for service organisations than others. Rather like the promotional tools which go to make up the promotional mix, many of these tools and concepts may be combined to create an overall pricing strategy which is most effective for the organisation over time.

Other issues, such as organisational objectives, will impact on the choices and decisions made with regard to pricing policy and are covered later in this chapter. Initially, however, it is useful to consider the various approaches to pricing policy and examples of the way in which pricing is used as a marketing mix tool. Some of the most commonly used pricing concepts can be described as follows:

Price skimming

Here the supplier 'skims the cream' off the market by offering a product or service at a high price on a low volume basis. This is particularly appropriate for new products in new market situations where a proportion of consumers are always prepared to pay more for new, innovative goods. The price skimming approach can help speed up the payback period. Frequently, the price reduces after a period as the products become more popular and sales volume increases. Mobile telephones are an example of this; the actual product (the telephone) has reduced in price over time since initial introduction to the market and the service (mobile communications) charges have also reduced, bringing the mobile phone within reach of ordinary consumers.

Penetration pricing

In this case the price is set at a low level in order to attract high volume sales, thus penetrating the market and gaining substantial market share. For new products and services the payback period is lengthy but with the advantage of establishing a strong market position. The strategy is especially suitable for use when entering highly competitive markets, such as the fast food restaurant business in the UK, or international airlines. New entrants would be unlikely to succeed by charging high prices; pricing would have to be attractive in comparison with the competition to penetrate the market.

Mixed pricing

This is based on the above two pricing strategies; begin with a price skimming policy then reduce the price as competitors enter the market to defend the organisation's position and attract new customers. The example given previously of mobile communications typifies this approach.

Cost-plus pricing

Here pricing is based on the costs of producing the good or providing the service. The total costs are computed then the price determined by adding on some required margin or 'mark up'. This approach has a number of weaknesses in that it considers neither the competitive situation nor the market potential. Prices may be set too high against those of competitors to attract customers or may not be set high enough to exploit demand, especially if the product or service is innovative, new, or distinctive in some way from competitive offerings.

Variable pricing

This is particularly relevant in industrial and business-to-business markets where individual contracts are priced according to specification. Service providers such as architects and consultants quote a price according to the needs of the project. Tendering is a situation which generally reflects this approach. Sometimes variable prices include some fixed element, such as hourly labour charges, but even these may be variable in line with the complexity of the work.

Marginal pricing

Marginal pricing is based on the concept of marginal cost and is particularly relevant for service industries. The marginal cost is 'the cost of the last unit of output' and may be very low. For example, a unit of output for an airline could be defined as a fare paying passenger so the marginal cost of the last unit of output – one extra passenger on a plane – will be very low in comparison with the overall costs of fuel, maintenance, staffing costs and so on. It is probably equal to the cost of the meal and drinks served on board. Therefore, when there is spare capacity on a passenger airline, empty seats which can be filled by passengers paying vastly reduced ticket prices are preferable to empty seats.

This is the principle behind 'standby' airfares where seats are offered at the last minute for a fraction of the normal fare – anything over the marginal cost is a contribution to the company's profits. Travellers arriving late at night can often negotiate reduced room rates in hotels, and holiday makers prepared to make a last minute reservation can book package tours at heavily discounted prices. The perishable nature of services means that empty seats on a plane or vacant bedrooms in a hotel represent a business opportunity which is lost. Such surplus items cannot be set aside for an end-of-season sale, for example, so any tactics (using promotional tools as well as reduced prices) which can help to maximise take-up of the service, thereby reducing any surplus, are extremely valuable.

Promotional pricing

Sales promotion techniques often use tactical pricing reductions as a means of increasing sales over a short period. Discounts, special offers, vouchers, rebates and even 'buy now pay later' schemes and interest-free credit are all examples of promotional pricing. It is useful to aid penetration or as a seasonal tool (hence the end-of-season 'sales') but should be treated as a short-term tactic, not a long-term measure. The overall effect of a price war between suppliers competing with one another can be to de-value the market.

'Loss leaders' are another example of promotional pricing used in retailing especially. A staple product is offered at a loss-making price to attract customers to the store where they will (hopefully) spend money on other products.

Differential pricing

Another form of promotional pricing of particular concern to service marketers is differential pricing, where different prices are charged for the same service at different times or to different customers. This tactic is used to attract more business in slack periods or to attract particular groups of customers to make up demand at particular times. Differential pricing may be seasonal, reflecting the different prices charged for the same holidays in low-, mid- and high-season or by time period, hence the price of rail fares in peak periods compared with off-peak periods.

Hairdressers or theatres might offer reduced prices to senior citizens or students on certain days or for certain shows, when demand is likely to be low. In these circumstances, the differential price charged may be based on marginal pricing, demonstrating again how more than one approach may be combined in creating the ideal pricing strategy for an organisation.

2. PRICING ISSUES FOR SERVICES

The overall pricing strategy will be influenced by the organisations' objectives but certain factors will impact on actual pricing decisions and the selection of appropriate pricing policies. The factors affecting pricing policy include the following:

Costs of producing the service and breakeven analysis
Competitor pricing
Demand levels and elasticity
Regulatory factors
Marketing mix
Positioning

Basic financial considerations need to underpin pricing decisions if a service provider is to operate profitably or survive in the competitive environment. Most service organisations are concerned with making a profit or, in the case of not-for-profit organisations, charities or services in the public sector, covering costs and possibly raising funds. It could be argued that there are exceptions; services which are heavily subsidised, such as museums, for example, but even subsidised services will generally seek to maximise possible sources of revenue and operate in a cost effective manner.

Some services which do not charge prices to the end consumer as a rule are, nevertheless, subject to pricing mechanisms within local and national government. State schools and National Health Service Hospitals are examples of these. Other services are constrained in their pricing policy because fees or prices are standardised at national level, as with student fees which are standardised to a large extent at UK universities.

Many public sector services traditionally supplied by local authorities such as refuse collection, school meals and janitorial services are now open to tender and public sector service providers are forced to compete for business against commercial service providers from the private sector. The costs of providing the service need to be analysed and prices set at competitive rates if the local authority is to continue to supply the service. In all the examples given, however, analysis of what the service costs to produce and deliver and other cost factors is an important task.

Costs of producing the service and breakeven analysis

In order to use costs as the basis for any formal pricing decisions, it is necessary for service organisations to analyse all costs accurately. Where organisations offer a range of services, the costs for each individual service must be assessed. There are three main components which make up the costs of providing a service: variable costs, fixed costs, overheads.

Variable costs fluctuate in relation to the level of service output. They include the costs of materials and provisions, staffing costs and other areas of expenditure such as advertising. *Fixed costs* are those costs which do not generally alter in line with the volume of output. They include the costs associated with buildings, depreciation of vehicles and machinery, rates and local taxes, for example. It is true to say that fixed costs may, in fact, change over time with increased levels of service output (e.g. if another branch of a restaurant is opened) but they do not fluctuate in the way that variable costs do. *Overheads* are the costs attributable to management and administration within the organisation.

Some costs may be *shared costs* which are allocated across the whole range of services. The costs of premises and vehicles are examples of costs which are likely to be shared but staffing costs may also be shared across a range of services unless service personnel are only involved in the production and delivery of individual service lines.

Breakeven analysis is a basic tool which can be used to calculate the minimum quantity of a service which must be sold in order to cover the costs of producing and delivering that service; in other words, to break even. Cost curves are plotted on a chart, then a revenue curve can be superimposed over them, thus creating a graph which depicts the profit/loss picture for several possible cost-revenue situations at different levels of service sales volume. The diagram illustrates breakeven analysis.

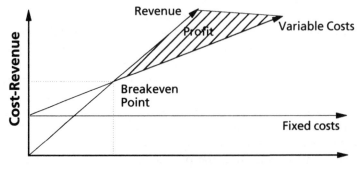

Level of Activity

Breakeven analysis is of limited value in determining pricing policy as it is based on very simplistic assumptions about the relationship between costs, price and demand:

- No account is taken of price elasticity of demand in relation to actual revenue.
- The breakeven point is derived from a calculation rather than from a forecast of the actual sales volume required to reach certain levels of profitability.
- In reality, variable costs within service organisations do not necessarily increase proportionately with levels of output and fixed costs do not remain completely constant irrespective of levels of output.

As with many marketing concepts and tools, managers should not rely on the breakeven concept in isolation in making pricing decisions. It is important to understand the concept, however, and its value as a simple method of evaluating different pricing options, especially where forms of cost-based pricing are involved. It should always be used in conjunction with other approaches which take into account the structure of the market, the potential demand for the service and the competitive situation.

Competitor pricing

Organisations need information about competitors' prices in order to make pricing decisions. This does not necessarily mean that organisations are going to set prices at the same level, nor to undercut competitors' prices even, although tactical pricing battles are often seen between rival organisations or brands. The effect of price cutting as anything other than a short-term, promotional tactic designed to gain short-term competitive advantage can be to de-value a market with the result that all competing organisations lose revenue eventually.

Competition-orientated pricing (or 'me too' pricing as it is sometimes known) occurs frequently in markets which are very price sensitive and where the core benefits sought are largely similar. Bank charges tend to be set at more or less the same level between the main banks and major airlines set their fares at competitive levels to survive in the market. Organisations operating competition-orientated pricing strategies will tend to attempt to influence consumer preference through other elements of the marketing mix such as service quality.

There may even be very valid reasons for choosing to set a price considerably higher than the main competitors if the service offered is of a much higher quality, or provides additional benefits. As stated previously, all marketing mix elements are interdependently linked, and price determination will take into account many factors besides competitor pricing. The key issue, however, is to analyse competitor pricing relative to the organisation's own pricing strategy and that of other competitors.

It can also be difficult to determine who competitors are, if indirect competition is included as well as direct competitors. A restaurant may compare its prices with those of other restaurants and eating establishments in the locality but in reality there are other choices available to prospective customers in terms of how they spend their leisure time and money. It may be necessary to consider how the price of a meal at the restaurant compares with the price of an evening at the bowling alley or a trip to the local cinema or leisure centre.

Demand levels and elasticity

The level of demand for a particular service offering will be a key influence on pricing decisions. Demand levels may vary for a number of reasons:

- economic conditions and trends in consumer spending
- the stage in the life cycle of a service
- seasonal variations
- busier times of day – peak periods
- level of marketing and promotional effort
- degree of substitutability of the product or service.

The key task is to forecast levels of demand and potential demand, taking price into account. The demand for some goods and services will go up and down in line with price increases and decreases, whereas the demand for other types of goods and services will remain more or less constant. Price elasticity of demand represents a measure of how sensitive demand is in relation to changes in price. Cigarettes, petrol, electricity and basic foodstuffs tend to have low elasticity while luxury or non-essential goods and services will tend to be more price sensitive.

Regulatory factors

Regulatory measures imposed by government and other bodies on many kinds of organisations affect pricing decisions and, ultimately, the price charged. In the services sector, UK public utilities prices are monitored by consumer 'watchdog' bodies set up by national government, such as OFTEL which monitors the telecommunications suppliers. These watchdog bodies bring pressure to bear on the service providers to supply at fair prices and to restrict price increases.

Charities and not-for-profit organisations are frequently subject to constraints laid down within the constitution of the organisation, or set down by the board of trustees or other governing body regarding what they can charge for their services. Public sector services such as leisure centres and school meals services are also similarly constrained in their pricing decisions. Frequently such services are subsidised to some degree so they are able to afford to operate at a level which might technically be loss-making.

Other formal regulatory factors influencing prices in the UK include legislation such as the Trade Descriptions Act and the Consumer Protection Act. Collusion between companies in price setting is not allowed and the Monopolies and Mergers Commission is established to prevent the creation of monopolies.

Marketing mix

As stated previously, the elements of the marketing mix are interdependently linked. Each element must sit congruently with the others to make the whole marketing mix offering credible and attractive. Some possible influences of the price on the other elements of the mix are as follows:

Product/service offering The price must reflect the value of the product accurately. Determining what value is associated with particular products or services is highly complex as perceived value is extremely subjective. What represents good value to one customer may not do so to the next. Many organisations offer a range of offerings at varying price levels in order to suit as many potential customers as possible. Offerings may vary in quality from the basic 'budget' range to a luxury range, at prices to reflect the different quality levels. Hotels frequently offer varying standards of accommodation across a wide price scale. Other services may be offered at a discount for quantity or regular purchase.

Promotion Price may or may not be a feature of promotion. Price sensitive goods and services often rely on attracting customers on the basis of price and will wish to communicate this to all potential customers. Similarly, organisations offering promotional pricing such as special discounts or vouchers will include this in promotion. Whether price is specifically referred to in the promotional message or not, however, it should accurately reflect the service quality and value to match customers' expectations. Price reductions and offers used in sales promotion represent a key part of the promotional mix.

Place Expensive products and services which can command premium prices will be distributed through selected channels which should reflect the quality and status of the offering. Location can also be closely linked to price. More expensive, exclusive professional services such as law firms and stockbrokers are likely to be located in upmarket city centre offices. Consumers expect to pay more for these services than they would for a similar service from a provincial practitioner.

People Service quality should, ideally, never be compromised by price. Differences in the level of service offered are, however, often clearly reflected in the price charged. More expensive services will often require higher levels of staff training and more specialist knowledge on the part of individual members of staff.

Process and physical evidence Physical evidence is important in determining what constitutes 'value for money' in the services sector. Facilities, decor and the physical environment in which the service exchange takes place (or is initiated) should reflect the price of the service. High street travel agents offer a combination of characteristics in respect of these marketing mix elements to attract customers; well trained staff in smart uniforms and pleasant, bright offices together with the latest in computer technology for on-line booking and information systems.

Positioning

The idea of positioning relates to the way consumers perceive and evaluate products and services. Specifically, it relates to the way in which consumers rank the features and attributes of a service against those of competing services. Consumers will perceive certain brands as being higher or lower in quality, for example, or of being more or less expensive than other brands.

They will also differ in terms of how important price is with regard to a particular product or service. Different target groups and segments will have different perceptions of price and some will be more sensitive than others. Consumers often rely heavily on price to make judgements about the quality of goods and services when they have little other information. For these reasons, it is critical for marketing managers to understand different customer attitudes towards price and their perceptions of quality in determining price levels.

3. ORGANISATIONAL OBJECTIVES AND PRICING POLICY

Many organisational objectives can be closely linked to specific pricing strategies and will play a large part in determining those strategies. Examples include:

Maximise current profit
Maximise current revenue
Maintain price leadership
Survival
Maximise growth

In price sensitive markets, price will have to be set relatively low to maximise revenue. To achieve maximum growth in sales, penetration pricing – where prices are sometimes set as low as possible – will be used. However, there may be other organisational objectives which are not so directly linked to price. A museum might have maximising the number of visitors as its primary objective. Enhancing the image of the organisation, discouraging new competitors from entering markets and building brand loyalty are all examples of organisational objectives which are in this category.

It is important for organisations to make decisions about prices which are compatible with the organisation's overall objectives. In services marketing, many organisations, especially in the charity, not-for-profit and public sectors, the task of balancing decisions about pricing and overall objectives is highly complex and may be subject to all kinds of non-business constraints. The important task, however, is to be very clear and explicit in specifying corporate objectives. These can then be analysed in the light of possible pricing problems and decisions made accordingly.

4. A FRAMEWORK FOR PRICING DECISIONS

Prices are not set once only; developing pricing policy should be a continuous process, always open to refinement and adjustment when the need arises. It is important to recognise problems which can arise from the failure or inadequacy of some pricing programmes so that steps can be taken to rectify the situation. As with all aspects of marketing planning, pricing should be monitored continuously and corrective action implemented quickly.

There are a number of key stages in price decision making which can be identified as follows:

- *Analyse organisational objectives in terms of pricing.*
- *Determine demand levels and customer characteristics.*
- *Analyse costs.*
- *Examine competitor pricing and positioning.*
- *Set prices utilising pricing concepts, e.g. cost-plus.*
- *Monitor market response to prices set and identify problems.*

Organisations should always be ready to adapt pricing to variable conditions in the market. Price should be used fully as a marketing tool – a key element within the marketing mix.

5. SUMMARY

Pricing is an important element in the marketing mix. It reflects the value attached to it by the service provider and it must correspond with the customer's perception of value. There are many pricing concepts and techniques which organisations may use in developing their pricing policy, including:

Price skimming
Penetration pricing
Mixed pricing
Cost-plus pricing
Variable pricing
Marginal pricing
Promotional pricing
Differential pricing

Various factors influence the overall pricing strategy. The organisation's objectives and degree of profit orientation are obvious examples but other considerations include:

Costs of producing the service/breakeven analysis
Competitor pricing
Demand levels and elasticity
Regulatory factors
Marketing mix
Positioning

In services marketing pricing decisions can be highly complex, especially in the public and not-for-profit sectors. Organisational objectives are major factors in deciding upon a pricing strategy and when objectives are set, the potential impact on pricing should be considered. Pricing policy will be subject to continual development as prices fluctuate over time. A framework for pricing decisions should be monitored continuously to allow for responsive action and adaptation when required.

Progress test 12

1. Why is 'price' such a key element of the marketing mix?

2. Outline the main pricing concepts which organisations might use in developing their pricing strategy.

3. List the main factors affecting pricing policy and explain why they are important.

4. For what reasons may the level of demand for a particular service fluctuate?

5. Describe how breakeven analysis is arrived at.

6. In what ways might pricing policy affect the other elements of the marketing mix?

7. Give an overview of the main stages in price decision making.

Discussion

1. It has been emphasised that organisational objectives will play a key role in determining prices and pricing policy. To what extent do you think this is true in the following examples:
   (a) a commercial service provider
   (b) a public sector not-for-profit organisation
   (c) a voluntary organisation

2. To what extent do you think price influences your perception of service quality and, ultimately, your buying decisions?

13

PROMOTION AND COMMUNICATIONS IN SERVICES MARKETING

INTRODUCTION

Promotion is used to communicate information about goods and services to target market audiences thereby facilitating the exchange process. It is sometimes argued that effective marketing – offering the right service at the right price in the right locations to meet target customers needs and wants – should not require extensive promotional activity as the products or services will 'sell themselves'. There is an element of truth in this, as the purpose of developing a finely tuned marketing mix is to match offerings and benefits very closely to the needs of identified target groups of customers. The result of this, in theory, is that customers will favour one particular organisation over competitors and will actively seek their service offerings.

However, in practice, it is difficult to imagine a situation where some element of promotion is not required to inform the customer of the organisation's existence or about the offering itself, even if this is simply by word of mouth. Promotion plays an important role in informing, educating, persuading and reminding customers. This role is even more important in services where there is a high degree of intangibility so there is no physical product or packaging to attract potential customers' attention.

Additionally, effective communications are needed to inform customers about their role in the service delivery process. They need to know where automatic cash dispensers are located and how they work, for example, or how to make reservations for a restaurant or a seat at the theatre. The highly competitive marketplace for both commercial services and, increasingly, services in the not-for-profit and charitable sectors has led to advertising playing a major role in services marketing today. This is, however, only one aspect of the promotion and communications process which is explored in this chapter.

1. INTERNAL/EXTERNAL COMMUNICATIONS

All organisations need to communicate with their customers (both internal and external) at various times and for a variety of reasons. Often, communications are also directed towards other groups such as the organisation's publics – local authorities, government bodies, shareholders, community and pressure groups, for example. Communications can be viewed as the transmission of information. Service organisations may need to communicate information for various purposes:

Externally

- to inform the target markets about current and new service offerings and benefits
- to educate customers
- to persuade existing and potential customers to buy
- to remind customers about the service and where it is available
- to publicise policy decisions, for example about environmental issues
- to make public announcements

Internally

- to inform employees about changes in the organisation
- to communicate plans and programmes effectively
- to keep all employees informed about company performance
- to publicise incentive schemes and other events
- to inform and educate employees about new products and services
- to disseminate marketing intelligence within the organisation

The above lists illustrate a variety of reasons why organisations need to communicate both internally and externally. Different forms of communication will be used to meet the different information needs of organisations and to find the most appropriate means of transmitting the information effectively. Different forms of communication and promotional methods will be reviewed later in this chapter, but it is necessary at this stage to understand the communications process.

2. THE COMMUNICATIONS PROCESS

Central to good communications is the need to be able to transmit messages accurately. This is not an easy task. There is so much room for misinterpretation or misunderstanding to occur in any communications situation. Even in personal, face-to-face communications it can be difficult to convey precise factual messages accurately. It can be imagined, therefore, that the difficulties involved in communicating a convincing, persuasive, unambiguous promotional message in a thirty second television advertising slot are immense.

The communications processes is typically illustrated as consisting of four main elements:

The source (the sender): encoding
The message (which is subject to noise)
The media selected to transmit the message
The recipient: decoding

The source

The starting point is the source – the person or organisation sending the message. The source must have a very clear idea of the objective of the communication, i.e. what is the desired outcome of sending this message. If this is not clear at the outset then the communications process is already in danger of breaking down.

Encoding

The source encodes the message by putting it into words, supported by images and pictures which will enhance the effectiveness of the message. Even simple direct communications go through this process of encoding; the right words have to be chosen carefully to avoid any misunderstanding. Essentially, the encoding process translates the thought and objectives of the sender into a message which will make sense to the intended recipient or audience.

The message

The message has now been encoded and may be in the form of a letter, a spoken announcement or a television or radio advertisement, for example. In reviewing the message, the sender must be certain that it accurately conveys what they originally intended.

The media selected to transmit the message

Unless the message is going to be transmitted directly to the recipient, either face-to-face or by personal letter, for example, some form of media must be selected. The most appropriate medium for getting this message across to the target audience will depend on several factors. The choice of medium itself can affect the way the message is received and interpreted. An announcement about company policy may carry more weight if it is published in the *Financial Times* rather than the *News of the World*. On the other hand, if the intended audience is more likely to read a popular tabloid newspaper than the *Financial Times*, then this will dictate the choice of media.

Noise The whole communications process is affected by noise. Noise, in this context, means anything which can detract from the message in any way by distracting the recipient. In the case of television advertisements, for example, noise can occur in the form of other advertisements, family conversations, the option of reading a book or a newspaper instead of watching television, and so on. Similarly, in newspaper advertising, noise arises from exciting editorials, interesting photographs, other advertising offers or sports reports which compete for the reader's attention. The reader may be introducing noise by listening to the radio as well as reading the paper.

Noise occurs in many ways, most of which are beyond the control of the sender. Direct mail is increasingly used as a more direct medium of communication for organisations to use in contacting their target customers to avoid the noise associated with other media forms. The sheer volume of direct mail now received by many consumers is in itself a form of noise, distracting the recipient from the intended message. For this reason, in using different media, it is essential to make the message as interesting or eyecatching as possible, in order to overcome such distractions.

Decoding

Decoding is the act of interpreting the message and forming an impression of what it is intended to convey in the light of the recipient's own understanding. Noise can have an effect on the message as not all the intended audience will pay full attention to the message, and of those who do, each will place their own interpretation on its meaning. The more complex the message, the more likely it is that distortion will occur.

The recipient

The receiver of the message can themselves affect the accuracy of the message. Their personal beliefs, attitudes and preconceptions will influence how they interpret the message. The anti-nuclear campaigner is unlikely to be anything but sceptical of messages sent out by the nuclear industry to raise its public image. Other recipients may find such messages reassuring, however.

Previous experience of the organisation will colour the recipient's interpretation of the message, as may cultural influences. Some famous advertising mistakes have been in the international arena, where the use of particular colours or symbols has led to rejection of the advertising (and the relevant products) because the connotations attached to those colours and symbols have been unpleasant or made the advertisement socially unacceptable.

The communications process ends with some form of feedback. Sometimes this is direct feedback, as in a personal sales negotiation, for example, while at other times it may be harder and take longer to measure the effectiveness of the communication, by monitoring increases in sales, for instance, or responses to sales promotions. One-way communications are the most difficult to monitor, especially as marketing communications compete with so many other messages and distractions in the crowded marketplace and there may be no direct form of feedback.

Ensuring the most effective communications for marketing and promotion is a complex task. External communications form a key part of the promotional mix, and internal communications are vital for effective marketing management. Internal marketing programmes encourage good communications within organisations, and these are explored in Chapter 8, while this chapter explores communications within the promotional mix.

3. THE PROMOTIONAL MESSAGE

The promotional message may be designed with one or more aims in mind:

to inform
to entertain
to educate
to persuade
to remind

The promotional objectives will dictate, to a large extent, the nature and form the promotional message takes and the type of appeal used to get the message across. The promotional objectives will themselves be determined by a variety of factors:

- the competitive situation
- the positioning of the brand or service
- the life cycle stage of the service offering
- organisational and marketing objectives

In launching a new service, the initial objective will be to create general awareness of the service, and the promotional message will be designed to inform consumers that it exists. Educating consumers in how to use the service and persuading them to try it, or participate in it, will follow. Once a service is established, promotional messages will serve to increase awareness or remind consumers about the service, and persuade new customers to purchase.

A variety of different appeals will be used to present the promotional message. The type of message and the media choice available will influence the nature of the appeal. The types of appeal under consideration include:

rational appeals
emotional appeals
fear appeals
humour appeals

The appeal used is designed to evoke some kind of reaction, in line with the promotional objectives. A mixture of more than one appeal may be used.

Rational appeals

Some messages need to be long and detailed and will contain a quantity of information to inform and educate customers about the service offered. The content will be presented factually and logically and will often rely on explanations and comparisons. Rational appeals are founded on the notion that, presented with all the facts about a superior service offering, consumers will make a rational decision to buy. They depend on fairly detailed information and are therefore more suited to newspaper and magazine advertising, although this type of appeal is also used in other media promotions. Industrial and business-to-business services often use this format in the trade and other press, as do certain financial and other consumer services.

Emotional appeals

By using emotional appeals, advertisers attempt to provoke a response via emotions and feelings. Evidence suggests that emotional appeals enhance messages because they make consumers feel more involved with the advertisement. Emotional appeals using animals, children and families have been used to sell everything from toilet rolls (the famous 'Andrex' puppy) to life insurance and airlines. In a highly competitive marketplace, it may be difficult to differentiate a service using rational appeals and so emotional appeals are used in campaigns. British Airways' efforts to differentiate itself on service and friendliness and a promotional campaign positioning BA as 'the world's favourite airline' have paid off, largely due to the success of its promotional campaign internationally.

Fear appeals

Messages containing fear appeals are used by marketers to encourage customers to act in a particular way. The Automobile Association has used the portrayal of dreaded situations – breaking down in the rush hour, or the lone female motorist being stranded in a remote area at night – to encourage people to become a member of its repair and rescue services. Fear appeals must not be too threatening and tend to work best when they present a solution to the problem within the message as in the Automobile Association campaigns mentioned. American Express use a similar format to promote their traveller's cheques, emphasising their quick replacement service in the event of cheques being lost or stolen – the tourist's nightmare.

Humour appeals

Humorous messages are used successfully in many advertising campaigns. They attract the audience's interest and attention more effectively than serious messages and can also have a mood-enhancing effect, which makes the recipient more responsive to the message. Humour should not undermine the product or service's image, or detract from the actual message. Humour has also been used successfully by the Automobile Association in some of their campaigns and this may help to alleviate the perceptions of anxiety associated with their service by customers, providing a balance between a service offering which is perceived as unwanted but a necessary evil, to be used in situations of dire necessity, and a service provider which is caring and friendly.

Campaigns in services marketing

Promotional messages of all types have been used successfully in services marketing, with campaigns often using a combination of appeals to get the message across.

When First Direct launched their revolutionary direct banking service, the first promotional messages were designed to create awareness of the new service. The first of its kind, a bank with no branches where all transactions and services were accessible by telephone, twenty-four hours a day, it used a provocative message – 'banking without branches. it's extraordinary.' – with a telephone number and pictures of household objects unrelated to banking. The message had a humorous quirky appeal which served to arouse consumers' curiosity; the message informed them that there was a radically new service being launched, but it did not attempt to explain the concept or educate the consumer about it in the advertisement because research had shown that it was simply too different for consumers to grasp quickly. Customers responding to the advertisement by telephone were then sold the new concept and its benefits in a personal, one-to-one situation.

In the services sector, promotional campaigns are undertaken by commercial organisations such as British Telecom's campaign – 'it's good to talk' – designed to remind consumers about the service and prompt increased usage. A celebrity delivering the message in a confidential, personal manner developed an emotional aspect to the appeal, while information on the low cost of calls at particular times presented a rational message. McDonalds' 'we've got time for you' message emphasised their customer service through warmth and a strong emotional appeal, using young children and family images to attract customers. Commercial organisations use virtually all media to get their message across.

Increasingly, promotion and advertising play a key role in the marketing strategy of not-for-profit and charitable service organisations. The National Canine Defence League's message, 'a dog is for life, not just for Christmas' has been well known since it was first used in the early 1980s, and is another example of an emotional appeal.

Public sector organisations use promotion to keep important issues in the public mind. The Health Education Authority's long-running AIDS awareness campaign has been the recipient of an award from the Institute of Practitioners in Advertising (IPA), as has the Health Education Board for Scotland's 'Smokeline' campaign, designed to help people give up smoking with the line 'You can do it. We can help.' Both of these have used a mix of appeals, including fear (showing the harrowing effects of AIDS or smoking-related illness) and rational appeals within informative and educational messages. Government campaigns based on similar mix of appeals are widespread and serve to inform and educate the public about road safety, fire prevention and against drink-driving, for example.

4. THE PROMOTIONAL MIX

The basic elements which serve to achieve organisational communications objectives form the promotional mix. This essentially brings together the various promotional tools used in the marketing programme in a coordinated and controlled way. The elements which make up the promotional mix are:

Advertising
Personal selling
Publicity/PR
Sales promotion

The promotional mix will be adjusted according to the organisation's promotional objectives and its marketing situation. Generally, however, in consumer services marketing, advertising will be by far the main component (and the most expensive) while in industrial and business-to-business sectors greater reliance is placed on personal selling, trade fairs and other promotional tools.

Advertising

Advertising is paid-for publicity, transmitted through a wide variety of media. The media space and time must be bought (although this is sometimes provided by the media for certain charitable or public information announcements) with the target audience in mind. In this way, advertising is distinctive in that the advertiser has control over what is to be said and when and how it is to be transmitted, by which means. This is in contrast to PR, for example, which aims to attract favourable publicity or editorial comment, for example, neither of which can be guaranteed.

All advertising is however subject to fairly strict controls and even government legislation, especially television advertising. 'Legal, decent, honest, truthful' is the slogan of the advertising industry's watchdog, the Advertising Standards Authority. Consumers are invited to write in if any adverts do not stand up to this code, or are offensive or misleading. Advertisements may have to be withdrawn or modified if the Authority finds that complaints are justified or rules are being breached. The Independent Broadcasting Authority also monitors advertising very closely and regulates what can be presented and at what time of day.

There are a number of advantages to using advertising over other forms of media:

- Control (as discussed earlier)
- Mass communication
- Cost-effective
- Supports other elements of the marketing mix
- Can be highly effective in creating strong brand image and appeal

Advertising is non-personal and involves mass media communication of messages to large numbers of people at the same time. Although company advertising expenditures can be very high, especially in the case of consumer goods and services, the cost of reaching vast numbers of people is often far cheaper than other promotional means. Where there is little tangible difference between service providers and service offerings within a particular market sector, advertising can play a fundamental role in differentiation and positioning. Advertising is an extremely powerful tool for developing a strong brand or organisational image. It can be used to create awareness and stimulate demand, and can successfully underpin the other marketing mix elements.

There are some disadvantages associated with advertising, however:

- High development costs
- Rising costs of media space and airtime
- Lack of immediate feedback
- Problems concerned with credibility
- Low attention focus of audience

The costs of developing and producing an effective advertisement can be very high, especially for television advertising. Advertisers are also dependent on the availability of suitable media and have to meet increasing prices for the best media. The majority of advertisements do not attract direct feedback so there are difficulties in monitoring the effectiveness of a poster campaign, television commercial or newspaper advertisement.

Advertising may also lack credibility with consumers who do not perceive it as genuine and are sceptical about claims made. Additionally, consumers frequently pay little attention to advertising, screening out those in which they have no special interest. 'Information overload' arises when consumers are bombarded by too much information from advertisers and other sources and they tend to switch off and quickly become unreceptive. This reinforces the importance of getting the right message across, in a way which will be well received and which is not at risk of being misinterpreted or misunderstood.

Personal selling

Personal selling takes many forms but consists of the seller engaging in some kind of personal contact with the customer or potential customer in order to persuade them to make a purchase (or become a member of a club, or to enrol at a college or become a regular donor to a charity, for example). It differs from advertising in that there is this personal contact, either face-to-face or by telephone, usually. There is an inbuilt element of flexibility in personal selling because the salesperson can judge the customer's responses to the message as the contact takes place and modify it accordingly.

Personal selling can be used to get far more information across than an advertisement can do, and is used very widely in industrial selling where complex specifications and technical details need to be discussed. It is also widely used in the financial services sector for similar reasons, in that both the customer and seller need to ask many questions and provide substantial amounts of information for the right service offering to be specified. Personal selling has other advantages in that it can be aimed at specific target markets and prospects and also provides more direct feedback than other promotional methods.

There are some disadvantages associated with personal selling. There is a very high cost per contact (when compared with advertising and other promotional methods) and setting up and training a sales force represents a significant investment for the organisation. Some organisations have developed a very negative image with the public for unethical practices using high-pressure sales techniques – timeshare holiday companies have attracted masses of criticism in recent years, as have some areas of the financial services sector – with the result that consumers tend to regard all salespeople with suspicion and distrust.

Telephone selling has also become widespread and, while it has a very useful role to play when the consumer has already shown interest, by responding to an advertisement for example, it is often done on a 'cold call' basis and is seen as irritating and intrusive by the consumer.

Publicity/PR

Publicity refers to communications about organisations, products or services, which is not paid for or sponsored by the organisation in question. Often it takes the form of news reports and announcements. Not all publicity is good publicity, as organisations find to their cost sometimes. Whenever there are health or safety scares over a particular type of product, dramatic media coverage will ensure that consumers find out about it. Organisations will then attempt to restore good public relations through the use and application of PR tools. These include:

- Publicity through the media
- Involvement in social and community initiatives
- Sponsorship of events
- Public announcements and special publications
- Corporate brochures and other publicity material

One of the main advantages afforded by publicity as opposed to paid-for advertising is enhanced credibility with audiences. Editorial features attract more attention generally than advertisements and are perceived as being more genuine and impartial. A company whose latest technological advance is featured on the famous 'Tomorrow's World' television series benefits from the kind of attention which would be both costly and difficult to achieve through advertising alone.

This impartiality also leads to a major disadvantage, however, which is lack of control over what is said, how it is presented and at what time, for example. PR managers will plan and distribute information on a systematic basis to try to ensure that the organisation is presented in the best possible light. PR has traditionally been viewed as playing a supporting role in the promotional mix, underpinning activities such as advertising and sales promotion, but it is gaining wider attention and recognition as a communications tool in its own right.

Sales promotion

Sales promotion consists of all those activities which can help to stimulate purchase of goods and services. Sales promotion activities can be aimed at the end consumer or at intermediaries in the channel, sometimes referred to as 'out of the pipeline' and 'into the pipeline' promotions respectively. Sales promotion tools include:

Free samples
Money-off coupons and special offers
Competitions

Point-of-sale displays

'Free' gifts and other incentives

Sales promotions play a useful role in helping to stimulate trial of new products, and maintaining interest in established brands. Many financial service providers offer free gifts of small electrical appliances, gift items and even weekend breaks to customers who take out life insurance and savings plans. Competitions are used by many types of organisation to attract new customers and keep existing ones – the free prize draw for big money prizes being a popular approach.

Sales promotions should be regarded as tactical methods of stimulating sales over a period whilst a particular promotion is running. They should not be used to replace other elements of the promotional mix as their effects are temporaryn nature and will not have longer-term impact on the consumer.

Trade fairs and exhibitions can be viewed as a form of sales promotion when they are used, like the Ideal Home Exhibition, to introduce products and services to consumers and stimulate demand. Trade fairs can also be treated as publicity for organisations in situations where appearances at trade exhibitions are seen as a tool for corporate image building rather than as a selling tool, as is often the case in industrial market sectors.

5. MEDIA CHOICE AND SELECTION

One of the key tasks facing promotional management is the selection of appropriate media for advertising and other forms of communication. The choice of media available for transmitting the message to the target audience is immense – in the UK alone there are hundreds of regional newspapers and consumer magazines and some sixty Independent Local Radio stations to choose from apart from the national daily papers and regional and national television stations. The choice of media will be determined by a number of factors including:

The available budget
Target audience factors
Level of coverage required
Exposure and frequency
Cost effectiveness
Desired impact

The amount of money available to finance a campaign may rule out the use of certain expensive media forms such as television and national press. The choice of available media will always be governed by budgetary considerations. The target audience profile may also rule out certain types of media or indicate clearly which might be most appropriate. Magazines use independent market research organisations to provide readership audits – detailed information about the number of readers frequently incorporating geo-demographic and other data about the profile of the readers. This information is a crucial selling tool for publishers trying to sell advertising space and is also very helpful to advertisers wishing to buy space in the most appropriate publication to reach their target audience.

It is unlikely, however, that one particular communications vehicle, such as a magazine, will reach all members of the organisation's target market. The level of coverage required to communicate the message to as many customers and potential customers will also be a key factor in media selection. Several different media will probably be used in order to maximise the level of coverage in communicating with the whole of the target audience.

Audiences need to be exposed to an advertising message several times for that message to be remembered. This level of frequency – the possible number of times any individual is exposed to the communications message – is another factor which governs the choice of appropriate media. If individuals ideally need to see a television advertisement six times for it to be effective, the actual number of times it must be transmitted will be far greater to allow for different viewing habits among the target audience and to ensure everyone has at least six OTS ('opportunities to see').

Advertising media will also be looked at in terms of cost-effectiveness before a decision is made. The number of people the message reaches will differ according to which medium is used, and the costs of using each media vary dramatically. For this reason, advertisers calculate the average CPT ('cost per thousand') to estimate the relative cost-effectiveness of different media.

The desired level of impact must also be considered. The CPT of outdoor poster advertising is only a tiny fraction of the CPT of cinema advertising, but the impact of transmitting an advertisement to an attentive audience sitting comfortably in a cinema is far higher than the impact of poster advertising to passengers and drivers in rush hour traffic.

The success of the advertising campaign will depend on the selection of the right combination of media to maximise coverage and frequency cost effectively and within the required budget. The available media will include:

Television
Newspapers
Magazines
Cinema
Radio
Outdoor

Each medium has distinct advantages and disadvantages. Media planning and buying has become a specialised management function and media planners are also responsible for scheduling the timing of the campaign. Advertising is the element of the promotional mix most likely to be passed to outside experts – advertising agencies and media buying services, for example. Its success depends on a mix of creativity and careful planning and scheduling in order to communicate the right message via the most effective media.

6. MANAGING THE PROMOTIONAL EFFORT

The development of an effective promotional campaign involves combining the promotional mix elements in the most appropriate way to meet the organisation's communications objectives. Promotional management is concerned with this task of coordinating and implementing promotional programmes, integrated within organisational marketing programmes. Controlling the promotional programme and evaluating its overall effectiveness are also key parts of the promotional manager's task.

There are essentially three stages in promotional management:

- *Developing the promotional mix*
- *Assigning the promotional budget*
- *Monitoring and evaluation*

In developing the promotional mix, advertising campaigns, publicity and PR, sales promotion and personal selling must be combined to create a comprehensive promotional programme. Interestingly, in many organisations, management of the sales force is treated quite separately from promotional management, and the promotional mix is not fully integrated. Organisations which seek a marketing orientation should ensure that promotional elements are treated as a cohesive whole, and the management roles and tasks structured accordingly.

The task of allocating the promotional budget most effectively can also be difficult, usually because the level of funding available never seems enough. In designing the most appropriate promotional mix, therefore, promotional management must include detailed costings of each proposed part of the promotional plan, to ensure that plans stay within budget and that the budget is allocated for maximum effectiveness.

Many factors will influence the design of the promotional mix:

The nature of the organisation
The service offering
Service life cycle stage
Type of markets the organisation is operating in
Customer characteristics
Buyer behaviour and decision processes
Channels of distribution

The main differences often lie between consumer markets and industrial markets. Organisations such as banks and package tour operators seek to attract as many customers as possible from a broad spectrum of the population. They are likely to choose mass advertising via television, radio and the national press as their primary means of communicating with large numbers of customers. In consumer goods marketing, the sales force often plays a key role in selling to the channel intermediaries. With expensive goods and services, such as cars, furniture, holidays and insurance, the role of the salesperson at the point of sale is also crucial.

Industrial organisations tend to deal with far fewer customers as they are dealing with other companies, not the general public. They will select personal selling and sales promotion through trade fairs and exhibitions, supported by limited advertising in specialist journals and trade publications. Personal selling is most suitable for industrial products and services where the supplier often acts as consultant and has extensive contact with the client over long periods. Advertising is likely to be used to promote the organisation and build a strong corporate image. It may also be used to generate awareness of the organisation and its services and stimulate sales enquiries.

Organisations can develop quite distinctive promotional strategies which become part of that organisation's differentiation in the marketplace. Communications programmes are clearly identifiable with a particular organisation's image, or certain types of products. Successful promotional programmes, however, will only be developed as a result of an integrated marketing programme and clearly defined marketing and communications objectives.

7. MONITORING AND EVALUATION

The final stage in the promotional management process is that of monitoring and evaluating the programme. In order to do this effectively, controls must be built into the plan to enable its effectiveness to be measured. This control stage is an essential part of all planning. It serves a number of purposes in relation to the promotional plan and helps to determine the following:

- Are communications objectives being met?
- Has the target audience received the message?
- Have they received the right message?
- Are budgets being adhered to?

There are several ways of evaluating the results of communications but there are many difficulties associated with measuring effectiveness – it might be impossible to say how much an organisation's image has been enhanced in one individual's perception as a result of a particular advertising or PR campaign because perception is highly subjective. Some communications are designed to elicit some action response, however. Prompting trial purchase of a new product or buying a product to enjoy the opportunity to participate in a competition are examples of this, and are obviously easier to measure in terms of sales volume and level of demand. Evaluation methods include:

Marketing research – awareness testing This is typically carried out before and after the campaign to assess whether awareness of the organisation or service has increased following the promotion.

Direct response Many advertisements, sales promotions and exhibitions are designed to elicit orders and response can therefore be measured by the number of responses received and orders placed.

Point-of-sale monitoring Developments such as EPOS (electronic point of sale) have made it possible to monitor the success of in-store promotions, for example, while they are actually taking place. Measuring sales response to special offers which have been advertised, such as a special McDonalds meal offer, is another important way of measuring results and also illustrates the way that promotional methods are often combined.

The central focus of evaluation methods must be the promotional objectives. How well has the campaign met these objectives? How can the campaign's success be quantified? Weaknesses and failings of the campaign must also be clearly identified and tackled, withdrawing the promotion if necessary. The monitoring and evaluation system must feed results and information back into the planning cycle to help decision-making later.

8. SUMMARY

Promotion is essentially about communications. Target audiences need to receive information about goods and services before they can begin to consider making a purchase. In addition to external communications, internal audiences need good communications if the organisation is going to function in a proper and marketing-orientated manner.

The communications process consists of four main elements:

source
message
media selected
recipient

The whole process is affected by noise or distractions. This distraction can take the form of competition for the recipient's attention from other advertising or entertainment, for example.

The promotional message may be designed with one or more aims in mind:

to inform
to entertain
to educate
to persuade
to remind

The promotional objectives will influence the nature of the promotional message and the type of appeal used to get the message across.

Promotional activity is organised in the form of the promotional mix within the marketing mix. The elements which make up the promotional mix are as follows:

Advertising
Personal selling
Publicity/PR
Sales promotion

One of the key tasks in designing and executing promotional programmes is the selection of appropriate media for advertising and other forms of communication. The range of possible media choice is extensive but will ultimately be governed by factors such as the budget available and the target audience profile.

The development of an effective promotional campaign involves combining the promotional mix elements in the most appropriate way to meet the organisation's communications objectives. Promotional management is concerned wih this task of co-ordinating and implementing promotional programmes, integrated within organisational marketing programmes. Evaluation and monitoring is also vital. Evaluation methods may include:

Marketing research – awareness testing
Direct response
Point-of-sale monitoring

All this activity should help to ensure that well defined communications objectives are met, the target audience receives the message correctly and the available budget has been utilised effectively.

Progress test 13

1. What is the role of promotion within marketing?

2. Why is it important for organisations to communicate both internally and externally?

3. List the four main elements of the communications process and explain what they mean.

4. What factors are likely to influence the promotional objectives and why?

5. Outline the different types of appeal which may be used in a promotional message and suggest in which circumstances they might be especially appropriate or effective.

6. What four elements make up the promotional mix?

7. Media selection is largely governed by which factors?

8. How can marketing managers evaluate the success (or otherwise) of promotional programmes?

Discussion

1. Think about the promotional activities you are exposed to as a consumer. What strikes you as being particularly effective or attractive? Try to analyse what the promotional objectives are in each case and how well they have been met.

2. Devise a creative promotional programme which is based on a very low budget for each of the following:
   (a) a local, council-owned textile museum/heritage centre
   (b) a wildlife conservation society
   (c) a charity set up to care for abandoned pets.

14

SERVICES DISTRIBUTION PLANNING

INTRODUCTION

Most producers of physical goods do not sell directly to their end consumers in today's market. They can make choices about where to produce the goods, based on lower labour costs and other considerations, together with decisions about which markets to sell the goods in and how to get the goods to the consumers. The inseparable nature of services means that such a range of choice is not open to service providers. In many instances, the quality and value associated with a service are dependent on the interaction between the service provider and the consumer at the point of exchange.

Consumers of services actually participate in the service delivery process and the method chosen by the service provider for service delivery will form part of the service itself. Whether the exchange is based on hi-tech automatic means or traditional personal service, the methods used will influence the outcome of the exchange and customer satisfaction levels.

Distribution, or the 'place' element, of the marketing mix is concerned chiefly with two main issues: accessibility and availability. As shown above, the inseparable nature of services means that services must be accessible to customers and potential customers in order for exchanges to take place. Accessibility must be a component of the actual service offering for it to have value. Additionally, the perishable nature of services means it is essential for the service to be available to customers – in the right place at the right time. The service cannot be stored until a later date; it must be available for consumption at the point of production. This chapter reviews the factors which service marketers need to take into account in determining a distribution strategy. The role of channel intermediaries is also discussed, together with channel management issues.

1. ACCESSIBILITY AND AVAILABILITY

Services must be both accessible and available to customers and potential customers in order for an exchange to take place and for the value of the service to be realised:

Accessibility refers to the ease and convenience with which a service can be purchased, used or received.

Availability refers to the extent to which a service is obtainable or capable of being purchased, used or received.

Both criteria must be met in order to achieve successful services marketing. This can be illustrated by the following examples:

The UK National Lottery, launched in 1994, was designed to be easily accessible to all eligible players throughout the UK. Entry forms were simple to complete and could be bought via a network of retail outlets such as grocery stores and newsagents. However, when the lottery was actually launched, many of the chosen outlets either had not got the correct computer network installed or it failed to work correctly, rendering the service *unavailable*. In urban areas it was not too difficult for customers to find alternative outlets but some rural areas with just one designated lottery ticket seller were left with no means of entering. Despite the very high entry numbers recorded in the first week, significant adverse publicity resulted from dissatisfied would-be entrants and custom was lost.

Many Government benefits which were, in theory, accessible and available to all eligible claimants were not being taken up by all potential payees. People were put off by the lengthy processes involved and their fear of having to deal with complex form-filling. Sometimes they simply did not know what kinds of benefits they were entitled to because of confusion over the different names given such as Family Credit, which some people thought was in fact a loan service rather than a benefit payment. In effect, the service was *inaccessible* for them. This led to the simplification of many of the procedures and the re-organisation of the various departments responsible for dealing with claims to make the whole process much more accessible.

2. LOCATION

These criteria – accessibility and availability – must be given priority in all decisions about services distribution. In this section the idea of 'place' will be considered in terms of the location and time of the service delivery. This needs to be considered before any decisions regarding the use and selection of channels of distribution (reviewed in the next section) can be made.

There are several key factors to be considered in decisions about service location:

Service inseparability
Perishability
The role of the consumer as co-producer of the service
Customer needs and wants
Importance of geographical location as part of the service
Target markets

Service inseparability

Some services are more inseparable than others; a hairdresser has to perform a service on a person-to-person basis with clients whereas credit card customers are happy to be able to use the credit card for cash or payments at vast numbers of locations without direct contact with the credit card company on each occasion.

The degree of direct access to the central service provider required will influence channel decisions. Many services are now provided using telephone contact and other forms of telecommunications and direct marketing:

> First Direct provide a complete telephone banking service as Direct Line does for insurance. Neither operation has actual branch offices on the high street; all contact is remote.
>
> Direct mail is used to promote the services offered by many service organisations and service exchanges can frequently be carried out by mail, such as applying for a loan or responding to a charity appeal.
>
> NWS Bank offers loan services by post or telephone with loan cheques being delivered direct to customers' homes by courier service within hours of the loan being approved.

Some of these developments reflect moves on the part of service providers to reduce the degree of service inseparability thereby increasing flexibility and reducing costs of providing the service. Additionally, the benefits to the consumer are frequently greater:

- The convenience and ease with which credit cards can be used at locations worldwide without direct contact with the card provider,
- The advantages of dealing with a bank which is open outside normal trading hours and which is accessible from any telephone.

Perishability

This is another area where services marketing differs quite distinctly from the marketing of physical goods. A key function traditionally performed by channel members is to hold inventory – stocks of physical goods held in warehouses for onward transportation to markets or, in the case of retailing, for example, stocks on the shelves for local customers to buy. Services cannot be stored in this way, so intermediaries play a different role in facilitating the service exchange and often form part of the service production and delivery process.

The role of the consumer as co-producer of the service

The role of intermediaries in the production and delivery of a service has already been noted but there is another vital issue to be considered – the role of the consumer. Many services require extensive interaction on the part of the consumer in order for the service to have any value; the audience must go to the theatre, the customer must study the menu and place an order to eat at a restaurant. Customer needs must therefore be given priority when making decisions about when and where the service will be available. Theatrical performances given in the mornings might be highly accomplished but would be of little value if there was nobody watching!

Customer needs and wants

As stated, customer needs are a key factor influencing decisions about services distribution. These are likely to differ between various customer segments using the same services and between different types of service offering:

- Some customers may be willing to collect their own take-away meals while others will always choose an outlet which offers delivery.
- Elderly or housebound persons may require home visits from doctors or chiropodists and will be the main consumers of specific home-based services such as 'meals on wheels' and home helps.
- Some consumers may rate 'convenience' as the key benefit sought in selecting a service whereas others may seek exclusivity. The latter group will be prepared to travel and put more effort into their participation in the service delivery by, for example, being prepared to queue to get into the best nightclub or to make a reservation weeks or months in advance for seats at the opera or a table at a gourmet restaurant.
- Bank customers may be willing to visit their local branch to conduct day-to-day transactions but may prefer a bank representative to visit them at home to discuss life insurance, pensions or mortgages.

Buyer behaviour and the factors influencing service choice between different target segments are essential considerations in location decisions.

The importance of geographical location as part of the service

Again, service providers frequently have very different criteria to consider here from those affecting manufacturers of physical goods. Manufacturers may choose to produce the goods at a location convenient for cheap labour or natural resources and then ship the products to the target markets for consumption. Apart from the inseparable nature of services making this largely infeasible as discussed previously, many services are dependent on geographical location as part of the service. Examples include:

Tourist destinations
Health spas (when located at real sources of spa water)
Historic or geographic attractions such as Buckingham Palace or the Grand Canyon.

In these cases, the idea of 'place' is largely pre-determined and the key task for marketing managers is to manage the other elements of the mix in such a way as to get the maximum number of visitors/customers to travel to the service.

Some services, such as those examples given above, do attract customers who are prepared to travel for the service. The same applies to services such as specialist medical treatment or education and training where the patient or student may travel long distances to consume the service. The importance of geographical location must be looked at in the light of the needs and wants of different customer segments, as discussed in the preceding section.

Some service providers need to travel to their customers, however. Electrical appliance repairs, decorating, plumbing and maintenance services frequently have to be carried out at the customer's home or business premises. Other services need to be available locally as customers will not be willing to travel long distances for them, especially if there is strong competition nearby. Tyre repairs and garage services, banks, hairdressers and take-away food outlets are all typical examples.

Target markets

Location decisions are influenced by all the factors outlined above. The key criteria, however, is to make the service accessible and available to all target market segments. Service providers can choose where to locate their service outlets, or where to provide their service in order to maximise their market opportunities, in all cases except those where to service is location specific (tourist destinations and historic sites, for example). Factors influencing such decisions include:

- Market size and structure by geographical region
- Location of potentially attractive consumer segments
- Organisational objectives
- Level of market coverage desired
- Number and type of competitors in region
- Local infrastructure; good road access, facilities, public transport network
- Distribution method

The distribution methods selected will have an impact on location decisions:

> First Direct offers an innovative telephone banking service to all its consumers throughout the UK with no branch offices and all transactions conducted by telephone. The service is made *available* to customers via a twenty-four-hour telephone line, staffed by highly trained customer service personnel. In order to make the service *accessible*, however, this type of distribution strategy relies on widespread promotion to attract and inform potential customers, rather than local branches.

3. DIRECT DISTRIBUTION

For reasons already highlighted, many service organisations choose direct distribution methods which do not use outside agents or intermediaries. The inseparable nature of services and the role of the service provider in the service delivery process make this a desirable option for the sake of quality and customer care. Quality standards may be difficult to maintain through a third party and the spirit or ethos of the service provider can be lost so that the customer does not benefit fully from the service exchange.

For direct distribution to be a feasible option, certain considerations must be taken into account. The practical issues influencing decisions to undertake direct distribution include the following factors:

Company resources/company objectives
Type of service
Geographic spread of the market
Legal and political restrictions on foreign operations
Levels of technical expertise or skill required to deliver the service satisfactorily
Customer preferences

Company resources The structure and size of the service organisation will influence the choice of distribution strategy, and this may change over time. As organisations expand, they may choose to continue to serve each of their customers directly and invest in additional personnel and premises accordingly. The organisation's objectives will also influence the distribution method selected. If the main objective is fast growth, then establishing a network of intermediaries may be the preferred alternative.

Type of service Perhaps the most relevant distinction here is that of people-based services and equipment-based services. Equipment-based services such as car rental, vending machines and dry cleaning do not involve such a high degree of personal involvement in the delivery of the service. Such services may be well suited to being operated through a network of agents, and frequently are. People-based services, however, which involve high levels of personal expertise or understanding, or which require very close contact with customers, tend to be much more suited to direct distribution.

Geographic spread of the market Locally-based service organisations operating in a limited area will probably be well placed to serve all their customers directly. Coverage of a wider market area will require further investment in setting up branches or the development of a network of intermediaries. Again the type of service and the organisation's objectives and resources will also be key factors. In some situations, it is appropriate for the service provider to travel to the customer's location, even overseas. Expertise-based services such as architects and consultants frequently operate in this way.

Legal and political restrictions on foreign operations In some foreign markets, restrictions apply to local investment and the setting up of overseas branches, in some cases actually prohibiting such activity. The only alternative may be to operate through local channels, making direct distribution impossible. Further discussion of these issues can be found in Chapter 23.

Levels of technical skill or expertise required to deliver the service satisfactorily People-based services, or other services which require a relatively high degree of technical skill or expertise for satisfactory delivery, are better suited to direct distribution. The costs of training channel members and monitoring quality need to be assessed against the cost of setting up branches to serve target markets. Some service intermediaries do provide personnel with the right skills and knowledge, however, especially in sectors traditionally served by agents or intermediaries, such as travel agents or insurance brokers.

Customer preferences The needs and wants of the customers must be considered in planning a distribution strategy. Different customer segments will exhibit varying buying habits, for example, which may influence their choice of service provider. For example, customers who are loyal to a particular bank or building society may be happy to consult them about all their financial service requirements. Other customers may prefer to shop around and look for a better deal by contacting independent financial advisors who act as agents or brokers for a number of financial service providers.

There are advantages for the service organisation operating direct distribution methods. These include:

- Greater control
- Customer service and satisfaction levels can be more easily monitored, as can service quality
- Management has direct control over all aspects of operations
- Internal and external communications can be handled more effectively
- Closer involvement with customers
- Direct contact with customers can allow databases to be established and used for target marketing
- Greater confidentiality can be maintained
- Commission costs and other fees are avoided.

Some of these advantages are far more important to certain types of service organisations than others. Banks and accountants, for example, do need detailed knowledge of their customers and have to maintain confidentiality. It is not so important for fast food restaurants or bus service operators to have such detailed information.

4. CHANNEL FUNCTIONS

The role and functions of channel intermediaries in services marketing varies somewhat from that of the marketing of physical goods. Some comparisons can be drawn by looking at the functions traditionally associated with channel members:

Storage and warehousing This is obviously not applicable due to the perishable nature of services.
Breaking bulk This again relates to taking quantities of physical goods so does not apply.

Delivery/transport Intermediaries would undoubtedly play a role in the service delivery process but not in the context of delivering physical goods from stock

After-sales service This is frequently linked to the marketing of physical goods although is also applicable to services; whenever dissatisfaction occurs, in fact.

Price setting

- In the sale of physical goods, each channel member will have applied some 'mark up' to the price of the goods and has, usually, some flexibility in deciding what to charge and whether to offer discounts. In services marketing, channels tend to be much shorter with either direct distribution or the use of one level of intermediaries being common.
- Agents may make a charge for providing the service, as is the case with banks cashing travellers cheques, or theatre booking agencies.
- Alternatively, the agent may be paid a commission by the service organisation, as with travel agents and insurance brokers (which will be incorporated into the price paid by end consumers) but will not themselves have any control over price setting. Prices published in travel brochures and charged for insurance premiums will tend to be set by the central service provider.

The degree to which intermediaries are involved in price setting will depend on the nature of the service and the distribution method (agent or franchisee, for example). Intermediaries will generally have less control over setting prices than is the case with physical goods.

Promotion Here the role played by local agents and distributors will be similar in both services marketing and the marketing of physical goods, especially in international marketing. This promotion may be as simple as displaying a 'Visa' sign for information to planning complex campaigns.

Personal selling This is likely to be of greater importance in services marketing because of the key role played by the service provider (whether that be the actual organisation or an agent acting on its behalf) in the service delivery process. The ability of an intermediary's personnel to interact satisfactorily with customers in facilitating the service exchange is a key consideration in selecting and managing channels.

5. CHANNEL SELECTION

Whilst it has been established that services organisations will not necessarily use channels in the same way as manufacturers of physical products, various types of intermediaries are used in many service situations. Care must be taken when selecting intermediaries or channel members. Their direct contact with the ultimate user of the service means that they can influence levels of quality and customer satisfaction. This is a more complex issue in services marketing because of the role of the service provider in the service delivery process and is the main concern of channel management in services marketing.

Factors which influence the selection of channel members include the standing of prospective intermediaries, their image, personnel and location. Channel members should be of sound financial standing and reflect the quality and image of the service offered. They need to have the appropriate facilities, resources and personnel to be able to deliver the service effectively. The special characteristics of services have led to certain types of channel being commonly used, while others, such as wholesalers and retailers, are not applicable in most circumstances.

There are two main groups of channel intermediaries which may be selected:

Agents and brokers
Franchise operators

Agents and brokers

Many services are offered via networks of agents or brokers. The agents often provide a chain of offices throughout various locations and provide relevant facilities and expertise. Developments in technology mean that it is very easy for service organisations to maintain very close contact with agents via on-line computer systems as well as telephone contact. Agents may have specialist local knowledge which can enhance the performance of the service in a particular market. The level of service they provide varies according to the nature of the service offered. Basic service transactions such as encashment of travellers' cheques may be all that is required, as opposed to more complex services such as financial advice.

Franchise operators

Franchising involves the sale of a successful business formula to an external buyer or franchisee who runs the operation in a specified location. The franchisor can benefit from this approach in several ways:

Low cost expansion Expansion, often on a wide scale, can be undertaken with little capital investment as the required investment comes from the franchisees when they buy in to the operation.

Rapid growth Franchising offers a means of establishing 'outlets' in many locations quickly, providing the franchise is successful and attracts investors. This is a vital factor in a competitive marketplace.

Local management expertise/personnel As individual business entrepreneurs in their own right, franchisees can provide excellent management coverage without massive central training and recruitment costs. The franchisors do not need to increase staff numbers in order to gain widespread expansion as local staff will be employed by the franchisee as part of the business.

Similarly, the franchisee benefits from the arrangement in several ways:

Reduced risk Buying into an established business formula with a well recognised organisation and brand name is less risky than starting up from scratch.

Business support The franchisee will benefit from services offered by the franchisor in staff training, for example, and the provision of business materials, technical and legal support and ongoing development.

Franchising is not without its drawbacks, however. A poor operation run by a franchisee will carry the organisation's name and reputation down with it. Some controls have to be built in to ensure franchisees do work to pre-determined quality standards and follow organisational policy. The franchisor makes less profit through this system of distribution than they would make through direct expansion but this potential loss can be outweighed by the benefits of franchise growth.

Franchisees can find that the promised profits do not materialise and become demotivated and let the business slide. Some may even have been the victims of the kind of unscrupulous trading practices which have been exposed from time to time. This can have the effect of creating a negative image of franchise operations which can deter would-be investors from buying genuine, well-run franchises. The success of franchising has been outstanding, however, with many household names in service industries being run on this basis. Dyno-rod drain cleaning services, Rentokil pest control and Prontaprint business printing and reprographic services are successful and well known examples.

6. SUMMARY

Distribution, or the 'place' element of the marketing mix, is concerned chiefly with two main issues: accessibility and availability. The inseparable nature of services means that services must be accessible to customers and potential customers in order for exchanges to take place, as customers form part of the service delivery process. Additionally, because services are perishable, they cannot be stored or sold on to a wholesaler to be sold on to consumers at some time in the future. For these reasons, the distribution alternatives open to service organisations are not the same as for the marketing of physical goods.

A key decision with regard to distribution is location. There are several key factors to be considered in decisions about service location:

Service inseparability
Perishability
The role of the consumer as co-producer of the service
Customer needs and wants
Importance of geographical location as part of the service
Target markets

Many service organisations choose direct distribution methods which do not use outside agents or intermediaries. The practical issues influencing decisions to undertake direct distribution include the following factors:

Company resources/company objectives
Type of service
Geographic spread of the market
Legal and political restrictions on foreign operations
Levels of technical expertise or skill required to deliver the service satisfactorily
Customer preferences

The role and functions of channel intermediaries in services marketing differ from the marketing of physical goods. Comparisons show these differences and illustrate the reduced involvement with channel management and reduced possibilities for channel conflict. The main types of channels seen in services marketing are agents and brokers with franchise operations also being widespread.

Progress test 14

1. Why is the distribution method particularly important in services marketing?

2. What criteria must be met with regard to distribution? Why is this so?

3. Outline the main factors which must be considered when making decisions about location.

4. Give examples of services which are wholly dependent upon geographical location together with examples of some which are not.

5. Why is direct distribution frequently the most logical choice for services marketing?

6. Describe the traditional functions of channel intermediaries and comment on their applicability to services marketing.

7. Which two main types of intermediary tend to be most commonly selected in services marketing?

Discussion

1. What market trends are likely to affect 'place' decisions for services marketers in the future?

2. A number of organisations have opted for direct distribution methods in fields where this has been a complete break with tradition (e.g. First Direct banking services). Could this be an appropriate route for other types of service? Suggest other innovative approaches suitable for consideration in relation to services.

15

PEOPLE – THE FIFTH 'P'

INTRODUCTION

In today's competitive environment, organisations in all industries have been forced to realise the importance of customer care and its key role in strategy. Nowhere is this more vital than in services marketing. Consumers are becoming increasingly sophisticated in terms of their expectations and make far higher demands of those organisations who serve them. Quality is judged by standards of service and the role of the employee in service organisations is critical in maintaining quality standards.

The inseparable nature of services means that the human element forms an intrinsic part of the service package. In some situations it *is* the service package, while sometimes it accompanies the more tangible elements which comprise the service offering.

'People' as the fifth element in the services marketing mix applies not only to service personnel, but also recognises the role that other people – the customers – play in service delivery. Sometimes the role of the customer is an important part of the service itself, as in education, for example, where the students must follow the learning programme or in car hire where the benefit – transportation – can only be achieved through the customer's driving. In many services like this, participation of some kind is essential to derive the service benefits.

Management of people within the organisation is a key task. The organisation's staff are its prime resource, and human resources management is the professional approach to finding and developing the right people. Central to successful service delivery is management of the customer/provider interface. Employees need to understand their role in the service exchange, and human resources management provides the programmes and strategies to ensure the highest standards of customer care.

1. THE ROLE OF THE EMPLOYEE IN SERVICES MARKETING

The role of the employee in services marketing varies according to the situation and the level of interaction. Frequently this depends on the degree of tangibility of a service. The level of contact can be determined by classifying the service according to whether it is a labour-intensive (people-based) service or an equipment-based service, as follows:

High Contact
People-based services:
education, dental and medical care, restaurants

Low Contact
Equipment-based services:
automatic car wash, launderette, vending machine, cinema

Additionally, people-based services can be further broken down in terms of the expertise and skills of the service provider:

Professional
Medical and legal services, accountancy, tutoring

Non-professional
Babysitting, caretaking, casual labour

This illustrates the variety which exists in the roles of people in service provision. These different roles may be grouped into the following broad categories:

Primary – where the service is actually carried out by the service provider, e.g. dentists, hairdressers.
Facilitating – where employees facilitate the service transaction and participate in it, e.g. bank counter staff, waiters, hotel porters.
Ancillary – where the employee helps to create the service exchange but then is not part of it, e.g. travel agents, insurance brokers, equipment hire.

Frequently, the overall service offering will be made up of a combination of the roles described. The dentist will perform the actual primary service, but a receptionist may arrange appointments and send out reminders. The restaurant staff are dependent on the chefs and kitchen staff, if they are to be able to perform the service. For every employee in a bank who has personal contact with customers, there may be a number of administrative staff behind the scenes. The important issue is that customer care is everyone's concern throughout the organisation. Successful service provision is dependent on interpersonal exchanges, between the provider and the customer, and between service personnel.

Customer perceptions of quality are frequently influenced directly by the actions of service personnel. Levels of satisfaction or dissatisfaction can be governed by the way in which personnel deal with the specific needs and requests of customers; by the steps taken by service personnel in the event that some aspect of the service goes wrong; and by service which goes beyond the customer's expectations, usually by the personal actions of an individual employee.

This important role played by employees in service organisations (or other people working for services, such as volunteers or members) is critical to long-term success. The image of a service organisation is often indistinguishable from that of its employees. For this reason staff selection and training take high priority in service management.

2. STAFF SELECTION AND RECRUITMENT

As the value of staff rates so highly in service organisations, careful recruitment of the right kind of personnel is an important step. *Internal marketing*, as described in Chapter 8, recognises that employees and potential employees are customers of the organisation's internal market and their needs and wants should be considered in the same light as those of external clients. Marketing activities should be aimed at these internal markets in the same way as when marketing to external clients.

Organisations seeking to attract excellent service personnel can consider using the same tools and techniques that they use to attract customers. Recruitment should not be left solely to the human resources management function but should be seen as a powerful tool in itself for enhancing and maintaining the organisation's standing and image. The human resources management function can support, advise and guide line management in this area. Programmes designed to generate interest in the organisation, through sponsorship and PR, for example, can also be used to attract the people who share the organisation's ideals and standards. While many sources of information exist detailing approaches and techniques for recruitment, the basic steps are as follows:

Preliminary stage

- Identification of vacancy (may be a new post or replacement)
- Develop job profile – review job description and person specification. The person specification can be adapted to place emphasis on customer and service orientation, a desirable or even essential quality for all jobs.
- Consider internal sources
- Consider using specialist recruitment agency
- Advertise – internally and externally
- Process applications
- Screen applications for shortlist

Selection stage

- Arranging interviews; venue, timing, date
- Determine process for selection; formal/informal interviews, use of pre-selection test, presentations
- Conducting interviews
- Testing
- Offer/Acceptance
- Formal appointment

Follow-up stage

- Induction
- Training
- Ongoing staff development and appraisal

Requirements for the job

Service employees frequently have significant personal contact with customers and responsibility for satisfactory service delivery lies on the individual's shoulders. Conflicting demands from customers and management over time spent on personal service versus efficiency and productivity, for example, may need careful handling. Coping skills, manner and demeanour will all be key factors in a candidate's ability to do the job, as well as their technical skills and qualifications. First Direct telephone banking, for example, look for empathy and ability to listen and communicate in their prospective employees, not just banking experience.

Basic requirements should be identified as a starting point and may include:

Qualifications/technical knowledge
Ability, specialist skills and aptitude
Experience
Personality and personal attributes
Physical characteristics

Recruitment issues in the service sector

Certain services have special aspects which may impact on recruitment. The so-called 'caring professions' are an example. Many caring services operate in traditionally low-paid sectors so a sense of vocation and commitment may be desirable personal attributes. Charities have sometimes experienced difficulties in attracting experienced managerial staff as applicants are sensitive to the moral issues involved in receiving high salaries from charitable bodies. To recruit appropriately qualified personnel, however, in, say, accountancy and marketing management, charities have to offer competitive salaries.

Some services obviously require staff with certain qualifications, such as teachers and lawyers. The degree of specialisation required will govern the potential marketplace for recruits. In a situation where demand for certain skills outstrips supply, which sometimes occurs, or in highly specialised areas, a different approach to recruitment may need to be found, such as in-service training for potential applicants, to bring them to the required standard.

The rate of legislative changes, for example, affecting organisations in the public sector brought about by compulsory competitive tendering, privatisation and the introduction of a quality culture geared to customer care has led to different personnel requirements. Such organisations are having to compete more and more in the external marketplace, not just in terms of maintaining their services against competing private service providers, but also in recruitment. They are often hampered or constrained in their strategy by existing practices which may be outdated or inappropriate and other influences including:

Traditional low rates of pay
Cutbacks
Tightly structured pay scales
Conditions of service.

3. TRAINING AND DEVELOPMENT

Training is needed on more than one level; at its basic level it may be needed to impart knowledge about a particular aspect of the organisation or job; at a broader level, it gives focus and direction for the future to employees and also plays a communications role within the organisation. The training opportunities offered by an organisation may be influential in attracting and retaining person- nel. Additionally, it can help create personal job satisfaction and can overcome difficulties associated with change, for example when introducing new technol- ogies. Essentially there are three stages in managing the training of the human resources – the staff – of the organisation. These are:

Identification of training needs Define training objectives, develop measures for evaluating training and decide on content/scope.
Implementation of training programmes Design training methods, materials and facilities, coordinate training programme and trainees.
Evaluation of training effectiveness Measure outcomes, compare performance – adjust and refine future training accordingly.

Staff development takes training a stage further. It should be ongoing, and form an integral part of the employee's progress, incorporating areas such as the following:

Functional training: specific job skills, technical skills
Personal development: assertiveness training, study for formal qualifications
Organisational development (cross-functional): quality initiatives, customer care programmes, corporate mission awareness
Appraisal systems: incorporating both employee and employer feedback

Training can be carried out in any number of ways. Workshops, team briefings, formal presentations and structured programmes are commonly used, together with work shadowing, job exchange schemes and project management. Different modes of training are more suited to different training and development needs; a formal presentation followed by hands-on practical exercises might be most useful for the introduction of a computer software package, while workshops are more appropriate for situations where participants are encouraged to discuss issues and make suggestions.

Induction training is designed to help new employees understand the or- ganisation and their role within it. This is a key area, especially in service organisations where a customer orientation is essential. These programmes introduce new employees to the culture of the organisation, emphasise the standards required and highlight company values at an early stage. It may be implemented in stages over a period, or take place as an intensive programme over one or more days.

If a new initiative is launched, such as Total Quality Management (TQM), training will be an essential part of communicating the new policy to all employees. The task of designing and implementing training and development programmes lies with Human Resources Management even though the commitment and initiation of such programmes must be led by top management and involve all line management and employees.

4. HUMAN RESOURCES MANAGEMENT ISSUES

When the people in an organisation represent its most valuable asset, then the task of looking after those people is equally important as financial, operations or marketing management. The managers who look after the people within an organisation may be grouped under the headings: personnel, industrial relations, or training and development. They are all concerned with human resources management. Typically, the responsibilities of human resources managers include the following:

Recruitment and selection
Training and development
Setting up new modes of operation, e.g. quality circles
Management of change
Team briefings, communications strategies
Staff suggestion schemes
Internal communications
Administration (pensions, insurance)
Appraisal schemes
Pay structures
Staff development and support
Trade Union liaison
Conditions of service
Discipline and grievance procedures
Termination issues (redundancy, ill-health)
Capability

Additionally, human resources management plays a very central role within an organisation. If the human resource task is to be handled effectively, managers need:

- *a thorough understanding of the needs of the directors, managers and employees throughout the organisation*
- *clear identification with organisational goals and objectives*
- *understanding of the needs and wants of external customers*
- *close co-operation with other functional managers.*

In practical terms, there are a number of ways in which these wide-ranging aspects of human resources management can be translated into effective strategies for service organisations. A customer orientation must be at the forefront of all policies, with customer care heading the agenda. An audit of human resources management activity can be undertaken and continuously updated to ensure programmes and procedures are implemented in line with organisational and employee needs. An action plan can be designed along the following lines:

Organisational objectives
Effective transmission of organisational objectives to all employees/members of the organisation.
Providing opportunities for employees to participate in developing organisational objectives.
Ensuring that all employees understand how performance against objectives is measured, and their role in achieving success.

Recruitment
Developing programmes for successful recruitment.
Building and promoting the organisation's image.
Conducting recruitment in a fair and professional way, in line with the guidelines contained in the code of conduct of the Institute of Personnel Development, for example.
Efficient response and follow-up procedures.

Induction
Establishment of effective induction programmes
Managing ongoing induction with feedback

Appraisal and review
Clearly defined job descriptions and person specifications and objectives.
Development of competency profiles for specific jobs.
Ensuring employees and managers share common understanding of the appraisal process.
Providing appraisal training for all line managers and others required to undertake performance review activities.

Training and development
Identification of training needs.
Development and implementation of training programmes.
Integration between training and other functions.
Support for individual staff development.
Management development programmes.
Evaluation.

Pay structure and benefits
Establishment of salary structure and reviews.
Reward systems for competence/qualifications/performance.
Provision and communication of benefits packages, pensions.

Communications

Internal marketing.

Publication of staff magazine and other internal communications.

Ensuring that staff are always kept informed and in touch, allowing for feedback from staff.

Transmission of new ideas and initiatives.

Quality

Liaison with functional managers on quality initiatives.

Involvement in implementing programmes for quality.

Communicating to employees the nature of responsibility for quality; instilling ownership for quality issues.

The above list contains suggestions for human resources management; the actual task will differ between organisations. Sometimes training and information programmes may need to be extended beyond the organisation's employees, to sub-contractors for instance. Nynex, the cable communications multinational, has suffered adverse publicity in the UK when installation work has damaged gas mains or created excessive disruption to homeowners in areas where installations have been carried out.

The work has largely been carried out by independent sub-contractors but the negative image has been associated with the Nynex name. In this situation, extending customer care awareness and training programmes to sub-contractors or agents, if feasible, may be worthwhile. The same may also be true in terms of channel management, where agents acting on behalf of a service provider need to be included in training and communications.

The broad nature of the function is clear, however, and its close relationship with customer service can be seen. Suggested elements for a customer service audit include evaluation and review of personnel issues and performance measures, together with personal and job goal specification – all areas where integration with human resources management is appropriate. Service organisations need to invest in human resources management to look after their most important investment – the people.

5. SUMMARY

The inseparable nature of services mean that parts, or sometimes the whole, of the service is made up of the human element in the service delivery. Management of people is a key task within the organisation but equally important is the management of the customer/provider interface. Employees need to understand their role in the service exchange process as well as to have the technical and knowledge capability required.

The level of contact within a particular service depends on the type of service. In some services, people play a far greater part than in others. The staff are the most important asset within the organisation, however, and recruitment and staff development are crucial. Internal marketing recognises that employees in the internal market are equally important as external customers and their needs and wants should be examined.

The basic steps in recruitment can be broken down into several key stages, illustrated briefly here:

Preliminary stage – identification of vacancy and requirements, processing applications
Selection stage – arranging interviews, offer/acceptance, formal appointment
Follow-up stage – induction, training, ongoing development.

Training is needed to impart knowledge and build expertise and also to give focus and direction for the future direction of the organisation and its employees. Staff development incorporates training but goes a step further in designing strategies for an holistic approach to getting the most out of people and helping them maximise their potential.

Human resources managers work alongside managers in other functional areas (including marketing) to look after the people in an organisation. Their responsibilities cover a wide area with regard to selection, training, industrial relations and other related issues. They also play a central role in the organisation in terms of enabling organisational objectives to be met successfully through the efforts and understanding of all the people in the organisation.

Progress test 15

1. Why is the 'people' element of the marketing mix so important in services marketing?

2. What is meant by the terms 'primary', 'facilitating' and 'ancillary' in relation to the roles of people in service provision?

3. In what ways can the actions of service personnel influence customer perceptions of quality?

4. How can internal marketing techniques help in recruiting the right personnel?

5. Outline the stages in the recruitment and selection process.

6. Suggest some of the influences which can hamper effective recruitment and human resources management in the public sector and similar areas.

7. What areas should be incorporated into effective staff development programmes?

8. List the typical responsibilities of the human resources manager.

Discussion

1. Develop a detailed proposal for a customer care programme within a public sector service, starting with an audit of human resources management activity and focusing on the action plan points covered in this chapter.

2. Look at some recruitment advertisements for service industries in the national or trade press. Putting yourself in the role of human resources manager for the organisations concerned, draft an ideal application for the job.

16

PROCESS AND PHYSICAL EVIDENCE

INTRODUCTION

The intangible nature of services mean that they are not bought and owned by consumers in the same way that physical goods are. A service is performed rather than handed over. The consumer receives benefits deriving from the service – a feeling of satisfaction after a good meal, pleasure and entertainment from a visit to the theatre perhaps or a car in good working order after repairs have been carried out. This means that the performance process – the way in which the service is created and delivered – is an integral part of the service offering and the ultimate consumer benefits.

Intangibility is also the reason for the importance of physical evidence in the services marketing mix. As discussed in previous sections, some services are more intangible than others. Some services are product based and service providers will focus on ensuring that any facilitating goods which form part of the service are of an appropriate quality and standard. The food in a restaurant must be of an acceptable standard and the surroundings clean, cars for rental should be well maintained and in a presentable condition. Services which are highly intangible, however, such as consultancy and financial advice are more difficult for the consumer to assess. In the absence of actual goods or products about which the consumer can make judgements relating to quality and value, for example, the consumer will look for other ways of evaluating the service. Corporate image and corporate identity play a key role in consumer perception.

These special aspects of services marketing are so fundamental to success that they represent two components of the marketing mix: process and physical evidence. *Process* is concerned with the functional aspects of service delivery such as queuing systems, timeliness and quality of delivery. *Physical evidence* includes facilitating goods, decor and comfort.

1. CORPORATE IMAGE

The image which organisations present to the world at large is made up of many different elements. Its reputation as an employer and its approach to social responsibility issues are examples of the factors which influence consumers' subjective and objective judgements about an organisation. These factors are often of equal importance in forming consumer attitudes and judgements as more obvious ones such as service quality, value for money, guarantees and luxury decor.

Image is, however, difficult to define as it is based on an individual's perception of the message and signals reaching them concerning a particular product, organisation or public figure. It is therefore of vital importance that organisations ensure that the messages, information and signals which they send out are consistent with the organisation's objectives and are positive and constructive at all times to protect the integrity of brand and corporate image. In order to do this, all the elements which make up the organisation's image should be managed as effectively as possible. This is also vital in terms of the association between corporate image and the concept of corporate identity.

Comprehensive corporate relations programmes which incorporate public relations can play a key role in determining how the organisation is perceived. Strategic programmes can be used to communicate effectively with target audiences which may include:

Customers
Potential customers
Consumer groups
The media
Local groups or campaigns
Special interest groups
Volunteers (e.g. charities or parent teacher associations)
Donors
Employees

From this list, it can be seen that effective corporate relations is a logical extension of relationship marketing, covered in Chapter 9.

The key to successful corporate relations strategy lies in setting clear objectives. The strategy to achieve these objectives can then be designed using a combination of communications methods and tactics. The objectives may revolve around increasing awareness and ensuring that the organisation is regarded favourably by target audiences or promoting certain aspects of the organisation's service which are innovative or which differentiate it from the competition, or probably a combination of a number of these. The benefits which can arise from a well planned corporate relations programme can include:

- Enhanced market reputation
- Increased market share
- Greater employee satisfaction/loyalty
- Better links with suppliers, intermediaries and other bodies
- Improved understanding of the organisation and its activities – internally and externally.

However, managing the information and messages sent out by the organisation is not the only route to improved corporate image. Customers' perceptions of an organisation are also strongly influenced by visual and other sensory signals as well as their experiences of a particular service or organisation. Some of these influences make up the 'physical evidence' component of the marketing mix. This is the evidence on which consumers base their opinions and it emerges from every interaction between the customer and the organisation at every level. The number of factors which can contribute to a customer's perception can be vast and can range from fairly small details to more obvious influences.

Using a fast food restaurant as an example, physical evidence could include:

the food itself –	taste, smell, presentation, temperature
its packaging –	style, colour, environmentally-friendly, convenience
seating –	comfort, layout, availability
overall appearance	hygiene, cleanliness, lighting, decor, attractiveness
of the restaurant –	(inside and outside), well maintained
accessibility –	car parking, location of entrances/exits, wheelchair access, geographical location
facilities –	toilets, childrens' amusements, customer information, payphones
staff –	personal appearance, dress code, manner, efficiency
corporate image –	attitude towards the company image, logo, advertising, brand loyalty, the individual's knowledge of the organisation and its activities
service delivery –	prompt, slow, slipshod, efficient
atmosphere –	welcoming, friendly, cold

Controlling so many variables is the key management task in developing a favourable image amongst customers and potential customers. Clearly it is more than a case of developing effective corporate relations and communications packages. The importance of other elements of the marketing mix can be seen, especially in relation to the service product and the role of people in the service delivery process. Managing these elements correctly is of crucial importance, as has been discussed in earlier chapters.

2. CORPORATE IDENTITY

One way in which organisations attempt to reinforce all the messages, signals and impressions which customers receive is the establishment of a strong and positive *corporate identity*. Corporate identity goes beyond corporate image in that it builds a distinctive and recognisable physical identity for the organisation. Corporate identity tangibilises corporate image by linking the values, benefits and qualities of the organisation's image with identifiable physical attributes such as brand names, logos, staff uniforms, house-styles and consistent standards.

Many organisations use corporate identity as a unique selling proposition in promotional strategy. This can be a powerful tool for differentiation, particularly when brand and/or corporate identity recognition is very strong, as the following examples illustrate:

Cunard advertises 'The one and only QE2' in a promotional campaign for the ocean liner of that name, stressing its 'legendary' elegance, entertainment and high level of personal service.

Marriott hotels advertise the uniform appeal and quality of their hotels with the slogan: 'Always in the right place at the right time'.

ITT Sheraton focus on their corporate branding in advertisements which announce that each of their 400-plus hotels is different and unique but based on Sheraton's extensive experience with travellers around the world.

Henley Management College ran advertisements featuring the date of incorporation (1945) and the award of a Royal Charter (1991), stating 'established in some twenty countries across five continents' under the copy 'Where in the world but Henley?', clearly establishing firm credentials as a leading business school.

An increasing number of organisations are paying particular attention to corporate identity to reinforce their image. The traditionally austere and imposing banking halls of the past have been refurbished in more attractive styles and made more welcoming. 'Corporate apparel', the term given to staff workwear and uniforms, is a booming business as the sectors which traditionally presented a strong identity through the attire of their personnel – airlines and security services, for example – have now been joined by banks, building societies, pub restaurant chains and retail travel agents, to name but a few.

Staff uniforms or workwear represent only one physical manifestation of corporate identity. Others include the visual images mentioned earlier such as logos, house styles, architectural design of outlets which are instantly recognisable and extend to monogrammed bathrobes in hotels, corporate gifts bearing the organisation's logo, in-house magazines such as those offered by airlines – anything, in effect, which can be used to strengthen the customer's awareness and favourable perception of the organisation.

3. CUSTOMER PERCEPTIONS AND PHYSICAL EVIDENCE

The examples of physical evidence described in the previous sections can be broken down into two main types, described by the following terms:

Peripheral evidence This type of evidence can actually change hands during the service transaction as in the purchase of an airline ticket or the issuing of motor insurance cover note or a hotel room key. The purchaser may become the owner of the item, but it is, in itself, worthless unless the airline does offer the flight required or the insurance company actually exists and has sufficient funds available to cover a claim and the hotel room is warm, reasonably furnished and so on.

Peripheral evidence includes those items which confirm the service, as in the examples mentioned but also includes items which are complementary to the service itself. This means that the service can be performed without these items but they enhance the organisation's identity and can help make the customer's experience more enjoyable or positive. Examples include books of matches, free house wine with a meal, toiletries and chocolate in hotel bedrooms, newspapers and magazines for airline passengers.

Essential evidence Essential evidence is integral to the service offering and includes, for example, the facilities offered by a leisure centre or the items on display in an exhibition or museum which make a visit worthwhile. This type of evidence will not normally be owned by or passed on to the customer, except on a temporary basis as in the case of car or equipment hire, or linen rental in catering. In all cases, the quality and standard of the essential evidence will be a major influence in the customer's purchase decision.

Both these types of evidence combine with the organisation's other marketing mix elements, especially promotion and people, to create an impression on customers and potential customers. They also help to make the service more tangible, in that it can be associated with clear mental images, colours, names and so on, in the mind of the consumer, as the following examples illustrate:

> The Automobile Association's handbook and membership card are permanent, physical reminders of the organisation's services, as is their distinctive livery on patrol cars and vans. The technical standard of the mechanics and the quantity of spare parts carried are examples of the essential physical evidence which forms part of the service.
>
> The monthly viewing guide, 'Sky TV Guide' mailed to satellite television subscribers, is a glossy, high quality magazine with articles and features as well as programme listings. This will reinforce the service image of quality when they are used on a daily basis in customers' homes, while the essential evidence – the quality of transmission – will also be closely regulated by the organisation.

Physical evidence, in its many forms, will help the potential customer or user to evaluate the service offering. As discussed in Chapter 10, service quality is not easy to measure in a precise manner. The customer's overall judgement of service quality can be an evaluation of both the process and the outcome, compared with the customer's own expectations and desired benefits. Their impression of quality will always be subjective and based on their individual perception of the physical evidence and other elements of the service offering. This leads to an important idea in assessing quality from a services marketing perspective:

perceived service quality

Perceived service quality represents the customer's judgement of an organisation's service based on their overall experience of the service encounter. A number of key criteria are used to make this judgement and the following list of examples shows clearly the importance of physical evidence and the service delivery process itself:

People: credibility, professionalism, efficiency, courtesy, approachability, accessibility, appearance, communications skills
Process: timekeeping, dependability, trusted performance levels, promptness, efficiency
Physical evidence: appearance of tangible aspects of the service, physical surroundings, smartness

The relative importance of the customer's perception of both essential and peripheral evidence in evaluating service quality has been highlighted but the impact of the service delivery process should also be considered. Customers are frequently active participants in the service process – they co-produce the service – so this must be taken into account in planning and management. The following section looks at the process element of the services marketing mix and some of the technological developments which have revolutionised service delivery in many fields.

4. PROCESS

The study of process – the way things are actually done and the steps taken to achieve desired results – has been given considerable attention over the years in the areas of manufacturing, engineering and computer programming. Indeed it has given rise to such revolutionary developments as 'just-in-time' and 'lean production' in manufacturing and production operations. It is only more recently, however, that the importance of the actual process in service delivery has been recognised and developed as a tool for competitive advantage. Developments in technology have also helped revolutionise many processes in the home, in industry and in the services sector.

The principles by which service delivery processes can be designed, implemented and monitored are really no different from those mentioned relating to the fields of manufacturing, computing and so on. There are certain specific characteristics of service process design and implementation however which should be considered. These include:

Customer participation in the process The level of involvement or participation of the customer in the service process – in a self-service restaurant, for example, as opposed to waitress service.
Location of service delivery Should the process be carried out at the service provider's premises or at the customer's home? For some services, this seems a simple decision – plumbing or carpet cleaning should be carried out 'in situ' at the customer's home while dry cleaning or a theatrical performance will be carried out at a specialist outlet or venue. In other cases, traditional practices may no longer be applicable as telephone banking and insurance services have shown, without the need for any branches on the high street. Travel arrangements can be made without visiting a travel agent and services as diverse as hairdressing, take-away food and financial consultancy can all be delivered to the customer at home if required.

The service itself   The service itself – is it process dependent (usually the case with highly intangible services such as legal representation) or equipment based (such as vending machines or dry cleaning).

High-contact or low-contact services   The level of contact between the customer and the service provider's personnel – this can range from nil (as in the use of automatic cash dispensers, vending machines or ticket booking machines of various kinds) to very high contact as in medical or professional services where the client or patient is being looked after by the organisation's personnel for varying periods of time.

Degree of standardisation   The degree to which the service is delivered in a very standard format (for example, the McDonalds fast food experience) or whether some customisation is catered for (as in professional services, where each client's needs will be slightly different and will be serviced accordingly). The extent to which the service can be altered from the standard to meet the needs of different consumers or users may be termed *divergence*.

Complexity of the service   This is measured by the number of steps or activities which contribute toward the service delivery. Ensuring that tourists have an enjoyable holiday will include many different steps incorporating travel arrangements, hotel operational management, high levels of customer contact and service and so on. Less intricate processes will include far fewer steps and sequences of actions to deliver the service – a bank cashier accepting a deposit and updating the balance in a pass book for example, or a motor garage performing a routine car service. Both these examples will be governed by standard procedures and guidelines which will be implemented with little divergence.

In designing the service delivery process, all these issues should be taken into account. The steps required to deliver the service and provide the appropriate benefit satisfactions to the consumer can be 'mapped' or 'blueprinted' in the same way that flowcharts are used to denote all the decisions, alternatives and actions required for a computer programmes to work successfully and carry out the tasks they are used for. Chapter 10 which looks at service quality contains some useful information about developing quality practices and processes for services, and in particular, about benchmarking for services and implementing the process.

The purpose of setting down clear outlines or blueprints for service delivery processes and transactions is as follows:

- *To ensure that the service is carried out in the fastest, most efficient and cost-effective manner possible*
- *To enable service quality to be monitored and benchmarks to be put in place thus allowing accurate measurement of both quality and productivity*
- *To facilitate staff training and enable individuals to carry responsibility for individual stages of the service transaction and delivery*
- *To reduce the amount of divergence thus enabling accurate budgeting and manpower planning etc. to take place.*

Sometimes, however, it should be noted that complete standardisation of the service delivery process is not the most desirable option either for the service provider or the consumer. In many cases, the personal element of the service which caters to customers' different needs is a key factor in differentiating a service from its competitors. Burger King have pioneered customer choice in allowing consumers to specify how they want their burger cooked and their own choice of sauces and accompaniments under the 'at BK you got it' slogan. This shows how some degree of customisation can be introduced into very simple service delivery processes and is in direct contrast with their arch rivals, McDonalds, whose range has been generally all offered as standard.

Some organisations choose to let their personnel have a certain amount of discretion to make decisions and take alternative actions to improve customer satisfaction. Traditionally this has been the prerogative of the senior manager who has been allowed to negotiate a waiver of bank charges, for example, or upgrade an airline seat or a hotel room to make up for some inconvenience caused to the customer by the service provider. Recently, however, the trend has been to allow greater flexibility to all staff, empowering them to use their own judgement to make decisions which will enhance the service delivery process.

This 'empowerment' of staff is very much in line with much of what has been said about people in earlier chapters (see Chapters 8, 9 and 15) and is said to lead to better staff and customer relations and higher levels of service quality through employee pride in the job and the individual ownership of problems and short-falls. It is even used in promotional material as a unique selling point as the following Marriott Hotels advertisement shows:

> "I arrived at Hong Kong airport without my case. Thanks to the foresight of the Marriott concierge, it managed to arrive without me."

The account then relates how the traveller was very relieved to find out that the concierge had spotted his briefcase and sent it after him. The grateful traveller then goes on to say:

> "His initiative saved the day. I understand that this kind of conscientiousness on behalf of their guests is typical of all Marriott staff. They call it empowerment. I call it remarkable."

A level of built-in flexibility in process design can help achieve greater customer satisfaction and a higher quality service overall. Changing attitudes towards staff empowerment and the increasing sophistication of the consumer and their demands are not the only factors to have impacted on service delivery processes, however.

5. TECHNOLOGICAL DEVELOPMENTS

The pace of technological developments in recent years has had a major impact on service delivery processes and practices. Computer networks and the use of modems mean that real-time information about bank accounts, airline seat availability and theatre bookings, on-line information for electronic funds transfer at point of sale (EFTPOS) can all be accessed instantaneously, leading to obvious advantages for service providers as well as customers or users of the service.

Automatic teller machines (ATM) are often cited as revolutionary technological developments in the services sector. These cash dispensing machines are a familiar sight throughout the UK on the high street, at supermarkets, shopping centres, motorway services and airports, while their numbers continue to grow. It would be virtually unthinkable to consider using a banking service which did not provide this facility, which is one of the reasons why their use has spread throughout all leading banks, finance houses and credit card issuers. The services provided by these machines, however, are constantly being upgraded. Innovations include multi-lingual options, where the user can specify a preferred language, instant statements and bill payments.

Many organisations have used technology to improve service efficiency and profitability or to improve the service to their customers.

> The Royal Mail, one of the most advanced postal groups in the world, offers a fast, reliable service but has also managed to keep the price down thanks to advances in automated sorting and the use of barcodes.
>
> The Meteorological Office provides weather and climatic information on a worldwide scale for both public sector use and as a commercial service to industry. The service is entirely dependent on up-to-the-minute data of the most perishable kind and rapid transmission and processing of information are essential to the process. The use of information technology and advanced telecommunications has led to tremendous advances in all aspects of the process. Telecommunications facilities play a key role in ensuring that observational data from all over the world are available promptly and reliably and then in delivering forecast products to consumers. 'Weatherfax' is another innovation in delivery which can provide hourly updated information on users' terminals. 'MIST' is another innovation which delivers continuously updated data from the Meteorological Office's central computer directly to users' terminals.
>
> Automated queuing systems in banks and post offices are another familiar innovation which have reduced customer frustration and improved service generally.
>
> Remote diagnostic tools can now be used to provide repair and maintenance services for computer equipment without the need for the engineer to leave base and spend time travelling to the client's premises.

Advances in technology have impacted on the 'process' element in the marketing mix in many different ways as the above examples suggest. This is in addition to the number of new services which have arisen directly from new technologies such as mobile telecommunications, satellite television, medical procedures such as scanning, laser treatments and keyhole surgery made possible by the use of fibre-optics, to suggest just a few examples.

6. ATMOSPHERICS

Another area which should be considered in reviewing the service process is that of atmospherics. This is the term given to the way in which marketers, notably in retailing, can plan for and provide an atmosphere within stores designed to be conducive to customer spending. This is a relatively new area of study and has been limited to retailing by and large, but has obvious applications for services marketing wherever the service exchange takes place at the service provider's premises, and especially in services retailing operations such as banks, travel agencies, hair and beauty salons and extends to include restaurants, hotels and many other possibilities.

Atmosphere can be used to create an image in the customer's mind based on the following types of sensory stimuli:

Sight – size, layout, lighting, colour
Sound – music, background noise, volume, pitch, tempo
Smell – fresh, heavily scented, appetite stimulant
Touch – temperature, comfort, soft/hard (seating etc.)

The importance of creating a pleasant or enjoyable atmosphere has been well recognised but what is now emerging seems to be that consumers will respond to different atmospheres with different types of buying behaviour. Colour, for example, can have a variety of effects on humans. Some colours are known to stimulate while others represent comfort, warmth or security. Music has also been recognised as a mood influencer. Different combinations of colours and music could be used to create a soothing warm atmosphere in a restaurant, or to attract teenagers to a busy fast food outlet.

The combined effects of atmospherics within the service environment and the role of the people participating in the service delivery process can affect the customer's mood and subsequent purchase decisions. It can, theoretically, be possible for the services marketing managers to control all of these influences, thereby inducing moods which will lead the consumer to act in a certain way with regard to purchase – linger in a restaurant and spend more on drinks, actually make a holiday reservation while in the travel agency rather than simply picking up brochures, for example.

Atmospherics is a developing area of study which is bound to be of potential interest to service marketers in all fields. Hospitals could aim for a brighter atmosphere to aid recovery, colleges could use colours and decor designed to stimulate concentration. Many steps have already been taken in this direction. Dentists have moved away from very stark, austere surgeries to more attractive decor, music and toys in an attempt to help patients relax and take a more favourable view of the experience, for example. Most of the research into the area has grown from retailing and developments in retail store and shopping mall design which can have a great deal of relevance for service marketers both now and in the future.

7. SUMMARY

The performance process relates to the way in which the service is created and delivered; it is concerned with the functional aspects of service delivery such as queuing systems, timeliness and quality of delivery. Physical evidence provides customers with a means of evaluating the service and includes facilitating goods, decor and comfort, for example.

Corporate image plays an important role in terms of physical evidence and this can be developed through corporate relations programmes. The benefits which can arise out of a well planned corporate relations programme include an enhanced market reputation and greater employee satisfaction and loyalty. Corporate identity takes corporate image a stage further by building a distinctive and recognisable physical identity for the organisation. Branding, house style and decor, staff uniforms and logos are typical examples of the physical means which can be utilised to to tangibilise corporate image.

Physical evidence can be broken into two main categories:

Peripheral evidence
Essential evidence

Both these types of evidence combine with the organisation's other marketing mix elements to create an impression on customers and potential customers and help to enhance perceived service quality.

Process has only recently been given much attention in the services sector, although it has been the subject of study in manufacturing for many years (hence developments such as 'just-in-time'). The principles by which service delivery processes can be designed, implemented and monitored are influenced by the following specific characteristics of services:

Customer participation in the process
Location of service delivery
The service itself
High-contact or low-contact service
Degree of standardisation
Complexity of the service

Processes are often designed around flowcharts or blueprints which set a standard sequence of actions which must take place in order for the service to be implemented. Sometimes, however, complete standardisation of the service is not the most desirable option either for the service provider or the consumer. Flexibility in both customer choice and staff actions can provide added benefits and help differentiate the service offering.

Perhaps the greatest impact on the process element of the services marketing mix has been due to technological developments, enabling automated service, for example, and using computerised systems to provide 'instant' service as with ticket reservations and so on. Some new services have arisen directly out of developments in technology, such as mobile communications and advanced medical techniques.

Atmospherics is the term given to the way in which marketers can plan for and provide an atmosphere at the service delivery location designed to be especially conducive to customer spending. Atmosphere can be used to create and enhance an image in the customer's mind based on sensory stimuli. Generally considered a specialist area in retailing, new developments in this area could be of great interest to services marketers.

Progress test 16

1. What is meant by the terms 'process' and 'physical evidence'? Why are they elements in the services marketing mix?

2. Why is corporate image hard to define? How can organisations ensure that the organisation's image is managed as effectively as possible?

3. Discuss the ways in which corporate identity goes further than corporate image in building a strong identity for the organisation.

4. List the two main types of physical evidence, giving examples of each.

5. Explain what is meant by 'process' in relation to services marketing. What specific service characteristics impact on process design and implementation?

6. Outline the main purposes of setting down clear outlines or blueprints for service delivery processes.

7. What is meant by 'empowerment'?

8. In what ways might atmospherics be helpful in developing the services marketing mix?

Discussion

1. What technological developments are you aware of in services you use? Discuss the impact of such developments and highlight the possibilities for the future.

2. In this chapter, examples of physical evidence relating to a fast food restaurant are given. Conduct a similar analysis of two or three other types of service you use and consider how both the process and physical evidence could be improved.

Part Four

SPECIAL ASPECTS OF SERVICES MARKETING

17

NOT-FOR-PROFIT SERVICES MARKETING

INTRODUCTION

To attract more students, universities and colleges undertake extensive and demanding promotion and recruitment campaigns. They utilise market research techniques and enter into new product development initiatives to ensure that they are offering the optimum range of courses to appeal to their chosen markets. Extra subject options covering topics such as languages or even 'green' issues may be included to increase the added value of some courses and distinguish them from the competition. New market segments are catered for by specially designed programmes offering direct access for mature students, or specialised tailored programmes such as MBA degrees for health care or public sector managers.

In the USA, and increasingly in Europe, churches and religious groups use advertising and promotional methods to raise funds and attract new members. Sophisticated communications through satellite television networks and other media channel the religious message.

Political parties employ state-of-the-art promotions to build their image and reinforce their political campaigns. The Presidential elections in the USA and the General Elections in the UK represent a demonstration of all possible media advertising and public relations approaches to winning votes.

The Scouts Association uses a combination of sponsorship and competitions as well as traditional fundraising methods which are far more advanced than their well known 'bob-a-job' activities (where Scouts carried out tasks such as gardening and cleaning cars in their local neighbourhoods in return for payment of one shilling). Famous brand name Flora is sponsoring cookery projects (the cook's badge) through its project for heart disease, while companies such as Rover, Esso and Texas Homecare assist in the running of fundraising drives and promotional offers. Local scout groups even have access by telephone to PR expertise to help them gain valuable publicity for their activities.

Each of these real-life situations illustrates organisations which have several things in common. Firstly they are all generally perceived to be non-commercial groups. Secondly they are all organisations whose overall goals are not financial profits; their mission might be defined in terms of educational standards, religious conversions, voting majorities or community service, for example. These organisations come under the general heading of 'not-for-profit' organisations. Finally, each organisation has used marketing activities to solve key problems and meet the challenge of today's environment.

In this chapter, services marketing management will be applied to non-commercial, not-for-profit organisations. Charities are generally considered to be not-for-profit organisations too, and are closely associated with this area of marketing. However, the range and scope of charity marketing activity is so extensive that it is dealt with separately in Chapter 20.

1. NOT-FOR-PROFIT ORGANISATIONS AND MARKETING

The underlying principles of marketing are the same for non-commercial, not-for-profit organisations as for business operations in the corporate sector. The task of marketing management in each case is to identify unsatisfied needs and wants, and to develop effective and timely marketing programmes to fill those market gaps with appropriate goods and services, thus achieving organisational goals through customer satisfaction. However, there are some key differences between commercial, market-driven organisations and not-for-profit organisations, especially relating to the constraints upon their activities arising from their traditions and development.

The not-for-profit business concept

It is useful to consider what not-for-profit actually means. Many non-commercial organisations may make a profit in basic financial terms on their business transactions. School fees may cover costs and allow a margin of 'profit'. However, the concept of not-for-profit is related to the organisation's overall orientation and long-term goals. The school may use the margin of profit to develop its facilities and enhance educational quality levels while a golf club which makes a profit on its membership fees may use the proceeds to benefit its members by providing a subsidised bar and social events.

Marketing can be broadly defined as an exchange process designed to bring about mutual benefits and satisfactions. Certainly it would be true to say that this applies equally to commercial business exchanges and non-commercial activities. Not-for-profit organisations are clearly involved in exchange transactions. Universities offer courses to students in exchange for fees while Performing Arts companies offer entertainment in return for an admission fee. It is the long-term goals of the organisation which define the nature of its business. Commercial organisations seek financial profitability and growth, while not-for-profit organisations have aims which are far more altruistic in nature, and which generally provide societal benefits as well as benefits to the individual organisation.

Types of not-for-profit organisations

There are many different types of non-commercial organisations ranging in size from small local concerns to large international groups. Generally, however, these fall into several main categories:

Cultural Opera, ballet, theatre and other performing arts, museums, historical societies, zoos and conservation societies.

Educational Private schools and colleges, universities, business schools and other educational establishments.

Political Political parties, political candidates, political organisations, trade unions.

Public interest Organisations campaigning for or against social issues such as fitness, health, drug abuse and smoking. Organisations offering a public service such as the Youth Hostels Association, Relate (the marriage guidance service) and the Family Planning Association.

Social Chambers of Commerce, social clubs and organisations such as the Scouts Association, the Royal Automobile Club, golf clubs and other membership groups.

Religious Churches, religious movements.

Healthcare Nursing homes, hospitals, health research bodies, hospices, cancer support groups, AIDS research and care trusts, such as the Terence Higgins Trust in the UK.

Charitable and philanthropic Local and international charities, Oxfam, Save the Children Fund, welfare groups, Barnardo's, the National Society for the Prevention of Cruelty to Children, Rotary International.

These categories do represent, in the main, not-for-profit organisations, although there are operators within many of the categories who do operate businesses designed as profit-making concerns. These may include health clinics specialising in cosmetic surgery on a full-fee basis, and independent secretarial colleges and training organisations, for example.

Characteristics of not-for-profit marketing

The major distinction between not-for-profit marketing and commercial business marketing is the idea of multiple publics. Commercially orientated businesses traditionally have one major public in that they view their market solely in terms of present and potential customers. Not-for-profit organisations, on the other hand, must typically direct their marketing efforts towards two main groups:

Sponsors, contributors or donors, as in the case of a charity. The organisation has to target marketing activity towards this group in order to raise funds and attract resources. Benefits are frequently offered in return; a company can receive favourable publicity for sponsorship of arts events for example, while fund-raising in the form of social events offers individual members of the public the opportunity to enjoy supporting various organisations.

203

Recipients, members or users These are the customers or clients of the organisation. They are similar in this way to the customers of a business. Frequently, the not-for-profit organisation will be faced with identical considerations with regard to this market as a commercial operation; how to attract more clients, or how to raise their image in the clients' perception, for example. These clients are not usually referred to as such, however. They may include students, patients, members or supporters.

This distinction is an important one as it impacts on the organisation's overall activities and direction. Not-for-profit organisations must develop dual marketing programmes to address these two markets. Marketing activities designed to attract support and funds should be designed and implemented for the sponsor market, while separate programmes will be used to attract new clients or users to the organisation.

It is possible that further groups must also be considered by the not-for-profit organisation. A hospice may have to deal with a board of trustees, or may be backed by a religious or other authority. It will probably also have to satisfy the requirements of Health Authorities or other Government agencies in its day-to-day operations. A University will be subject to controls from various governing bodies, and may also have to address clients other than the ultimate users, or students – education authorities, school and college teachers, overseas education councils for example, as these bodies will have power to influence and sanction student choice.

The role of marketing in not-for-profit organisations

Traditionally, writers in marketing and strategic management have concentrated on commercial business operations, and have paid little or no attention to the issues affecting not-for-profit organisations, or public sector agencies. At the same time, not-for-profit organisations have only gradually accepted business management techniques. There may be a number of reasons for this, including a reluctance to be seen to adopt an overtly commercial approach. However, as not-for-profit organisations now represent some very major institutions indeed, in terms of size and financial turnover (both nationally and internationally), strategic planning is essential.

Not-for-profit organisations are faced with the same strategic tasks as business concerns:

Mission definition
Objectives setting
Strategic planning
Implementation
Monitoring and evaluation

Not-for-profit organisations need to be dynamic and flexible to move with today's changing environment. This may mean that their mission needs to be changed over time:

The former Girl Scouts of America would probably not survive today with its former mission which was to prepare young girls for motherhood and wifely duties.

The Youth Hostels Association in the UK has had to re-define its original mission to meet the needs of the market it now serves. Initially set up to provide country holidays for underprivileged young people, it now caters for families, students and anyone seeking low-priced basic accommodation in the countryside.

They also need to run operations of considerable size, in terms of personnel, range of services or activities and finance, efficiently and effectively. The gradual acceptance of business management techniques which has taken place has largely been reactionary, and evidence suggests that marketing has not been widely adopted.

Marketing, and in particular promotion and advertising, is not widely accepted by many areas in the not-for-profit sector. It is perhaps perceived as being opportunistic, and not in keeping with the ideals of organisations dedicated to the public good. However, as the examples at the opening of this chapter illustrate, more and more attention is being directed towards marketing techniques.

2. STRATEGIC MARKETING PROGRAMME DEVELOPMENT

Similar procedures exist for developing strategic programmes in both commercial business companies and not-for-profit organisations. The target markets must be identified and analysed. Market research should be undertaken to aid decision making and ensure that market needs are correctly identified and met. Strategic programmes should then be developed through effective use of the marketing mix.

Target market identification

As noted earlier, not-for-profit organisations need to address two distinct markets – the *sponsor/contributor* market and the *client/recipient market*. These markets must be explored, and characteristics of attractive segments defined.

Market segmentation is equally important in not-for-profit marketing as it is in commercial business markets, and the procedure is the same. This section will consider market analysis and segmentation issues for the two markets:

Sponsors/contributors Market research will enable organisations to assess who makes up this market. Some organisations may deal primarily with corporate bodies and trust or grant foundations, while others may receive the bulk of their funding and resources from individual members of the public. Many organisations may combine these two possible sources. Research will also help in determining how to address the sponsor/contributor market. Formal sources of funding such as trusts may require official applications which leave no real scope for promotional initiatives designed to attract interest. Corporate sponsors, however, will be far more responsive to creative promotion and public relations. Members of the public may respond to various appeals, such as direct requests for donations or the opportunity to participate in events. They may prefer to donate by paying for a service designed to raise funds, or to sponsor specific activities such as sponsored walks.

Segmentation issues Sponsors/contributors may be segmented according to similar methods used in business marketing. The corporate sector may be segmented according to size and location of company, for example. Individuals may be segmented on the basis of age, or area of residence, and other geo- demographic characteristics. Nature of employment, and even level of education, may be highly relevant in attracting funds for organisations in the arts, or for organisations operating in related fields. Frequency or size of past donations can help to identify active segments.

Clients/recipients Many not-for-profit organisations have been guilty of failing to understand their client/recipient markets and have offered goods or services which met their view of what clients wanted. They have also tended to adopt a mass approach, with little or no differentiation between distinct customer groups. Market research-type investigations should be undertaken among current clients, and, as far as possible, potential clients, to determine needs more accurately. Secondary research using government statistics, for example, should also be undertaken in order to assess future trends.

Segmentation issues Organisations are now trying to segment their markets more accurately in the interests of efficiency and effectiveness. Political parties have developed separate appeals to attract different voting segments such as pensioners and the unemployed. Universities and colleges may segment students on the basis of home or overseas, age (as with mature students or women returners), company-funded or self-funded. Most not-for-profit organisations will adopt some sort of geographical approach to segmenting their client/recipient markets, and this is likely to reflect the geographical area(s) served by their activities.

For market research to be carried out effectively, not-for-profit organisations need to utilise modern, professional research methods. Increasingly this is happening. Political parties have for many years used opinion polls (with varying degrees of accuracy for forecasting results), and public and private organisations in the fields of healthcare, leisure and education are undertaking major market research initiatives.

The decision to segment both the sponsor/contributor market and the client/recipient market means that not-for-profit organisations need to refine their marketing to develop tailored marketing mixes for each target segment identified. This is where effective marketing management is critical.

Competitor analysis

There is substantial competition in both client/recipient markets and in sponsor/contributor markets. Youth groups and associations have to compete with other forms of entertainment aimed at young people. Healthcare clinics have to compete with other private and public institutions, and also, increasingly, with alternative health practices. The competition for sponsors'/contributors' money is strong. It comes both from other not-for-profit organisations in direct competition and from other areas – in times of recession, people may only be able to afford necessities, while companies may cut back any non-essential expenditure.

Not-for-profit organisations need to establish ongoing competitor analysis and monitoring. This information should form part of the marketing information system and is collected through marketing intelligence sources.

All organisations have to make decisions about what products/services to offer, how to promote them and how they will be distributed and priced. Issues such as positioning and branding need to be considered. Not-for-profit organisations are no exception, but they have to develop sets of strategies for each of their markets – the client/recipient market and the sponsor/ contributor market. These marketing mix decisions are considered next.

3. PRODUCT

The product element of the marketing mix must focus on the services or benefits which the organisation wishes to offer to its two distinct markets:

Client/recipient product decisions

The product offered by non-profit organisations to client/recipient markets can take many forms. Typically it will take the form of a service with varying degrees of intangibility, as the following examples show:

Highly intangible
Political ideas or philosophy, campaigns, counselling, religion
Education, the Arts
Healthcare, Social Clubs
Community Services, Youth Hostels
Food and clothing for the needy
Highly tangible

Product decisions will depend on how the organisation views its business and the markets it wants to reach. If a university views its mission only as providing degree courses then this will dictate its product offering. It may, however, follow a broader mission, as a provider of community education programmes, management development courses and vocational teaching. If this is the case then it will offer a broader range of products or services to more markets.

Sponsor/contributor product decisions

Once the sponsor/contributor market has been identified and analysed, the best way to address this market can be determined. The key task is to identify the benefits which potential sponsors/contributors will seek. This is difficult in terms of product decisions as the organisation is asking people or companies to give money for a cause. In order for the exchange process to be completed, the donor must receive benefits in turn.

Again, the benefits or products provided can range from highly tangible – as in the case of physical products sold to raise funds – to highly intangible benefits. These could include the following:

- The feeling of 'doing good'
- Social prestige
- Membership of an organisation or club
- Tax benefits
- Publicity/public relations

The main marketing management task is to develop a 'product portfolio' of benefits to match the needs and wants of the sponsor/contributor market segments.

Product management

Product management involves product mix decisions concerning the range of products or services to be offered. Additional services can be offered in order to attract more segments in both markets. The client/recipient product range can be expanded to include new or related services. Universities may offer evening courses, health care centres may offer 'well-woman' screening services. Benefits offered to sponsor/client segments may be updated to include newsletters and magazines in return for subscriptions, affinity credit cards, gift catalogues or personal gifts and awards.

Product differentiation can be another useful strategy in not-for-profit marketing. Organisations can seek to differentiate their product or service from that of the competition. Schools and colleges may offer special facilities or areas of excellence (for example in sports) which can help to distinguish them from the competition. Health clinics and hospitals may introduce upgraded rooms and offer restaurant-style menus of top-class cuisine.

The product life cycle concept applies to services in the not-for-profit sector just as much as to products and services in commercial markets. Services can become outdated as new services are developed, and part of the product management task is to monitor service performance and demand trends. New services need to be developed and introduced at the right times, and services which are no longer efficient or for which demand is declining should be phased out.

4. PRICING

Pricing is a complex issue in not-for-profit organisations. Very often, the organisation exists to provide its services free of charge to its client/recipient market. In organisations which operate fee structures, which are more closely aligned to commercial enterprises, fees must be set at a level which will cover costs (or costs less subsidies), and provide enough revenue for service levels to be maintained or to grow.

There are a number of elements to the 'price' issue of the marketing mix which do not relate solely to price setting. These include:

Method of payment
Credit terms
Payment frequency
Sliding scales

At first glance it may seem that these do not apply to organisations in the not-for-profit sector. However, it is worth considering each of these in turn, as they cover some important issues.

Method of payment

In sponsor/contributor markets, payment methods available can help to influence levels of support. Market research may identify segments of this market who may be more willing to pay (or to pay more) by some direct means such as standing order.

Certain methods of payment can attract tax benefits, either for the donor or the organisation. Deeds of covenant, where money is paid on a contractual basis over a set period, attracts income tax relief which is paid to the organisation on top of the sum contributed. In this way the donor can see their money being put to highly effective use, and they may be encouraged to contribute in this way. Churches regularly use this method to attract revenue from their members.

Payment does not have to be in the form of cash. Companies can be approached to provide goods or services – ranging from products to be auctioned to raise funds, for example, to providing expertise and time. Providing products or sponsoring the purchase of certain items (such as football strips for local teams) can bring benefits in terms of favourable publicity. Again, thorough research into the sponsor/contributor markets should identify these kind of opportunities.

Credit terms

The client/recipient market may need some form of credit or extended payment period to enable users to take advantage of services being offered. Clubs may allow membership fees to be paid over long periods or colleges may arrange credit schemes to spread the cost of tuition fees. Credit cards may be accepted, both in payment for their service, and in making donations. These aspects need careful consideration.

Payment frequency

In addressing the sponsor/contributor market, organisations need to consider how they can most successfully achieve their objectives. Will single, one-off payments result in more revenue than steady, smaller sums? There are many reasons why it can be preferable to receive slow, steady payments rather than ad-hoc cash injections. Encouraging contributors to make regular payments (through one of the direct payment methods available) makes strategic sense.

Subscriptions may be elicited, perhaps in return for newsletters or membership benefits. 'Friends of' schemes are used by many organisations, where subscribers pay a modest fee to become a 'friend' of an orchestra, or a hospice, for example. In return, they may be invited to participate in social events, or receive discounts on standard ticket prices.

Membership subscriptions may also be paid by clients, especially in relation to clubs and associations. These may be due weekly, monthly or annually. In all these cases, care must be taken to select the payment frequency most likely to be accepted, both by contributors and users.

Sliding scales

Charges for services in the not-for-profit sector can be based on sliding scales related to individual ability to pay. Membership or subscription fees for contributors can be similarly designed, with reductions for pensioners and students, for example.

Pay scales can also be used to optimise service usage through periods of high or low demand. Mid-week or daytime concert tickets may be reduced in price, with further concessions for pensioners. Museums and cultural centres which charge for admission may offer advantageous rates for school parties during term time, reverting to higher-priced individual and family tickets in the holidays.

5. PROMOTION

Promotion is perhaps the most well-developed element of the marketing mix as far as not-for-profit organisations are concerned. Advertising, sales promotion, publicity and personal selling – all the elements of the promotional mix – have been used regularly. However, promotion has frequently not been designed as part of an integrated marketing programme, with the result that it has been less effective than it could be.

Advertising and promotion in not-for-profit organisations is generally aimed at the sponsor/contributor market more than the client/recipient market. Campaigns to raise funds utilise mass and specialist media advertising, as well as direct mail and other methods to attract interest.

Television appeals with celebrity backing are widely used to generate funds, often with telephone hotlines for instant donations by credit card. Direct mail to selected target groups who may be past donors or who belong to special interest groups can be a very successful means of raising funds.

Organisations also target advertising and promotional efforts towards their client/recipient markets. It may be necessary to inform potential users that the service exists, as in the case of counselling and advice services such as the Citizens' Advice Bureau and the Samaritans. It may also be necessary to attract new users or members. Universities advertise their courses to prospective students; health clinics advertise their services widely.

Personal selling is undertaken at many levels. Specialist professionals deal with major organisations who are potential donors while door-to-door and street collections are regularly used.

Whatever the means and promotional tactics used, however, the campaign should be planned and implemented with the same care and efficiency as in commercial business. There are seven steps which should be followed in designing a promotional programme:

Budget decisions
Objectives setting
Target audience identification
Message selection
Promotional means/media selection
Implementation
Monitoring and evaluation

Promotional planning is examined more fully in Chapter 13. The design and implementation of promotional campaigns is a key marketing management task in any organisation which needs to communicate with its market(s). Not-for-profit organisations can utilise methods and techniques from commercial sectors which have been researched and shown to increase the chances of success, as part of their integrated marketing programmes.

6. PLACE (DISTRIBUTION)

Not-for-profit organisations typically deal directly with their markets and therefore decisions relating to channel selection and channel management are not common. In some instances, agencies such as public relations outfits may be used to frontline major campaigns, or professional agents who arrange corporate sponsorship may be retained. However, the major task in distribution management is to ensure that services are available and accessible:

Clients/Recipients – Sponsors/Contributors
AVAILABILITY – ACCESSIBILITY
Services – Benefits

There can be circumstances where not-for-profit organisations are faced with distribution decisions which are business-like in nature. Many organisations sell physical goods as part of their fundraising activities, or provide catering and refreshment services for their clients. These organisations must deal with the issues of storage, inventory control and physical distribution in relation to these activities.

Whatever the scope of the distribution task, however, the most important factor for most not-for-profit organisations is to establish themselves in locations where their clients and potential clients can reach them, and where they, in turn, can reach their contributors. This may mean setting up a network of branches to serve the client/recipient market, and having central bases in major cities to manage fundraising and other activities.

Not-for-profit organisations can be creative in their distribution strategy to meet the needs of their markets. Universities have established distance learning courses to meet the needs of students who live too far away to attend normally; while religious groups are taking their message to potential followers by holding televised services and religious broadcasts.

7. SUMMARY

The concept of not-for-profit is related to organisational long-term goals, rather than the possibility (or otherwise) of any profits ever being generated. Not-for-profit organisations can be categorised as follows:

Cultural
Educational
Political
Public interest
Social
Religious
Healthcare
Charitable and philanthropic

The main distinction between not-for-profit marketing and commercial business marketing is that of multiple publics. Commercial organisations may view their main market quite simply as current or potential customers. Not-for-profit organisations, on the other hand, must direct their marketing efforts towards two main groups:

Sponsors, contributors or donors
Recipients, members or users

Similar procedures exist for developing strategic programmes in both commercial business companies and not-for-profit organisations. The target markets must be identified and analysed. Market research should be undertaken to aid decision making and ensure that market needs are correctly identified and met. Strategic programmes should then be developed through effective use of the marketing mix.

The 'product' or service offered to the client/recipient in not-for-profit marketing will typically take the form of a service with varying levels of intangibility:

- Political ideas, campaigns or counselling (highly intangible)
- Youth hostels, food and clothing for the needy (highly tangible)

Sponsors and contributors, on the other hand, may be offered various types of benefit as follows:

- Goods sold to raise funds (highly tangible)

- The feeling of 'doing good' or social prestige (highly intangible)

All the elements of the marketing mix are important in not-for-profit marketing and require management attention. Some aspects need to be looked at from a new perspective, such as price and place due to the special characteristics of not-for-profit organisations.

The marketing concept is equally applicable to organisations operating in the not-for-profit sector as it is to commercial businesses. The key difference lies in the two distinct markets which the not-for-profit organisations serve, and the constraints which can impact on marketing and business decisions due to the high levels of public scrutiny they face. Marketing management techniques can help these organisations serve their markets more effectively.

Progress test 17

1. List possible goals and objectives of non-commercial organisations.

2. Describe how a not-for-profit organisation actually makes profit in the short term, and how is this reconciled in the long term?

3. Explain the concepts of 'multiple publics' and 'dual marketing'.

4. Why, in the past, may 'not-for-profit organisations' have been reluctant to adopt a marketing orientated approach?

5. Outline methods of segmentation where:
   (a) A political party is fund-seeking.
   (b) An operatic society is promoting a forthcoming performance.

6. When might a non-commercial organisation use product differentiation in its marketing mix?

7. Explain how different methods of payment available may influence both the donor and the client?

8. For what reasons are promotional strategies often not fully utilised in the not-for-profit sector?

9. What is *the* most important consideration that a non-commercial organisation must make in its distribution strategy? Consider the consequences of a failure to do so.

Discussion

1. Assess the fine line between 'purely' non-commercial organisations and those typically considered to be within that sector, but who in reality exist for profitable purposes (either overtly or under false pretences).

2. Give examples of not-for-profit organisations you regularly contribute to or benefit from. Consider the situation if these (and other) services became commercially driven.

18

LEISURE SERVICES MARKETING

INTRODUCTION

The concept of leisure, and the freedom to choose individual pastimes and leisure pursuits, is a 20th century development for the mass population. Historically, only the wealthy could divide up their time to engage in activities of their choosing. The working classes had neither the time nor the money to enjoy leisure activities on a broad scale. The development of leisure is seen predominantly in westernised cultures, where it has become increasingly sophisticated.

There have been a number of factors contributing to the growth potential of the leisure 'industry':

- Technology has reduced hard labour in the working day, to the extent that people need to seek physical exercise for its own sake.
- Labour-saving devices allow freedom from domestic drudgery.
- People generally have more free time due to a shorter working week, and longer holidays.
- Disposable income has increased dramatically.

All these factors help to influence a growing trend towards a more leisure-oriented lifestyle for the mass population. Leisure services have mushroomed accordingly. Leisure activities follow their own specific fashion trends, and marketing must play a key role in understanding and providing for the needs of the leisure consumer.

Many of the aspects of services marketing outlined in earlier chapters apply to leisure services marketing, especially some of the areas associated with tourism marketing, covered in the next chapter (for example, heritage parks and museums are frequently classed as leisure facilities as well as tourist attractions). This chapter will, therefore, focus on specific characteristics of leisure and the leisure market. Key considerations for marketers will be identified, particularly in the context of market research and marketing planning.

1. SCOPE OF THE LEISURE MARKET IN THE UK

Some idea of the scope and range of the leisure market can be gleaned by considering the different types of leisure service providers and the range of leisure services offered. The following only covers services which are specifically provided for leisure purposes. Indirect competition for consumers' leisure time and spending include activities such as shopping and eating out, for example.

Retailers have long been aware that for many consumers shopping is not only perceived as a task, to obtain essential purchases, but a leisure experience. Hence the development of shopping malls like the Metrocentre at Newcastle and Merryhill at Dudley, which combine shops with amusements and other attractions, designed to attract families for a day out. Hospitality services such as restaurants and holiday breaks also represent competition for leisure consumption.

Leisure services are offered by four types of provider:

Public sector
Commercial providers
Voluntary provision in the non-public sector
National agencies

To a certain degree, the extent to which marketing is embraced is determined by the type of service provider; as may be expected, commercial providers tend to lead the way in effective marketing, while public sector and voluntary bodies may be constrained by the way in which they are managed, and by an obligation to provide some services for altruistic or historic reasons. The wide range of services provided can be explored by examining each of the service providers' activities.

2. PUBLIC SECTOR

Public sector leisure services provision covers many areas including for example:

Outdoor leisure and recreational activities
Cultural recreation
Education-related services
Entertainment

Within the sector there are different types of providers such as metropolitan county councils, district councils or parish councils. There may be overlap in the provision of services, and they can be affected by political change.

These issues can impact on the effectiveness of managing these services. Marketing, in terms of market research, marketing planning and the marketing mix, may not be utilised in cases where, for instance, decisions are made at council level about the number and types of amenities which will be provided with no heed to the needs and wants of local consumers.

Increasingly, however, marketing management methods are being embraced in the provision of these services. Public leisure services are faced with competitive pressure from commercial sources, and limitations of public funding which makes profitability a key concern.

Some examples of public sector leisure services include:

Sports and recreation:

Leisure centres
Municipal golf courses
Swimming pools
Playing fields
Parks
Entertainment – public halls, catering

Countryside recreation:

Camp sites
Nature reserves and nature trails
Picnic sites

Education-related:

Library services (branch, mobile, main)
Evening classes in recreational/hobby subjects
Youth clubs and community centres

Cultural activities:

Concert halls
Theatres
Art galleries

Heritage:

Museums
Historic monuments
Places of interest.

This list reflects the scope of public sector leisure provision and illustrates the complex task faced by local authorities in providing leisure activities to suit the needs of the local population.

3. COMMERCIAL PROVIDERS

Commercial providers recognise leisure and recreational activities as potential sources of profit. They provide services which fall into the following categories:

Leisure in and around the home
Sporting activities/facilities
Tourism and holidays
Entertainment and social activities

An additional area which is attracting increased interest is that of sponsorship of cultural and other events. Baileys, the liqueur brand manufacturers, sponsor a series of summer promenade concerts at National Trust venues. Snooker tournaments and other major spectator sports events are sponsored by well-known brand names. The Football League attracts this kind of sponsorship, having been sponsored on an annual basis by firms such as Canon and Barclays.

This is another aspect of commercial involvement with leisure services. Sponsorship as an element of the promotional mix has been important for many years, and many marketing texts explore this idea. It is useful to note its significance in leisure marketing.

Commercial providers of leisure services operate the following types of activities:

Home-based leisure:

There is a lot of competition for peoples' time in the home. TV, radio, video/audio, reading (book clubs, publishers) even pets, compete for individuals' time and money.

The home itself can be a leisure object; DIY, gardening, cookery can all be viewed as leisure activities. The growth in garden centres and DIY superstores reflects these trends.

Recreation in the home; off-licences and take-away food outlets provide a service here, 'party-plan' direct marketing activities combine leisure with sales by catering to this desire for recreation in the home.

Leisure outside the home:

There are a number of categories of leisure services which are designed to take place outside the home:
Alcohol and gaming
Pubs, social and bingo clubs
Entertainment and the arts
Audience and spectator events
Cinema – now rising again in popularity with the provision of modern, multi-screen complexes offering a range of facilities (restaurants, fast food, speciality shops).

Outdoor sport:

Golf
Water sports: jet-ski, windsurfing, boating
Tennis
Adventure sports: 'paint ball' battle games, hot air ballooning, sky diving

Indoor sport:

Snooker
Gymnasia and health clubs
Ice and roller skating
Ten-pin bowling

Commercial leisure provision also extends to the area of leisure goods and equipment supplies. There is a growing market for sportswear (especially in the area of 'designer' wear, for womens' exercise classes, and for men), home computers, video films (both for hire and for sale) and take-away foods. Some providers combine leisure equipment provision with a leisure service. A jet-ski school may have a retail outlet selling watersports gear; a garden centre has a nature trail, pets' corner and restaurant facilities. Boating and yachting is a very high-value market, and the annual Boat Show provides a sales exhibition – a leisure service in itself.

In considering the idea of indirect competition introduced earlier, it is important to assess to what extent driving, or motorcycling, for example, are leisure activities. This opens up the commercial leisure services market even further; providers of driving accessories, motor cycle fashion items, organisers of rallies, even the Automobile Association (through its publications on interesting drives and touring) contribute to the overall market.

4. VOLUNTARY PROVISION IN THE NON-PUBLIC SECTOR

This covers a vast area, but typically it is dominated by membership-type clubs and associations. The main categories of activity can be broken down as follows:

Sport
Informal outdoor recreation
Arts and cultural groups
General recreational and leisure
Special interest groups

Within these categories, the range of activities is very broad, so it may be useful to consider some examples:

Sport:

Local league football clubs
Rugby Union
Local cricket teams and other sporting associations

Informal outdoor recreation:

Cycling clubs
The Ramblers' Association
Ornithological clubs
Archaeological societies

Arts and cultural groups:

Choral societies
The British Brass Band Club
Dramatic groups
Community arts

General recreation and leisure:

The Womens' Institute

The Scout and Guide movements
Pub quiz leagues
Church groups

Special interest groups:

First aid – St John's Ambulance
Pressure groups – Campaign for Real Ale
Environmentalist groups
Animal interest, Photography, Embroidery, Cordon Bleu Cookery, Writers' circles, etc.

Most of the above services tend to provide for the interests of their members exclusively. Sometimes the outcome includes the provision of a leisure service for the general public, however, as in the case of a brass band concert or an amateur dramatic production. Many groups host community events; fairs, festivals, exhibitions and demonstrations, for instance. They are engaged in leisure service creation and provision.

There are some institutional and private bodies which make some leisure provision, usually managed on a local voluntary basis. These include service organisations clubs such as the British Legion, or Soldiers' and Sailors' clubs. Firms may provide premises and facilities for sports and recreational activities for their employees and their families. Schools may run childrens' activity clubs in the holidays, while many universities now offer educational activity vacations, and frequently open their leisure and sports facilities to the public.

5. NATIONAL AGENCIES

In the UK there are a number of national agencies concerned with leisure services provision. Similar organisations exist in other nations. Some examples of these are as follows:

The Arts Council
The Sports Council
The National Playing Fields Association
The Countryside Commission

National agencies are generally able to provide various forms of resources, financial aid and technical support to leisure activities. Their roles, however, are not all identical. The Arts Council, for example, aims to improve accessibility to the Arts, and is grant-aided. It also helps in securing and managing sponsorship of major events. The National Playing Fields Association is a national charity.

The Countryside Commission does not exist solely for the purpose of providing recreation and leisure services; it is primarily concerned with conservation and maintenance, as is the Forestry Commission. Their roles have been extended, however, in recognition of the increasing demand for leisure services, and to ensure that leisure is managed in such a way that the natural environment will not be harmed.

This chapter so far has illustrated the extent and diversity of the leisure market, and has shown a number of characteristics which can influence marketing activities. There are a number of key questions concerning leisure services provision in the various market sectors:

- *Local authorities are duty-bound to provide a broad range of facilities for all on limited funds – they are not able to opt for the most profitable or financially feasible option.*
- *Voluntary organisations need to raise funds to provide the service for their members.*
- *National agencies have to prioritise grants and funding between many worthy applications.*
- *The commercial leisure providers may be more subject to risk from fashion trends, as they tend to lead in investment in new activities. As activities become more popular, local authority leisure services invest in their provision and may offer lower prices, as happened with squash courts and saunas.*

These points highlight some of the complexity of leisure services provision and the tasks facing management. Marketing is seen as being very well developed in some sectors, while it may hardly have entered others. There is evidence, however, that even the most traditional leisure providers are putting the needs of their customers first.

The following sections of this chapter focus on understanding the leisure services consumer, and designing appropriate leisure programmes and products (the leisure offering).

6. UNDERSTANDING THE LEISURE SERVICES CONSUMER

Marketers need to understand consumers in order to design and implement marketing programmes to satisfy consumer wants and needs. The main areas which are of interest are concerned with the buyer decision-making process: motivation to buy, and choice or selection. Understanding these behaviour patterns and influences can help in segmentation: dividing the overall markets into groups which have similar needs or interests, and then selecting target segments for marketing attention. A number of demographic factors may be taken into account in building up consumer profiles:

Age, and family life cycle stage Age plays a key role in participation in leisure activity. The type of activity selected and usage patterns change as people grow older, or reach different stages in the family life cycle. Time is important, and the age groups with the most 'free' time are child/adolescent and retired age groups. Single people tend to participate in different leisure and social activities than families with young children. Working people's leisure time may be centred around evenings and weekends, while retired people may seek leisure activities during the week. Leisure service providers recognise these differing needs and cater for them by offering off-peak discounts, for example, or more activities during school holiday periods.

Gender There are both similarities and differences between the leisure interests and buying patterns of males and females. While some activities are traditionally more 'male' or 'female' orientated, such as football, netball or Bingo, many are enjoyed by both sexes; swimming and the cinema are examples.

Availability of time can differ between the sexes, and this is recognised by the provision of creche facilities, for example, during the day. Some leisure activities demand a certain degree of segregation and many health clubs offer separate facilities for men and women, or devote different days to their activities. Ladies' cabaret nights featuring male entertainers such as the Chippendales represent a new trend in leisure provision.

Education and social factors Level of education is closely linked to a large degree to social class and income. These factors can all impact on participation in, and selection of, leisure activities. Certainly it is true that, while leisure and sports facilities are now available to much broader segments of the general population, and usage is increasing, participation in the Arts and cultural events tends to be limited to the educated classes. Use of library and education services also reflects this socio-cultural influence, while many of the more social forms of leisure (pubs and Bingo halls) attract quite different segments.

Income levels can dictate the type of leisure activities which may be pursued; polo and yachting, for example, require considerable expenditure while visiting museums or rambling may involve little or no expenditure. The level of discretionary income (the remainder after tax, national insurance and major living expenses) is of most interest to leisure marketers, as it is this income that the consumer may choose to spend on leisure.

Lifestyle Lifestyle is an important concept in consumer markets. It relates not only to the 'lifestyle you lead, but also to the lifestyle to which you aspire'. Accordingly, an individual's motivation to join a golf club, for example, may be connected with social factors rather than a desire to take open air recreation. Exclusive health clubs provide luxury facilities and decor to reflect an image which is affluent and successful. Visits to the opera or ballet may be an indication of social status rather than love of music. As standards of living improve, so must standards of leisure services provided. The old-style, functional swimming baths in many towns have been closed and replaced by attractive modern leisure pools, often combined with other leisure facilities.

The above represents an outline of some of the key factors influencing leisure services buying decisions. It is important to establish, through market research, which factors are the main influences in decision making with regard to particular service offerings. By building profiles of different segments and developing an understanding of their needs, leisure services marketing stands a far greater chance of success.

7. THE LEISURE OFFERING

Leisure programmes can be classified in a number of ways. It is important to distinguish between the types of leisure service offered when communicating with the marketplace. Generally speaking, however, leisure programmes are comprised of one or more of the following elements:

Activities – activities can be defined according to their degree of formality. Some activities are highly structured and may involve complex scheduling and programming. These include team and local league sports, educational courses, and events/series of events such as promenade concerts or theatre productions. Informal activities may be conducted spontaneously and may require only the combination of available time and space to take place. Examples of such activities include rambling or visits to the park.

Facilities – these may be purpose-built, such as swimming baths, or may be simply places available for leisure such as parks, or natural amenities such as beaches. In the case of natural leisure areas, some adaption may be required to enable users to enjoy them for leisure purposes. Car parking and toilet facilities may be required at local beauty spots or places of interest, while beaches may require cleaning and safety services. Facilities can range from the basic (village halls or the local parks, for example) or they can be luxurious and 'Hi-tech' (exclusive health clubs and gymnasia, or multi-screen cinema complexes, for example).

Services – this refers to the services which enable users and potential users to participate in leisure activity. These include information services, educational services, lending libraries and transport.

Designing the leisure offering means integrating and combining these elements in a way which will best meet the needs of the target market segments. When programmes are developed, they may be classified in the following ways:

Function – many services are classified by function. They are defined by the actual activities offered, and communications focus on this aspect.

Facilities – many leisure programmes can be distinguished by the nature of the facilities which are offered. Most potential users will have an understanding of the services offered by a leisure centre, or swimming baths, for example, and will be likely to respond to communications detailing the facilities available. Problems arise when users are not aware of what is being offered in any particular facility, and need to be educated or informed. This again should be considered in communications planning.

People – many leisure programmes are provided with distinct sets of people in mind. Activities are divided by gender or by age group. Some leisure activities are also directed at people sharing common interests, or people with special needs. In leisure services programme formulation, there is often a need to classify by ability levels, so that there are activities for beginners, intermediate levels and so on.

Outcomes – classifying leisure offerings in terms of outcomes can be very important as it links in closely with motivation and the buying decision process. Sometimes the same service can be advertised with different outcomes designed to appeal to different target groups. A luxury health club may identify that some customers join to get fit, while others join to socialise. Sometimes services which are apparently similar need to be distinguished by their outcomes to avoid frustration for users. Somebody seeking to improve their conversational French may need a different course to somebody wishing to take a French course simply to pass another GCSE.

8. SUMMARY

The concept of leisure on a broad scale is relatively new. A number of factors have helped to influence a growing trend towards a more leisure-orientated lifestyle for the mass population. The scope of the leisure market in the UK is vast and incorporates many different types of activity, largely catered for by four types of service provider as the following examples show:

Public sector

Sports and recreation
Countryside recreation
Education-related
Cultural activities
Heritage

Commercial providers

Home-based leisure
Leisure outside the home
Outdoor sport
Indoor sport

Voluntary provision in the non-public sector

Sport
Informal outdoor recreation
Arts and cultural groups
General recreation and leisure
Special interest groups

National agencies

The Sports Council
The Arts Council
The National Playing Fields Association

A number of demographic factors are important in understanding the leisure services consumer and are evident in patterns of consumption of such services. These include:

Age and family life cycle stage
Gender
Education and social factors
Lifestyle

The leisure offering is generally comprised of one or more of the following elements:

Activities
Facilities
Services

Designing the leisure offering means integrating and combining these elements in a way which will best meet the needs of the target market segments. When programmes are developed, they may be classified in the following ways:

Function
Facilities
People
Outcomes

Leisure service providers need to adopt a marketing orientated approach ensure long-term survival and success. In the increasingly fierce competition for consumers' discretionary income, leisure offerings must meet higher standards of quality and desirability. Understanding the needs of the leisure services consumer, and providing the best means of satisfying those needs, is the first step. Other aspects of leisure marketing management – implementation and evaluation, for example – are covered elsewhere in this book. Internal marketing can be very important, especially in the public and voluntary sectors where it is not necessarily possible to reward staff by traditional means (for example, through financial incentives). The role of internal marketing in successful strategic implementation is explored in Chapter 8.

Progress test 18

1. Account for the growth in activity in the marketing of leisure services.

2. Explain why retailers are increasingly concerned with the leisure experience.

3. List some examples of public sector leisure services, and the constraints these examples often suffer.

4. Briefly describe the extensive choice which exists within the field of commercial leisure services.

5. What tends to occur with regard to the provision and pricing of leisure services as popularity increases?

6. Outline the influence of demographic factors on the marketing strategy of:
   (a) a multi-screen cinema
   (b) a local tennis club.

7. What are the main elements of the 'Leisure Offering'?

8. Why can it be important to stress a variety of 'outcomes' when promoting some leisure activities?

9. Explain the long-term role of the marketing function in leisure provision.

Discussion

1. Describe how you organise and prioritise your leisure time; and consider the key factors which influence your final decisions.

2. How do you see your leisure requirements altering as you grow older and your lifestyle changes?

3. Consider the reasons why, in the past, you have discontinued/failed to pursue specific leisure activities. How do you think 'leisure providers' can best deal with such behaviour?

19

TOURISM MARKETING

INTRODUCTION

Tourism is a major industry throughout the world today. Developments in international travel mean that more people travel further, and more frequently, than ever before. The importance of tourism as an industry, and as an economic activity, is reflected by statistics such as these:

It is estimated that 15 million Europeans will stream through the Channel Tunnel annually (a figure equivalent to the total number of foreign visitors worldwide to Britain in 1988). English Tourist Board figures reflect this upsurge: a total investment of £924 million on new hotel developments in the first six months of 1989 alone, with a further £210 million spent on extending and improving existing properties.

In Hong Kong, tourism has drawn a steady flow of income to the economy over the last twenty years. Not only has it injected much needed funds into the economy, it has also been significant in creating employment opportunities in Hong Kong. Out of the 2.7 million labour force, 250,000 are employed in the tourism industry, thus providing 9.25% of the total jobs in Hong Kong. In 1990, tourism earnings were found to be over 6.5% of imports and contributed over 15% to the counterbalance of trade, according to Government statistics.

Tourism is also an industry operating on a massively broad scale; that is to say, it embraces activities ranging from the smallest seaside hotel, for example, to airlines, multi-national hotel chains and major international tour operators. The travel agency business together with holiday shops (which deal exclusively with package holidays) represent a significant retail market sector in the UK. However, tourism marketing concepts and strategies focus on certain unique characteristics of the tourism industry which are relevant to all tourism service providers.

1. TOURISM MARKETING

The concept of tourism marketing is based on the marketing concept in that it is the process of:

- *identifying and anticipating* consumer demand (and desire) for tourism products and services

- *developing* a means of *providing* products and services to fulfil these needs
- *communicating* this to the consumer, thereby motivating sales, consequently *satisfying* both the consumer, and the organisation's objectives.

Through marketing planning, segmentation and marketing research, a tourism marketing mix can be developed to achieve the tourism organisation's goals through strategic marketing.

2. THE TOURISM INDUSTRY

The tourism industry has traditionally comprised three main and distinctive sectors:

Transportation
Accommodation
Tour Operators (travel agencies represent a subset of this sector)

Increasingly, however, there is evidence that a fourth sector is emerging:

Tourism Destination Operators

It is useful to examine what makes up these sectors, and how the influence of tourism marketing can be seen:

Transportation

Airlines, Cruise and Ferry Lines, Passenger Railways, Coach and Bus Travel, Car Hire:
The range of airline services has increased considerably, not only in terms of frequency of flights and number of destinations, but also in terms of different services, and differing levels of service to meet different passenger needs. This shows the important role marketing plays as competition and demand intensifies.

Passenger rail services have also changed, and their role in tourism is wide as with, for example, Eurorail tickets allowing extensive international travel at a basic (service) standard for students and budget tourists, to the luxury of the Venice-Simplon Orient Express – where the train voyage is the holiday.

Cruise lines are operating different services tailored to consumers' budgets, and other shipping lines involved in the tourist industry, especially the car ferry operators, are broadening and upgrading their range of services and facilities to meet consumer expectations, and to remain competitive.

Coach and bus companies have acted in a similar fashion and these, together with car rental companies, are also included in this sector.

Accommodation

Hotels, Inns, Apartments and Club Resorts:
Accommodation includes hotels, ranging from the biggest international chains recognisable worldwide such as Hilton and Holiday Inn to small independent establishments. In order to gain recognition in an increasingly competitive

marketplace, many smaller independent hotels have grouped together, adopting a consortium approach. Under a central brand name, they can offer central reservations services, for example, and present a recognisable identity to consumers which enables them to compete against the larger, more established chains.

Other types of accommodation are also well established in tourist markets, notably self-catering apartments and 'club'-type complexes. Centre Parcs are today's answer to the Butlins-type holiday camps of the 50s and 60s, while Mark Warner Holidays are also successful in their inclusive 'club' formula.

Tour operators

Package Tours, Speciality Tours:
Tour operators are the firms which specialise in providing the whole holiday package, incorporating travel and accommodation needs for the consumer. They range from highly specialised operations such as Abercrombie and Kent who take small groups on safari or expedition-type holidays, to large operators offering services at all different levels to cater for budget, family, or singles holidays to 'near' or 'faraway' destinations.

Thomas Cook is one of the best known of such operators; they also offer travel agency and financial services to their consumers. An independent local coach firm may also be a tour operator, and indeed, many transportation companies also offer holiday packages.

Tourism destination operators

Theme Parks, Heritage Centres:
This is a new category in many senses, as it is an area of the tourism industry which has seen massive growth in the development of theme parks and other types of artificial tourist destinations in recent years. However, Disneyland and Disneyworld in America were the forerunners of this development in tourism marketing, and they have been well established for decades.

It is due to the recent growth, and the continuing trends, which make it an area which should be considered separately as a tourism industry. The new EuroDisney theme park in France is an example of a tourism destination operation. On a smaller scale, heritage parks which are being developed from Britain's industrial wasteland such as Wigan Pier, which attracted over half a million tourists in 1991, and similar attractions now represent a significant amount of tourism activity.

All the above sectors of the tourism industry, while quite distinct in themselves, have many aspects in common. There are certain features of tourism marketing which differ from other industries. The impact of environmental forces, for example, can provide different pressures or opportunities for tourism than for other service sector industries.

3. MAJOR CHARACTERISTICS OF THE TOURISM INDUSTRY

There are four main characteristics which distinguish the tourism industry from other service providers.

Inflexibility The tourism industry is highly inflexible in terms of capacity. The number of beds in a htel or seats on an airplane is fixed so it is not possible to meet sudden upsurges in demand. Similarly, restaurant tables, hotel beds and airplane seats remain empty and unused in periods of low demand. The seasonal nature of tourism activity exacerbates this problem.

Perishability Tourism service products are highly perishable. An unused hotel bed or an empty airplane seat represents an immediate loss of that service as a means of earning profit. This has an impact on overall industry profitability.

Fixed location Tourism destinations are fixed locations so effort must be concentrated in communicating the facility to the potential consumer. A consumer can conveniently watch a Hollywood movie at the local cinema but has to be persuaded to travel to India to see the Taj Mahal.

Relatively large financial investment Every modern tourist establishment and facility requires large investment, frequently over a long time scale. This means that the level of risk and the rate of return are critically important to tourism management.

General factors

There are a number of factors which can influence growth in tourism activity. There has been massive growth in international business giving rise to growth in international travel and hotel accommodation. The concept of the 'global village' where destinations worldwide have become much easier to get to has led to a far higher amount of long distance travel, both by business travellers and tourists. Overseas conferences, trade fairs and exhibitions have become commonplace.

Consumers in most developed countries are enjoying greater amounts of leisure time and relatively high levels of income, so can choose to travel more often. Holidays are very 'public' goods, which means that they carry a status value in the consumer's perception. Airlines provide business travellers with a range of higher-grade services which appeal to their status.

Safer and cheaper air transport has led to massive increases in the number of flights taken. It costs little more to fly long haul from the UK to Western Canada in the early 1990s than it did 10 years ago. This, coupled with the fact that package tour operators offer a far wider range of options to suit all tastes, and that their operations are more closely monitored and have an enhanced reputation, has led to overall growth in the market.

There are a number of reasons why consumers seek tourism services, and these factors also influence the demand for such services, and how the consumer makes a buying decision. The range of motivational factors which influence consumer choice include leisure and recreation, sporting interest, social interests such as family reunions or visits to friends, religious factors (pilgrimages, visits to places of religious significance) and business needs. Understanding consumer motivation and consumer needs is a major part of tourism marketing.

4. THE TOURISM MARKETING ENVIRONMENT

An environmental analysis should form one of the first stages in any marketing plan. In marketing, we are concerned with two types of environmental analysis: the micro-environment and the macro-environment. The micro-environment is the internal environment of the organisation which should be scrutinised by management to identify strengths and weaknesses in the company. This is as true for companies in the tourism industry as any other, but what we are concerned with here is the external or macro-environment which may affect the whole industry.

The objective of analysing the environment is to:

- identify influences
- control those (if any) which can be controlled
- use any which can be used for best competitive advantage

The main environmental factors with which we are concerned can be broken down under four main headings; Political, Economic, Social/cultural, Technical (PEST). Some examples of the main environmental factors which will impact on the tourism industry are as follows:

Political Political influences can affect tourism in many ways. Perhaps the most extreme example is when war, or civil unrest caused by political instability, breaks out:

The Gulf War had a tremendous impact on tourism in many countries in the region, even where the danger on holiday makers was negligible (in any real sense). Turkey, for example, lost a massive proportion of its annual tourism revenue, as many operators simply withdrew bookings altogether. The worry is that the losses may be long term, as confidence in the country as a 'safe' destination rebuilds. Yugoslavia is currently experiencing the same problems due to political unrest. Add to these problems affecting holiday destinations the impact that the Gulf War had on international travel of all kinds, including business travel as many USA companies refused to let executives fly overseas to any destination for fear of terrorism, and the true scale of the impact can be envisaged. The hotel industry in Hong Kong suffered at the time of the Gulf War for this reason.

The government's attitude to tourism can be another major factor here:

In countries such as Morocco, where tourism is seen as an under-developed, high value industry, government support is being given to tourism projects. In other areas, however, attempts are being made to curb tourism on grounds such as environmentalism. In the Antarctic, for example, it has become popular to take pleasure cruises to observe the wildlife and the landscape. However, there are now fears that ecological damage may result, and tourism is being discouraged.

Economic Economic factors can be seen to impact on the tourism industry in many ways:

Currency fluctuations are an obvious example, and in countries where the currency is highly unstable, the opportunities to develop tourism may be limited. Economic wealth, both in the country where tourism destinations are to be developed, and in terms of the potential consumers of tourism products, is another important aspect. Will a country be able to afford the infrastructure required for tourism; airports, roads, facilities? Will people be able to afford expensive holidays abroad, or, in times of recession, will they seek out cheaper alternatives, or opt to forego holiday travel?

Social/cultural factors Social and cultural factors are a major influence in consumer buying decisions, and this applies to tourism products and services, just as other products and services. Over time, changes do appear which will affect consumers' buying habits:

In the UK, the relative wealth today of what were formerly the 'lower' classes means that expensive holidays are no longer the prerogative of the rich. Working people from all walks of life expect a lifestyle which includes a choice of holiday options. The growing 'grey' market of comfortably-off middle aged and retired people represents a rapidly growing segment in tourism and leisure markets.

Fashion is another cultural variable which influences tourism. It has become very fashionable to go skiing, and long haul destinations have gained their own popularity among the British. But holiday habits differ from country to country. As Britain is an island (or a group of islands), British tourists tend to want to travel abroad for ski or sun holidays, and will therefore tend to fly a great deal, and use other overseas holiday packages and services. The French, in contrast, can get ski and sun holidays in France, and this is reflected in their holiday habits.

The above examples illustrate how macro-environmental factors may impact on tourism. The tourism marketing manager's task is to analyse current environmental factors, and to try to forecast and anticipate what future trends will be. This is perhaps the most important aspect of the analysis and probably the most difficult. The internal or micro-environmental analysis was mentioned earlier, with the idea that strengths and weaknesses should be highlighted.

Similarly, in conducting the external environmental analysis, one aim should be to establish what opportunities and threats lie in store for the organisation. This step is a fundamental stage in the planning process, and forms the tourism SWOT analysis.

Understanding and monitoring these macro- and micro-environmental forces is essential if the business is to achieve its objectives through optimum development and use of internal resources, and through accurately targeted effort in the external marketplac Tourism marketing management is responsible for all aspects of marketing planning and goal setting.

5. MARKETING PLANNING

There are a number of stages in the planning process which will be explored in this section from the tourism marketing viewpoint. In the first instance, considering the marketing concept and its applicability to tourism marketing, it is vital to know and understand the consumer of tourism products and services if the organisation is to satisfy its objectives profitably. Market research plays a major part in this management task. It is important to assess consumer needs, desires and motivations towards tourism services in order to establish levels of market attractiveness, to determine key market segments and to plan the most effective marketing programmes (the marketing mix) accordingly.

The tourism consumer

Tourists are not homogeneous – that is, they are widely differing in many ways. Their basic motivation for choosing to travel can vary enormously. The main motivators can be broken down as follows:

Physical: the consumer has a physical need to travel to attend a business meeting, or to reach a suitable climate for whatever preferred activity.
Cultural: holidays abroad have become the custom in much of Western culture.
Interpersonal: travelling to socialise with friends or for family reunions, for example.
Status/Prestige: certain sectors of the market seek travel as a status or prestige good – in certain social or business circles fashion dictates when and where people visit. Upgraded resorts, hotels and airline services reflect this sector.

Similarly, the tourism consumer will not have just one set of needs when they are travelling; some will require stability, whilst others may deliberately seek change and novelty, maybe even a certain level of risk or daring. Some will be satisfied with total peace and relaxation, while others will look for activity and sports, for example.

Market research needs to be employed to answer two key questions:

- What influences consumer choice?
- How do consumers perceive tourism goods and services?

This type of research will enable the tourism marketing manager to identify groups of consumers who share more or less similar tastes, and consider these groupings as potential market segments.

Segmentation

The idea behind segmentation is to divide a market into subsets of consumers who share some similar characteristics, thus enabling the organisation to target these subsets, or segments, with a tailored marketing mix. The target market segments should be sufficiently large to warrant substantial investment and attractive, therefore, in terms of profitability. Ideally, there must be potential for future growth, and competition which is not too intensive. If possible, the aim is to seek unsatisfied consumer needs which can be met by the organisation's operation.

Segments may be categorised according to varying criteria. In tourism marketing, these are likely to be in terms of age, frequency of travel, education, occupation or income. Typically these variables are aspects of lifestyle. Other bases for segmentation of tourism and travel markets include purpose (of trips – business, vacation, convention, social/family); psychographic segmentation (where behavioural aspects of motivation are used); and benefit segmentation (where the benefits being sought by the consumer are the key variable).

For segmentation to operate successfully, selected target segments must be:

accessible
substantial
measurable

Segmentation is important to tourism marketing managers in several key ways. Effective market segmentation can:

- enable the service provider to identify gaps in the market
- help in terms of achieving a stronger competitive position for existing destinations
- identify potential new consumers in the tourism market
- in product positioning, effective segmentation can enhance the image of existing destinations.

Setting objectives

The objectives set will obviously vary between individual organisations, but in tourism marketing there are several industry characteristics which impact on management decisions in setting objectives. The key issues are:

occupancy rates
profitability
satisfying tourists' needs.

The service provider will be concerned with not only maximising occupancy, but also with achieving stable occupancy as a priority. Similarly, because of the usual high levels of investment required, maximising return on investment (ROI) and also maximising total profit will be crucially important. However, none of this will be achieved if the consumers' needs are not consistently satisfied and fulfilled.

In essence, at this stage, it is clear that tourism marketing management is faced with several distinct tasks in the planning process.

Tourism marketing planning

- Development of *market research* systems in order to determine what consumers want.
- Investigation of how the market is made up and the best way to break it down into groups or subsets which are most attractive to the organisation through a process of *market segmentation.*
- Design and development of suitable tourism products and service offerings to appeal to the chosen segments – *product planning* to enable the organisation to meet its chosen goals, determined through a process of *objective setting.*
- *Communication* to the consumers and potential consumers to inform them of the services which are available and, if appropriate, to remind or persuade them by means of *advertising and promotion.*
- Ensuring that the service offering is available and accessible to consumers via an effective *distribution* programme so that they can buy the service at a value *(pricing).*
- *Monitoring and evaluation* of the above programme implementation to measure effectiveness against profitability targets and assess success in achieving *organisational goals.*

The above represents a brief outline of the tourism marketing planning task. Much effort relates to the design and development of an effective marketing mix. The tourism marketing mix will be explored in the next section. Marketing strategy and the marketing process will be summarised again later in this chapter.

6. THE TOURISM MARKETING MIX

The marketing mix refers to the blend of ideas, concepts and features which marketing management put together to best appeal to their target market segments. Each target segment will have a separate marketing mix, tailored to meet the specific needs of consumers in the individual segment.

The product mix

The product here refers to the tourism service offering. Although service products are essentially intangible, there are certain physical characteristics which consumers will assess in their evaluation of the product choice. These are:

- Attractiveness of the offering in terms of physical features, suitability of climate etc,
- Facilities available, and associated levels of quality and service,
- Accessibility in terms of ease of getting there for the potential consumer – are there adequate air services, road and other transport considerations?

Package tour products will be broken down into different types to suit the identified needs of consumers. Typically, these will fall into the categories of escorted and unescorted tours, and group tour bookings. Package tours have evolved considerably since their popularity in the early 1970s waned, as tourists' tastes became more sophisticated and the package tour image of mass holidays, with herds of people crowding to over-commercialised destinations, lost its appeal to consumers. Today's package tours cater for varying tastes, offering levels of refinement to suit both the 'cheap and cheerful' budget tourist, and the seasoned traveller seeking more exotic and exclusive services.

The tourism product should evolve over time to reflect changes and developments in the tourism marketplace. This is essential for successful marketing, which depends in the first instance on satisfying consumer needs and wants to achieve organisational success.

The idea that service products are intangible is an important one, but increasingly firms are trying to make their offering more tangible, thereby increasing their recognition amongst the target buying groups, and enhancing the value of the offering. Physical details such as hotel furnishings are replicated throughout certain chains so that the service offering has a strong, easily recognised physical identity which appeals to the security needs of many travellers, and encourages a feeling of being at home in the hotel. Tangible gifts such as toiletries, flight bags, even bath robes, bearing the company logo or brand, are another way of making services more tangible to the consumer.

Branding plays a very important role in tourism marketing. Car rental firms, hotel chains and airlines in particular employ tremendous efforts to ensure that their name is widely recognised and synonymous with quality, value or some other characteristic. Travel agents and tour operators depend on reputation to a large extent, and so it is imperative that they have a strong, recognisable identity.

Branding is interesting in tourism marketing, however. Usually the main reason for trying to build brand loyalty is to encourage repeat business. However, consumers' desire for novelty, change, and the wish to visit different destinations means that the opportunity for repeat business must be limited. However, this is not necessarily the case, and tour operators, travel companies and hotel chains recognise this fact. If consumer preference can be built up for a particular brand, then the opportunities for repeat business are high. The tourist who always stays with Hilton and rents a car from Hertz will do so whether in Bangkok or London or New York.

The promotional mix

The aims of the promotion fall into three main categories: to inform, to remind and to persuade. It will always be necessary to inform prospective consumers about new products and services, but other issues may also need this type of communication to consumers; new uses, price changes, information to build consumer confidence and to reduce fears, full descriptions of service offerings, image building (of destinations) are examples. Similarly, consumers may need to be reminded about all these types of issues, especially in the off-peak season. Promotion designed to persuade consumers will be in line with specific objectives, for example to encourage switching or to build preference.

It is vitally important to recognise that promotion, or marketing communications generally, may not always be aimed at the potential consumer or end-user of the product or service. In many business areas it is necessary to design promotional programmes aimed at channel customers to complement end-user promotions. Channel customers are all intermediaries in the channels of distribution – in tourism this will most frequently be the tour operator or travel agent, for example.

Hotel owners and airlines will need to promote their services to tour operators (who are, in effect, wholesalers of travel services and products) as well as promoting their service to end users and independent travellers. Similarly, tour operators will want to ensure that travel agents sell their services in a positive manner, and will therefore want to advertise to the agents the benefits of selling their tours (perhaps in terms of higher commissions), whilst advertising a totally different set of benefits to the end user. This type of promotion is referred to as 'into the pipeline' promotion. The crucial task is to assess accurately the needs and wants of intermediaries, as opposed to actual consumers and design promotional messages accordingly.

There are a number of promotional tools available to the tourism marketing manager which can be combined to create effective promotional programmes. Sales promotion (via brochures, point of sale displays and even video cassettes) plays a very important role as does advertising. Visual media is perhaps the only way to advertise tourism destinations properly. Whatever means are used, it is important to focus on the following:

- clearly identified segments
- a unique selling proposition
- well defined target audiences
- creative use of media and media scheduling to reach audiences
- monitoring and evaluation of promotional effectiveness.

Tourism promotional messages should always focus on the benefits attainable by the consumer of choosing a particular resort or tour operator, for example, rather than relying too heavily on descriptive presentations of features. Careful selection of attractive market segments at the earlier segmentation stage should lead to greater chances of choosing the right message to target.

Pricing

Pricing in tourism is a fairly complex issue because the price eventually paid by the consumer may be made up from the prices charged by various independent service providers in the case of, say, a package tour. Variations in the level of demand cause further complications in tourism pricing, particularly due to seasonality.

Pricing policy decisions will be directed by strategic objectives. If the objective is market penetration then prices must be set very competitively to appeal to the largest possible number of potential consumers. If, on the other hand, a firm is pursuing a niche strategy, catering for the luxury market in high value, exclusive tourism services, then prices should reflect this; promotion and advertising can be used to differentiate the product on an exclusivity basis and premium prices may be charged.

Providers of tourism products and services will almost always be faced by high levels of fixed costs, leading to variants of cost-plus pricing or return-on-investment as key determinants of pricing levels. It is also important, however, to have a clear understanding of factors affecting price sensitivity, and to include pricing tactics which exploit such sensitivities fully. For example, it may be possible to differentiate service levels and offer higher priced 'value added' services, as in business class air travel. Similarly, seasonal demand variations should be considered in price setting.

Distribution

Distribution management is concerned with two things: availability and accessibility. If tourism marketing management is to be certain that their products and services are both available and accessible to the target market, they must design a channel strategy that will be effective. In order to do this, research must be undertaken to determine *how* and *where* potential customers prefer to buy tourism products and services. Channels, which consist of all the intermediaries between the original service provider and the consumer, must be chosen to maximise distribution effectiveness.

Different distribution strategies may be selected to reflect the company's overall objectives, and even firms in the same area of market operations may not have the same distribution strategy. Most tour operators sell their services through travel agents or holiday shops but Portland operate a direct marketing policy, where consumers deal directly with the company – there are no middlemen. Interestingly, Portland is the direct selling arm of Thomson Holidays, a major package tour operator. As well as their direct selling activities, Thomson have pursued a vertical integration strategy through their ownership of Lunn Poly, the retail holiday shop chain.

Other companies may also utilise more than one method of distribution. Airlines, for example, sell tickets through travel agents, and sell seats on flights to tour operators, whilst also operating direct marketing by offering travellers the opportunity to make reservations through their own booking offices.

Besides travel agents and tour operators there are a number of possible intermediaries in tourism marketing channels. These include automated reservation services, central reservation systems and specialist air ticket agencies. The main decision is based on maximising the opportunity of selling the product or service to the tourism consumer.

Whichever distribution strategy is selected, channel management plays a key role. For channels to be effective in selling to the consumer they need reliable updated information. For this reason, information technology has been widely adopted in the tourism industry, and high street travel agents have on-line systems linking them into tour operators' and airline computerised booking systems. Point-of-sale information and promotional material must always be supplied in sufficient quantities to all channel members.

7. TOURISM MARKETING MANAGEMENT

Tourism marketing is essentially a three-stage process, starting with market research to accurately analyse consumers' needs. Tourism services and products must then be designed to fulfil those needs at an appropriate price, and then the availability of these products and services must be communicated effectively to potential consumers. Market research is the critical starting point – the success of subsequent marketing planning and policy decisions is dependent upon a clear understanding of the market.

To develop an effective marketing strategy, the market should be segmented and target segments selected based on a careful examination not only of the attractiveness of the segments, but also on the basis of company resources and strengths. It is important to recognise possible constraints at this stage. This analysis will enable the tourism marketing manager to formulate marketing objectives to maximise exploitation of marketing opportunities, and in line with overall company objectives. Marketing planning, and the allocation of the company's resources in designing an effective tourism marketing mix, can then take place.

To achieve strategic growth through tourism marketing implementation, three major strategic alternatives are available:

Market penetration – the aim is to gain market share at the expense of the competition. There are three ways of achieving this:

- Encourage existing customers to buy more of the company's products and services, in other words encouraging them to travel more frequently, or to choose more high-value holiday destinations.
- Persuade non-users of tourism products and services in the existing target markets to try the products and services.
- Attempt to get competitors' customers to switch to your offerings.

Market development – this means seeking new target market segments in which to offer existing products and services.
Product development – this strategy calls for product ranges to be upgraded or increased to attract a wider customer base.

8. SUMMARY

Tourism is a major industry which continues to grow in size and importance throughout the world. Tourism is a massive industry within itself comprising many activities:

Airlines
Cruise Liners
Multi-national Hotel Chains
Tour Operators
Travel Agencies
Holiday Shops

Certain aspects of the tourism industry are relevant to all operators within the tourism industry and these are covered in this chapter in relation to service marketing.

The tourism industry has traditionally been made up of three main sectors but a new sector has recently started to emerge:

Transportation
Accommodation
Tour Operators
Tourism Destination Operators

The industry also has a number of distinctive characteristics:

Inflexibility
Perishability
Fixed location
Relatively large financial investment
General factors

Tourism marketing should focus clearly on the needs of the consumer, and on a sound approach to marketing strategy and planning. Tourism is a dynamic industry, subject to constant change caused by consumer and societal trends. It is worth pointing out here that the tourism industry does not escape environmentalism and the trend towards consumer-led pressure for 'greener' practice throughout all industries. The publication of *The Green Tourism Guide* by Sustainability, and the adoption of a green rating for holidays on TV holiday programmes, have played a part in increasing consumer awareness about the environmental issues involved in their personal decisions about holidays and travel.

This is just one example illustrating why it is so important for tourism marketing managers to have a clear and full understanding of consumer trends and macro-environmental forces if marketing management is to lead to successful programmes and policies.

Progress test 19

1. How have developments in international travel increased activity in the tourism industry?

2. Briefly describe the three main sectors of the tourism industry, and also highlight the fourth emerging category.

3. What are the financial consequences which can arise as a result of the perishability of tourism services?

4. Explain the external environmental considerations affecting:
   (a) A tour operator specialising in holidays to Hong Kong.
   (b) A large 'white-knuckle' attraction theme park in the UK.

5. To what extent do the motivations of individual tourists vary?

6. Outline the importance of brand image and reputation in the tourist industry.

7. Should all tourism promotional activities be directed at the end-user? Give reasons for your answer.

8. Explain the effect that seasonal variations have on the pricing strategy in the tourism industry.

9. How can effective tourism marketing enable an organisation to achieve strategic growth?

Discussion

1. Consider the importance of lifestyle in the tourism decision-making process relating, where possible, to personal experience.

2. Why is tourism considered a dynamic industry? Evaluate the shifts you have witnessed within your lifetime, and suggest future developments.

20

CHARITIES MARKETING

INTRODUCTION

Charities represent an increasingly important area of business-orientated activity. In the UK alone, there are over 175,000 registered charities. Between them, these charities generated over £3.5 billion in revenue of various forms in 1990; it is not easy to estimate exact overall figures as many donations are in the form of personal and professional time and activities, and goods, rather than cash.

In recessionary times charities can be affected on two levels: greater demand for charitable services arising from increasing levels of homelessness and poverty, for example, and falling levels of donations caused by the economic downturn. The Charities Aid Foundation estimates that average donations per head in the UK fell by approximately 35% from £2 to £1.30 in 1990.

There is also evidence that increasing levels of competition due to the growing number of charities is contributing to the pressure faced by charities management. This growth in the number of charities has been partly fuelled by Government policies which have led to a greater dependence on charities to provide care in what were formerly areas provided for by the public sector.

International aid is also faced with increasing problems; over-population coupled with famine and drought on an unprecedented level, and the growing numbers of victims of war and natural disasters, are just some of the sources of need. Charities involved in overseas aid are particularly pressed in recessionary times due to the traditionally held value that 'charity begins at home'. When domestic problems increase, and the need for charities provision is perceived as being very high in the UK, this is often accompanied by a reluctance to donate to more remote causes.

In coping with these intense demands and pressures from a business and economic perspective, and when also faced with the need to be publicly accountable and to maintain a strong image, charities are adopting the marketing concept on a widespread basis. The management tasks of fundraising and building awareness, and distribution of funds and resources, for example, can be helped by effective marketing management techniques and programmes. This chapter explores the role of marketing in relation to charities, and includes an insight into the special nature of charities marketing, together with examples of effective strategies.

1. THE ROLE OF MARKETING IN CHARITIES

In common with other types of organisation, charities have marketing problems and need marketing skills. The scope of marketing generally has been broadened to cover not only 'business' organisations but also charities and other not-for-profit organisations in both the public and private sectors. Marketing may enhance a charity's performance, which is desirable, but, increasingly, it may be essential for survival.

Marketing management, with the procedures and ideas which have developed throughout the evolution of modern marketing in profit-orientated organisations, is now recognised as being equally applicable to charities marketing:

> *The underlying philosophy of marketing – that of creating satisfaction through mutually profitable exchanges – can apply to the act of giving and receiving, as well as buying and selling.*

Relationship marketing, where the marketing organisation designs strategies and programmes to address the needs of suppliers, employees and shareholders, for example, as well as its external customers, is especially relevant to charities marketing. Charities have more than one type of 'customer'. There are typically at least three major participants in the charities marketing process:

The Charity itself
Donors
Clients or recipients

There can be many more participants who influence or regulate the process, or who contribute a significant role within the charities management decision making and activities, for example:

Governing bodies
Foundations
Trustees
Outside bodies such as the Church
Affiliated organisations
Missions

Services marketing management tasks which play a critical role in charities marketing include:

Marketing audit
Market analysis
Market segmentation
Marketing planning
Designing the marketing mix:
    Product
    Price
    Promotion
    Place

These tasks will be reviewed throughout this chapter, and specific examples applicable to charities marketing will be highlighted.

2. 'BUSINESS FUNCTIONS' IN CHARITIES MARKETING

It is important to take an overall view of the closeness or similarity between charities and other organisations. Whether or not an organisation embraces marketing and adopts marketing management principles, there are certain functions which all organisations must undertake. All organisations providing products or services have the following in common:

Financial/Resourcing Every organisation, from the smallest local charities to international concerns must perform a financial function. Money and/or resources must be raised somehow and managed according to sound business principles and budgeting.

Production Inputs to the organisation, whether resources in the form of goods or funds, must be arranged, processed or managed in some way so as to provide the necessary outputs to satisfy the needs of the end-users or recipients. In its simplest form, a local church may hold harvest festival celebrations with a collection of produce for onward distribution to the sick and the needy. The food must be collected, sorted and made up into parcels before it can be delivered.

Personnel Every organisation is concerned with recruiting and managing people, whether volunteers or paid employees. Personnel need training, tasks must be assigned, and lines of authority and control laid down (even when control is shared by all members, as in co-operatives and many self-help groups). In today's environment, the need to operate as a competitive, viable and cost-effective commercially-styled concern has led charities to seek professional business managers and employees. In order to recruit good managers, charities have to undertake large-scale recruitment and promotion campaigns. There is evidence to suggest that this task is not an easy one as social embarrassment is caused through the notion of paying (or receiving) the high salary levels associated with high-calibre personnel within a charity. In fact, charities may experience difficulty in coping with this management task, before they dedicate specialised activity to marketing.

Purchasing Materials and supplies must be acquired efficiently by comparing and selecting potential sources of supply. Promotion and advertising are two examples of services which may have to be bought in.

These management tasks traditionally lie in the realm of the business enterprise. However, they apply to all types of organisations such as hospitals, political parties, and other public sector and not-for-profit groups. As charities themselves grow in size, and their activities grow in complexity, the importance and significance of these activities is clear.

Save the Children Fund, for example, raised £52 million in donations in 1990. Christian Aid is involved in diverse activities in over 70 countries, including the provision of artificial limbs, shoe-making classes, agricultural aid and health care. The extent and complexity of their management task is clear, in relation to all the areas described above.

3. MANAGEMENT TASKS IN CHARITIES MARKETING

The marketing audit

A starting point in assessing overall marketing needs, and the effectiveness of existing marketing practice, is the marketing audit. Organisations which are new to marketing, as many charities are, need to undertake a marketing audit to establish the current position.

A marketing audit represents a comprehensive examination of the organisation's market environment, objectives, strategies and activities. It should focus on problem areas and opportunities and lead to an action plan to improve marketing performance.

Carrying out a marketing audit can bring dual benefits:

- It can provide drive and direction to the organisation in the realisation of its (business-like) goals.
- It has an educational benefit, raising the awareness levels of the charity's administrators and managers of the business issues facing them, for example: competitive situation, budget setting, planning, forecasting.

As charities progress towards an enhanced marketing orientation, the marketing audit is a key stage. However, it should not be a one-off activity. It needs to be undertaken on a continuous basis, and become part of the management control and monitoring system.

Market analysis

Understanding the market is a fundamental aspect of services marketing. Many charity organisations have now become extremely large international and national organisations serving diverse markets across different cultural and geographical boundaries. Charities such as Oxfam, Barnardo's and Christian Aid are serving the needs of many different markets and segments. Their task is comparable to that of any major multi-national or national consumer goods manufacturer, for example. They are also in competition with other charities for donations.

The competitive situation needs to be studied, and programmes devised to gain competitive advantage. Many charities operate commercial activities to boost funds, and they need to undertake market research and competitor analysis in exactly the same way as commercial companies.

This can be seen in the case of the Royal Society for the Protection of Birds (RSPB) and the National Society for the Prevention of Cruelty to Children who run extensive commercial operations in the form of gift catalogues, at Christmas and at intervals throughout the year. The RSPB also sells its merchandise through its own shops at bird sanctuaries and nature reserves. They operate under business conditions and need to adopt sound marketing practice.

Unlike many commercial organisations, charities, however, must understand the needs not only of their end-users – the people who ultimately benefit from their services – but also the needs of their donors. As identified earlier, charities marketing transactions inevitably involve both of these groups; two distinct sets of customers, in fact, with distinctive needs and wants. Clearly, each of these 'markets' will require separate marketing programmes and policies.

Market segmentation

Segmenting the end users of charity services is important as relief aid must be given at the right time and in the right form to those who need it. Needs differ greatly, and scarce charity resources must be utilised with optimum efficiency. However, segmenting and then targeting potential donors is of the utmost importance.

Many of the smaller charities have adopted this approach. In the face of massive competition for attention and donations from well known charities such as Save the Children Fund, smaller charities have developed niche marketing strategies and directed their efforts at specialised donor segments. On a broader scale, many charities operate within two main segments as far as donors are concerned – individual members of the public, and corporations.

Through sponsorship and charitable donations, corporations are a major source of charity revenue. Their involvement stems from the expectation of some mutual benefit – enhanced public image of the corporation and attractive publicity, for example. Even in the area of sponsorship, however, charities are in line with competition from sports and the arts in particular. Companies will only undertake sponsorship where they can perceive some return on their investment in terms of exposure or positive publicity. This has resulted in charities researching the needs of companies and developing marketing programmes which have been finely tuned to attract sponsorship.

The idea of mutual benefit extends also to individual donors. However, this is perhaps less likely to be in the form of public exposure (although some individuals take pride in their own charitable generosity). Benefits sought by individual donors tend to be highly intangible and are related to emotional satisfaction, and the sense of 'doing good'. This is recognised by charities and, in many cases, something is offered in return for donations to reinforce the favourable emotion, and to create continued awareness.

Many charities invite subscriptions rather than donations, and subscribers then receive certain benefits such as newsletters, badges and other membership gifts. Charity programmes based upon the adopt-a-child scheme involve the donor as well as the recipient in the benefits of the exchange:

> The recipient, usually a child in a developing country, receives a contribution to their education and health care through the regular funds provided by the donor, who in turn receives letters, photographs and bulletins on the child's progress. In this way the needs of the child (welfare, education) and the needs of the donor (emotional satisfaction, sense of 'doing good') are satisfied

thereby meeting organisational objectives (to obtain steady funding from donors to provide education and welfare aid). This is true marketing in practice.

Segmenting potential audiences for marketing communication is very important in charities marketing. Media choice and promotional methods can increase in effectiveness when targets are accurately identified and understood. Different advertising appeals can be made to different segments of donor markets. Market research should be undertaken to find out what motivates people to donate, and their preferred method of giving. Programmes can then be designed accordingly.

4. MARKETING PLANNING AND THE MARKETING MIX

Charities need to undertake strategic marketing planning to achieve their objectives. Building on the marketing audit and market analysis and segmentation stages already discussed, marketing planning is an important step. The process of planning itself can help provide direction and focus and ensure that the organisation is 'pulling together'. Monitoring and evaluation ensures that it stays on course.

Strategic planning at the corporate, or organisation, level is equally relevant for charities as for business corporations, and marketing planning then takes place along with other functional divisions, such as finance. The following outline illustrates some of the organisational aspects of planning, and the linkages within stages of marketing planning.

Marketing planning in charity organisations reflects very close links to marketing planning in general for not-for-profit business areas, discussed in some detail in Chapter 17. A checklist covering the main aspects of the planning process is useful, however:

Charities strategic marketing planning

Development of market research systems in order to determine:

- how donors and sponsors perceive the charity and to what extent they may wish to become involved
- what 'rewards' or satisfactions they seek
- the ways in which they prefer to donate or contribute

Research systems must also be established to define parameters of the recipient market served. In times of international crisis or natural disasters the needs of the recipients, or clients, may be obvious, but in other situations a clear understanding of the nature of the aid sought – and the best way of delivering that aid – is essential.

Thorough market and competitor analysis to see how the market is made up. Internal and external environment analysis to identify SWOT:

strengths
weaknesses
opportunities
threats

Market segmentation – Investigation into the best way to sub-divide the donor/sponsor market into groups or subsets which are most attractive to the organisation through a process of market segmentation. Similar sub-division of the recipient market should be undertaken, especially in terms of nature of needs, to target efforts most effectively.

Development of organisational and marketing objectives

Having identified and analysed the target markets, programmes must now be designed to provide want-satisfaction to those markets. This is the development of a strategic marketing mix.

Charities marketing mix

Product Design and development of suitable campaigns, promotions and other service offerings (for example gift catalogues, or affiliated credit card services) to appeal to the chosen donor/sponsor segments and generate the required results for the organisation. Development of the service offering for the recipient/client market to satisfy current and future needs. One of the major tasks can be to make the process of charity giving more tangible, to increase the satisfaction of the donor and enhance the success of the exchange relationship. Charity products or services aimed at the donor/sponsor market may include:

- membership benefits – newsletter, physical goods or gifts publicity, such as the name or corporate logo of a sponsoring company on the charity's literature, or on an event programme
- personalised information updates on 'adopt-a-granny' schemes (which aim to sponsor the poor elderly in need of aid overseas).

Price Assessment of suitable levels for all aspect of pricing. This could include:

- Setting desired contribution levels for sponsors of charity programmes
- Commercial-type pricing of fundraising efforts such as goods and services for sale (for example gift catalogues or entrance fees to benefit concerts)
- Financial target-setting, and costing of fundraising activities
- Payment methods to facilitate donations by target segments (for example wages donation schemes, deeds of covenant or annual subscriptions by direct debit)
- Determining subscription levels and rewards where membership of a charitable organisation is desired
- Where a charity subsidises a service, such as a housing association, subsidy amounts and recipient contribution levels need to be assessed.

This illustration demonstrates some of the range of tasks involved in developing the 'price' element of the charity marketing mix. As with all the elements of the marketing mix, the complexity of the task will be determined by the scope of the charity's activities.

Promotion Again, charities are faced by twin tasks in developing their promotional mix – promotion to donors and potential donors and promotion to the recipient/client market. Charities have come a long way from the 'begging bowl' approach, and many have also moved away from the shock tactics designed to attract maximum attention. In international aid fundraising advertising campaigns, for example, the aim is to portray no harrowing pictures, but to treat the poor with dignity and show them how to help themselves.

Some charities, including the Royal Society for the Prevention of Cruelty to Animals in the UK, on the other hand, have deliberately introduced aggressive, hard-hitting images in their advertising campaigns. Charities, like commercial business operations, must undertake advertising research in order to establish the type of advertising message and image most likely to evoke the desired response. This research should be ongoing and is integral to the task of designing a successful promotional mix.

Public relations (PR) can play a vital role in charities promotion and is an important tool in the promotional mix. Good PR items – news, articles, events – tend to attract greater chances of publicity and media attention than PR for commercial concerns. Royal patrons are one way of helping to focus the media spotlight on a charity's activities, as is the involvement of celebrities and people in the public eye. Local radio stations will often host and publicise charity fundraising events in the local community, while the success of Band Aid and Live Aid is due to the use of international media coverage.

Charities need to use promotion not only to raise funds and to address their public but also to inform their clients in many cases. Many charitable organisations offer counselling services, for example, and clients needing these services must be aware of their existence. Advertising which can be most effective is often also costly, and the costs of providing advertising for the service competes within the charity's budget with the costs of providing the service itself.

Sales promotion can be a useful tool in charities promotion. In its simplest form, recognition of donations can take the form of a sticker, or a poppy for Remembrance Day. Prize draws, where tickets are sold in aid of a charity, are another successful and widespread form of sales promotion.

Place It is important that charities ensure that their services are accessible and available in the right places at the right time. Recipients/clients must be able to gain access to the service immediately it is required, and that need is often urgent, as in the case of disaster or famine relief. The charity service product is quite clearly highly perishable, and distribution or 'place', therefore, is a crucial part of the marketing mix.

For the donor/sponsor market, the effort to attract interest and funding must also be arranged at the right time and in the right place. Similarly the charity must be accessible so that donors and potential donors find it easy to approach the charity they wish to support.

5. SUMMARY

Many of the areas of activity associated with marketing management in the service sector can be studied and implemented from the point of view of the charity, as well as commercially-driven organisations. All organisations are concerned with offering the right product or service within selected target market segments, and are looking for the tools which provide the means for building successful exchange relationships.

In the case of a charity the task of identifying and ultimately satisfying potential customers is intensified due to the fact that charities must typically serve two distinctive market groups – *donors/sponsors* and *clients/recipients*. Each of these groups seeks certain benefits from the charity. In addition, charity management must address itself to another important group: governing bodies or trusts of various kinds who hold power over the organisation's activities.

Charities need to respond to changes in the environment and develop dynamic, professional management styles. Barnardo's charity has changed with the changing needs of the times and has undertaken significant publicity and image re-building to show that they now help all sorts of children and young people in many different circumstances – not just destitute boys as in the days when the founder, Dr Barnardo, started his good works.

Marketing management and planning processes need to be taken on board by charities in today's highly competitive climate, in order for them to be successful. Charity marketing is not only concerned with the securing of funds, but also with their distribution, and because of this special aspect of charity operations, pressures of public scrutiny and answerability are highest in this field.

The emphasis in this chapter, in marketing terms, has been on fundraising and the commercial areas of activity undertaken by charities today. This is because this is the area which is most affected by increasing competition and economic recession, and it is also the area in which many charities are only just starting to develop their strategies. In no way does this diminish the importance of the overall aims of a charity and its work in specialist fields; many charities are experts and leaders in the areas in which they work and they have full knowledge of their client/recipient markets, and how to serve them. They must focus on the donor/sponsor market, and achieve success there in the face of increasing competition if they are to survive and to continue to be able to satisfy the present and future needs of their clients.

Progress test 20

1. What are the reasons for the adoption of a greater marketing orientation by charities in the current day climate?

2. How can the 'buying and selling' exchange relationship be directly translated to charitable operations?

3. List the major participants detailed in the charities marketing process diagram and suggest further categories.

4. Briefly describe the overlaps in business functions between a large national charity and a major industrial company.

5. Explain the importance of obtaining competitor knowledge in the charities marketplace.

6. 'Mutual Benefit' is a key concept in a charity's operations. Outline the reasons for this in its relationships with:
   (a) Individual donors
   (b) Large corporations.

7. Relate the marketing mix components to a charity organising:
   (a) An international series of pop concerts to provide famine relief.
   (b) A campaigner for the repair of the town hall roof.

8. Why is the distribution of funds as equally an important concern for charities as their procurement?

Discussion

1. Examine your reasons for donating to charitable organisations. Can it often be explained by a 'sense of duty' or is it a genuine concern?

2. Consider the use of 'emotive' messages in charity advertising. At what point does such a policy become unethical and are such 'scaremongering' techniques justified by a needy cause?

3. How far do you believe modern charities have progressed from the 'begging bowl' approach? Are you dissuaded from donating when pressured?

21

FINANCIAL SERVICES MARKETING

INTRODUCTION

The financial services industry in the UK has experienced massive change since the early 1980s. Prior to this time, banks and building societies served different customer needs, often catering to different sets of customers. Regulatory frameworks and traditional business practices meant that there was virtually no competition between types of institution. Building societies offered savings and mortgages while banks provided current accounts, loans and business finance. Insurance and investments were also largely dealt with by specialist brokers.

The removal of many barriers to competition has been brought about through deregulatory legislation such as the Building Societies Act of 1986, which broadened the scope of building society business activity. This has led to intense competition as the boundaries between banks and building societies have faded. Additionally the size of the market continues to grow, as does the range of services available, due to the increased sophistication of consumers and their willingness to buy or invest in complex financial 'products'.

As well as traditional life insurance and other types of insurance and savings policies, higher-risk products such as Personal Equity Plans, shares and Unit Trusts are in demand from a far greater number of consumers than ever before. The Financial Services Act of 1986 brought in some safeguards to regulate the financial services industry and protect the consumer. It remains a highly lucrative business area in which financial institutions compete fiercely.

This chapter reviews some of the special characteristics of financial services marketing and developments which have taken place. The legislative changes referred to are also considered together in the light of the competitive environment.

1. SPECIAL CHARACTERISTICS OF FINANCIAL SERVICES MARKETING

Services tend to share four important characteristics which distinguish them from physical products and impact on marketing programmes, namely:

Intangibility
Inseparability
Heterogeneity/variability
Perishability

Financial services share these characteristics to a degree but also exhibit certain differences. Some of these similarities and differences are included in the following discussion:

Intangibility

Financial services are generally intangible, but the service providers go to considerable lengths to 'tangibilise' the service for customers. A building society passbook, regular bank statements, 'gold' credit cards and insurance policies are all examples of the way in which financial services are presented to consumers. They can enhance the image of the service and the provider and even bestow status or implied benefits upon the user as with a 'gold' card. Physical reminders of the service product, brand name and value serve to reassure the consumer and help the organisation's positioning.

Inseparability

The degree of inseparability depends on the type of service and the actual supplier. Whilst the service will frequently be inseparable from the service provider, such as the quality of service received by a customer visiting their bank to pay some bills, the situation is frequently less clear. Many everyday transactions are carried out now via automated services – the automated teller machines (ATMs) which are now so familiar. Because access to these systems has broadened to allow use of any particular machine by customers of other institutions, the customer will often not be dealing directly with their own provider.

Additionally, many financial services are sold by brokers and agents of various kinds and this has led to difficulties and dissatisfaction when consumers have been sold unsuitable products or been wrongly advised. Pensions providers, for example, have been left to resolve the problems caused by thousands of people being encouraged to leave company schemes and buy personal pension plans by commission-hungry agents with no formal standing in the company. Other services are frequently handled by agents overseas such as credit card agencies and other currency/traveller's cheque encashment. The good name of the actual service provider, for example the credit or charge card company, will be wholly contingent upon the efficiency and reliability of these services.

Heterogeneity/variability

In this case, the complexity of the service transaction process will determine the extent of variability and this can differ to a large extent between institutions and even within one institution. The greater the degree of automation within any transaction process, the greater the degree of standardisation. Thus, simple transactions may be carried out via ATMs and completely standardised or via a branch counter where they might be fairly standardised but subject to some variation in quality.

Total standardisation is not necessarily desirable from the consumer's point of view. A friendly greeting or being addressed by name can enhance service delivery and while an ATM cannot arrange an emergency overdraft facility when funds are low, branch staff can look at the standing of individual customers and make arrangements where appropriate, satisfying the customer and profiting from charges applied to the account. Some customers may want transactions to be handled as speedily and efficiently as possible while others may prefer a caring approach and a friendly chat. Customer care is the key for organisations whether engaging with customers in a simple 'free' transaction such as paying a bill or a long-term commitment such as a mortgage or pension. Tailoring the approach to the needs of the individual customer as far as possible may be the best policy.

Perishability

Again, the degree of perishability depends on the type of service. If a cheque needs to be cleared by a certain date and the system causes a delay then the benefits to the consumer are lost so the service could be said to be perishable. By and large, however, money and financial services are enduring in nature. If a bank's reserves are not fully utilised profitably through lending or investment they will still retain their worth and may be utilised again at a later date. A bank branch which does not have any customers at all on a particular day may actually gain rather than lose profit as staff may be able to use the peace and quiet to catch up on other work.

Similarly, customers perceive many financial products to be enduring or long-term commitments. An insurance policy becomes perishable the minute it expires, but for the whole of its active duration it represents an ongoing service. Production and consumption is frequently not simultaneous with financial services. Whilst a customer ordering a meal in a restaurant does so on the understanding that their needs will be satisfied the same evening, a customer signing for a savings plan may expect benefits in five or ten years, or even longer. There may be no immediate benefit – on the contrary having to make regular payments may easily be seen as a disadvantage or a cause of worry. Even financial services which offer a benefit such as a loan or mortgage which enables the customer to purchase something which they otherwise could not afford are not usually produced and consumed simultaneously, although very fast or 'instant' decisions on loan facilities within certain limits are increasingly offered as a benefit by finance companies.

A key task in financial services marketing is to create awareness of long-term benefits and helping customers to recognise the need for financial services such as pensions which they may not see themselves needing for many years, or needs which they may not want even to consider at all such as life insurance. Financial service providers also need to reduce cognitive dissonance in consumers who might back out of a commitment due to second thoughts. Regulations decree nowadays that most financial services are sold on the basis that customers have a short 'cooling off' period, in case the customer changes their mind or to offer them protection if heavy-handed sales pressure has been used. Everything which can be done to tangibilise the services by offering clear and attractive documentation, for example, and offering reassurance and confidence to the consumer should be looked at by the service provider.

Other characteristics

There are other characteristics which apply to many types of financial services and which must be taken into consideration by marketers. These vary between type of service and type of service provider but the following examples illustrate key ideas:

High involvement purchases/complex products Many financial services are high involvement purchases. This will mean that the customer will shop around for the best advice or the best offer and will generally take a long time to plan the purchase, for example with a mortgage or a pension. Information will be sought about competing brands and products, usually from a variety of sources including advertising, the press, informal advice from colleagues or family, perhaps, and formal advice from the bank manager or a financial consultant.

The process can be likened to buying a car or any other major purchase, except that the customer often perceives greater risk as financial services are frequently highly complex and it is difficult for the layperson to assess their value/potential. Someone buying a car is usually happy to rely on the supplier's guarantee that any faults will be put right but a customer looking for a good investment has no such guarantee – often a warning instead that investment products may go down as well as up in value.

High levels of brand loyalty Customers tend to stay with financial service providers and use them to satisfy their different needs at different stages of their life. Banks recognise this well and are keen to provide student overdrafts in the hope of retaining a professional salaried account holder for many years. Many people choose the same bank or building society as their parents because the parents open an account for them. Children and teenagers are a key target market for banks and building societies because of the possibilities of future business. Insurance companies emphasise in their advertising that they offer services to meet a whole lifetime of needs from a first-time mortgage, life insurance and household insurance for family protection, savings and pensions for old age and even funeral costs cover. Customer retention is the aim for financial service providers. Customers will, and increasingly do, change providers if they are very dissatisfied, however, or if they perceive better value elsewhere, thus increasing the competitive pressure between institutions.

Financial services also tend to be joint purchases, very often, with decisions made by more than one person. The nature of many products mean that repeat purchase is very low or infrequent so the service provider needs to maintain contact with the customer over time whenever possible through annual statements, sales follow-ups and so on. Service providers need to keep abreast of significant changes in their customers' circumstances as far as possible so that they can offer new services as required and safeguard both their own and the customer's interests in case of financial difficulty.

Many areas identified above are not unique to financial services but must be taken into consideration when planning effective marketing programmes. Other similar characteristics include the following:

- The importance of advertising in creating strong brand image and positioning.
- Distinct market segments and the use of target marketing, especially in growing markets (for example career women, the over 55's).
- Increasing price sensitivity and heavy price competition (for example car and home insurance, bank and credit card charges).
- Growth in the importance of customer care in service differentiation.

2. FINANCIAL SERVICES REGULATION AND LEGISLATION

The 1986 Financial Services Act

The Financial Services Act of 1986 was largely brought about to prevent some of the difficulties already highlighted within this chapter and to protect consumers. Recognition that the financial marketplace would become increasingly competitive following the de-regulation of building societies led to change in the way the entire investment industry was monitored and allowed to operate. The most fundamental shift lay in moving the industry from its former self-regulating status to legislative regulation industry-wide. Banks, building societies and other financial organisations including insurance companies have to abide by the regulations set down.

Investment advisers or financial consultants have to make it clear whether they operate on an independent basis, offering a variety of services from a range of organisations or whether they are tied to one provider, such as a leading bank. The Bradford and Bingley Building Society makes a feature of its independent financial advice in its advertising, stressing that its advisers are not tied to any single organisation; the implication being that independent advice will match the most appropriate offering to the customers needs, regardless of who the actual provider is.

There has been concern however that some sources of independent advice (and this does not relate to the example cited above) have actually been less than independent in nature but quite biased in fact – in favour of the organisations offering the highest commission levels. This has meant that customers may not have received the most suitable advice or financial product and may have actually been duped into buying more expensive or inferior products. Further legislation has been sought to implement full disclosure whereby advisers are obliged to reveal sources and rates of commission when selling services and this will apply to both tied agents and independents.

De-regulation and building societies

Traditionally, building societies' business activities were constrained by legislative and regulatory measures dating back to the late nineteenth century and they operated solely within the savings and mortgage business. Pressure for change was brought by the societies themselves in the light of increased competition from banks, affecting mortgage lending especially, during the early 1980s. The 1986 Building Societies Act brought about vast changes to the entire organisation of their business operations.

The Act brought about the following changes:

- *Expansion of the product/service range offered*
  current accounts
  investments
  insurance
- *Expansion of business areas*
  foreign currency exchange
  estate agency
  financial service subsidiaries
- *Organisation and structural change*
  assets and liabilities
  funding sources
  public limited company status potential

The Building Societies response to the 1986 Act was prompt and resulted in swift moves into new areas of business:

- *Services previously dominated by banks* – current accounts
- *Services previously dominated by banks and other financial institutions* – credit cards, insurance, personal loans
- *Diversification* – estate agency networks

The rationale for moving into the estate agency business appeared very sound as it provided a means to tie in new mortgage and insurance business at the point of sale, as customers of the estate agency would be ideal prospects for new business. Additionally, the housing market was very buoyant at the time and highly profitable for agents. Other types of financial institutions also ventured into the estate agency business, including banks (for example Lloyds Black Horse) and insurance companies such as Prudential and General Accident. The end of the property boom, however, and the ensuing slump in the market led to many companies facing financial difficulties and, in some cases, major losses such as the £80 million loss experienced by Nationwide prior to selling its estate agency chain to Hambro Countrywide. Rationalisation, closure of branches and even complete withdrawal from the business has been the result in the 1990s.

The Building Societies Act of 1986 did not clear the way for the societies to enjoy complete business freedom within the competitive environment, however. A major constraint is the restriction on the amount of funds which they can raise in wholesale markets – a restriction which does not apply to banks. The Building Societies recognise that this reduces their competitiveness alongside banks and continue to campaign for new legislation to go beyond the 1986 Act and broaden the scope of their strategic business activity. The Abbey National has relinquished its building society roots by becoming a Public Limited Company and acquiring bank status.

The Single Market

A number of European directives have had an impact on UK banking institutions and there will be further changes. The main development brought about by the single market is the establishment of a means by which banks and other financial institutions can offer a whole range of services to customers throughout the European community. This offers substantial opportunities to UK organisations, many of whom already operate within other member countries. Specific directives governing capital structure and aspects of funding and solvency are in place but changes are likely to be ongoing especially in those areas where there is considerable difference in existing national regulation.

3. THE MARKETING AND COMPETITIVE ENVIRONMENT

Environmental analysis and monitoring is of critical importance in any industry especially in the dynamic financial services industry with its proliferation of products and services and changing industry structure. External environmental analysis usually involves assessing influences on the organisation's business activity under the following main headings:

Political/legal
Economic
Socio-cultural
Technological

Some key influences in each of these categories and the competitive environment will be reviewed here:

Political/legal Some major political and legal developments have been reviewed in the preceding section which have highlighted the radical changes which have been brought about by these influences. Other influences which can have an impact on financial services and consumer confidence include the following:

- Government attitude towards home ownership
- State provision of pensions
- Government encouragement of savings and investment (via tax benefits, for example)
- Regulatory control and protection (to prevent the collapse of financial institutions and protect investors' money).

Economic Economic factors are key variables which will impact on activity in the financial services sector. The level of consumer activity is governed almost entirely by income levels and personal wealth. As income levels grow, more discretionary income is available to spend on financial services. Consumer confidence in the economy and in job security also has a major impact; if lean times are foreseen ahead, savings will take priority over loans and other forms of expenditure. Consumers may also seek easy access savings and be unwilling to tie up their money for longer periods with potentially more attractive investments.

The main economic factors which should be monitored with regard to financial services marketing are as follows:

- Personal and household disposable income
- Discretionary income levels
- Employment levels
- The rate of inflation
- Income tax levels and taxation structures
- Savings and investment levels and trends
- Stock market performance
- Consumer spending
- Consumer credit

Socio-cultural Many demographic factors have an important bearing on financial services markets. Certain factors have been particularly noticeable in recent years such as the growth of inherited wealth through property ownership and changing attitudes towards consumer credit and debt. Key influences include:

- Changing employment patterns
- Numbers of working women
- The ageing population
- Number of first-time housebuyers
- Changes in the number of households
- Marriage/divorce/birth rates
- Consumption trends

Technological Technology has had a major impact in many industries including financial services and banking in particular. ATM services which not only provide cash but allow for bill payments, deposits and instant statements are widely used. EFTPOS (electronic funds transfer at point of sale), where cards such as Switch and Delta are debited automatically when payment is made for goods and services without the need for cheques, is a clear example. From the customer's viewpoint, technology has played a major role in the development not of the financial product itself but of the process whereby the service is delivered. Automated queuing systems have made visits to the bank easier and more convenient. Telephone banking and insurance services such as First Direct and Direct Line are examples of telecommunications technology being used to innovate in place of a traditional branch-based service process.

Technology has also played a major role within organisations, bringing about far greater efficiency through computerised records and transaction systems and also in business development, through the setting up of detailed customer databases for effective segmentation and targeting. The Bristol and West Building Society has implemented a highly sophisticated customer database which provides staff with customer profiles so that cross-selling opportunities across a range of services can be maximised when staff are in contact with customers, or later, via direct mail for example.

The main technological developments fall within these categories, therefore:

- Process developments
- Information storage and handling
- Database systems

Product technology is of relatively minor importance within the financial services marketplace as product innovations are usually in the form of a change in the terms of services offered or slightly different services at lower charges or higher rates of interest. It is easy for competitors to follow suit or make other changes and, once the decision has been made, promotion and advertising the new or revised service will help to make it successful rather than any kind of technological refinements. Some physical developments relating to technology in the production of credit cards have taken place such as the imprinting of a hologram on cards to help prevent forgery.

The competitive environment

The financial services industry has undergone major changes, as discussed earlier. During the 1980s the industry expanded considerably and the number of financial products available proliferated. The trend since the early 1990s, however, is towards more streamlined business structures through rationalisation to produce greater efficiency and higher profitability in a market suffering from the setbacks of the recession.

The gap between banks and building societies has narrowed, leading to more intense competition in a saturated market. The only gains to be made are via product and service differentiation, building brand loyalty and customer retention. De-regulation has had the dual effect of widening the scope of building society business to include new products and activities and also increasing the levels of competition, placing building societies under competitive pressure which previously did not exist. This pressure is especially strong in the mortgage market but the increased range of savings and investment products available from a wide number of sources has also hit the building society passbooks.

The retail banking industry has been dominated by four major clearing banks for a number of years: Midland, Lloyds, Barclays and National Westminster. The number of smaller banks had reduced dramatically by the early 1970s as larger institutions emerged through mergers and acquisitions. A similar pattern seems to be developing within the building society market as the total numbers of societies has been falling while the largest organisations have grown. Indications show a strong possibility that the market will be dominated by as few as five or six main mortgage lenders by the end of the 1990s. Several major mergers have taken place including the Halifax and the Leeds, acquisition of Town and

Country by the Woolwich and, in another direction, the Cheltenham and Gloucester Building Society has been acquired by Lloyds Bank, while the Abbey National has acquired bank status in its own right.

4. THE FINANCIAL SERVICES MARKETING MIX

The challenges facing the financial services industry mean that greater emphasis than ever before must be placed on developing and implementing successful marketing programmes to create and foster a customer orientation. True differentiation of financial products is virtually impossible to achieve because they are intrinsically the same, offering similar benefits and services to consumers. The degree of substitutability between brands is correspondingly very high at the outset (for example, at the supplier or product selection stage). Once a financial product has been sold, however, the customer is frequently tied in over a long period and may even face penalties if they wish to change supplier (as in the case of fixed rate mortgages) or if they wish to discontinue the service (terminating endowment or insurance agreements before the full term has expired for example).

The key objectives for financial services providers are:

- attracting customers in the first place
- retaining customers through high levels of client satisfaction and by providing a portfolio of financial services to meet their changing needs over time.

Some key issues which must be taken into consideration in designing the most effective financial services marketing mix are as follows:

Product

As mentioned previously, there is little or no room for innovation in product design due to the ease by which competitors can make similar offerings, for example by altering charges or interest rates to meet those of competitors. Additionally, many financial services are affected by other restrictions, such as government directives relating to income tax and investments or constraints on the amounts which can be invested. Differentiation, therefore, can best be achieved through the other elements of the marketing mix. Current accounts are dominated by banks, although the building societies' share of this market in which they could not compete until recently is growing. They hold the majority of mortgage accounts, however, but this stronghold is increasingly under pressure from banks.

Price

The price in financial services terms relates to the costs involved to the customer in, say, bank charges or credit card interest rates. These prices seem to evoke low levels of customer sensitivity as many customers enjoy 'free' banking, by maintaining their current accounts in credit, for example, or paying their credit card balances off each month. The introduction of new charges, however, such as the annual credit card fee had a noticeable effect initially, however, and sparked off competitive reaction from lenders prepared to offer cards with no annual charge.

Price also relates to the value of the product to the customer and, as such, can be highly sensitive. This can be in terms of interest rates charged on a mortgage, where reductions in interest for first time buyers or preferential rates for existing customers of other services (for example current account holders) are standard promotional tools in the industry, representing a form of discounting. The rates of return offered to investors is another element of the price and different products within the range are frequently priced at differential rates, to attract long-term savers or large lump sum investors, for example. Pricing can therefore be used to differentiate the offering and is likely to be used by customers in selecting a service.

Promotion

Major advertising campaigns are undertaken continuously by banks, building societies and other major financial institutions such as insurance companies. The main purpose of the advertising is to strengthen awareness of the brand and company image and to inform the market about the services available. The Midland's 'listening bank' campaign and the TSB's 'yes' campaign are successful examples. The trend has also been towards developing more below-the-line promotional activities using highly sophisticated databases to target direct mail campaigns at distinct market segments and using publicity, sponsorship and other promotional means. Successful advertising campaigns have contributed to the growth of First Direct's market share although advertising has been used creatively to attract interest but not to sell the service. That has been done through personal selling over the telephone once the initial enquiry has been made and staff skills and customer care have been developed to enable a strong personal selling strategy to work.

Another area where personal selling is a strong tool is in the area of insurance products and the emergence of 'bancassurance' – the product offered through links between banks and insurers, commonly with banks as the controlling partner. The insurance organisation's expertise in personal selling and the strong customer loyalty and extensive customer base of the banks make for synergy in business development. The importance of personal selling is now widely recognised and many institutions offer home visits by financial advisers.

Place

Place or location has always been regarded as critical in retail financial services where high street positions are maintained by most of the large institutions. For transaction services where regular and frequent branch contact is required this can be important. First Direct, however, the telephone banking service, has proved that a bank without branches is possible though its customers still need access to convenient ATM outlets. Some consumers prefer personal, face-to-face contact within a branch and may be more likely to use a local branch or building society. Direct Line and other telephone insurance services are also moving away from the traditional large networks of branches and brokers or agents. Changes in distribution systems, technology and consumer demands are all key influences on the evolution of the 'place' component of the marketing mix.

People

Customer care is at the forefront of both quality and differentiation in the financial services industry. Staff need to be highly trained not only in customer care but in how to respond to the rapidly changing market environment. Personnel can be used to develop competitive advantage in the marketplace and to build and maintain relationships with customers. These topics are explored in more depth in other chapters (see, for example, Chapters 9, 15 and 24).

Process

This is the main area where technological advances have led to major change. Improvements in the process stem not only from the automation of many transactions and data handling within organisations but also from process re-engineering to reduce delays in processing mortgage applications, for example, or the installation of automated queuing systems to cut down on waiting time. North West Securities, a finance company specialising in consumer lending, offer existing and previous customers same-day acceptance of loan applications and will also arrange for courier delivery of a personal cheque for the loan amount to the customer's home if required.

Physical evidence

The environment in banks is changing, moving away from austerity and formality to a more friendly approach reflected in more attractive branch layouts and decor. Other physical evidence plays an important part in financial transactions such as the documentation which must be presented by salespeople to prove that they are authorised to offer investment advice. This creates confidence and helps to build the relationship between customer and provider. Physical evidence is also widely used to tangibilise the service. Attractive brochures and policy documents, presented in glossy folders, cheque book and credit card holders, 'gold' credit cards, chidren's 'collectable' money boxes are all examples of physical evidence being used in this way.

5. SUMMARY

The financial service industry has undergone considerable change since the 1980s and this trend looks set to continue with the gap between banks and building societies becoming much narrower and the emergence of large organisations dominating the marketplace. De-regulation, the single European market and other legislative and economic changes have broadened the scope of financial institutions and led to increasing competitive pressure.

Financial services share many of the characteristics of other services and yet are not dissimilar to some other types of goods in some ways. For example, many financial services do not appear to be perishable and also they are not necessarily simultaneously produced and consumed, with the customer waiting perhaps many years to receive benefits from the transaction. Other characteristics of financial services include:

High involvement purchases/complex products
High levels of brand loyalty

Key areas which have impacted on the financial services industry include regulation and legislation in various forms. The 1986 Financial Services Act was brought about to regulate the industry and offer some consumer protection. The 1986 Building Societies Act allowed vast changes in the way societies operate and broadened the scope of their business activity in the following ways:

Expansion of the product/service range offered
Expansion of business areas
Organisation and structural change

The dynamic nature of the financial services industry makes environmental monitoring and analysis essential. The competitive environment is continuing to change and is also under increasing pressure due to the effects of the economic recession on customer spending and confidence. The main factors likely to influence the financial services marketing and competitive environment are reviewed and consideration given to likely marketing mix implications.

Progress test 21

1. What factors led to the dramatic changes in the financial services industry?

2. Outline the main characteristics financial services share.

3. Why was the 1986 Financial Services Act brought about?

4. Which new areas of business did building societies move into following de-regulation?

5. How might the single European market affect (or how has it already affected) the UK financial services industry?

6. List the main economic and socio-cultural factors which are likely to influence the financial service market.

7. What trends are evident within the competitive environment? What are the indications for the future?

Discussion

1. Think about how you selected the financial services you have bought or currently use. What factors most influenced your decision? How satisfied or dissatisfied are you with your choice in terms of value and service quality?

2. Design a brief for a customer care and relationship marketing programme for:
   1) a bank
   2) a building society

   Highlight the most important factors in each case and discuss the possible differences between the two.

22

PROFESSIONAL SERVICES AND MARKETING

INTRODUCTION

Professional services such as accountancy, consultancy, medicine and the law make up a substantial proportion of the service economy in the UK and many other markets. These services represent the extreme end of the scale with regard to service tangibility, being highly intangible, high-contact, people-based services with a high degree of expertise. Examples of professional service usage can be found in all market sectors; solicitors may look after the needs of both consumers and business clients, architects and project managers operate within industrial and other markets while some professional services operate in various sectors including the business to business sector, such as accountants.

All professional service organisations seek to attract and serve clients in order to generate revenues and profits. Marketing can play a key role in making businesses more effective through identifying customer or client needs and wants and matching the organisation's offering to those needs. This is at the core of a successful marketing organisation. It is surprising, therefore, that some professional service sectors largely ignore marketing or, at best, pay lip service to it via limited promotion and public relations campaigns. The reasons for this appear to be largely traditional: the self-regulating professions have banned advertising in the past although a relaxation of these rules has come about. The prohibition of advertising and promotion seems to have led to a rejection of all marketing activity.

Understanding and utilising marketing concepts and strategies can make organisations more able to cope within the rapidly changing social and market environment especially during recessionary periods. This chapter explores some of the difficulties associated with marketing within professional service organisations and considers the implementation issues involved.

1. MARKETING AND THE PROFESSIONS

Professional services encompass a broad range of activities but can all generally be defined by certain common characteristics:

- Professional service providers are highly trained and knowledgeable in a complex specialist area of expertise.
- They will hold qualifications and accreditations within their field of expertise; entry into the field is not possible without the appropriate credentials.
- Typically, membership of a professional society or governing body is also required.
- Professional services are sold to individual clients – either business or private – on a confidential basis.
- The service is tailored to meet clients' needs.

There are several clear reasons why professional service organisations should embrace marketing:

- to understand client needs and wants
- to develop and operate the most appropriate service offerings to meet those needs
- to communicate the offerings to the clients and attract interest and custom
- to become more business and marketing orientated in the highly dynamic competitive environment
- to enhance service quality, thus ensuring client satisfaction and goodwill and safeguarding and building the organisation's reputation
- to create the potential for growth

In essence, sound business and management practice calls for the implementation of proactive marketing programmes and strategies. In addition, some of the special characteristics of professional services strengthen the argument in favour of the adoption of marketing, for example:

- The individual nature of the service, typically performed on a one-to-one, client-professional basis can lead to high levels of variance in service quality. It can also allow for greater customisation, tailoring the service to clients' needs.
- The service is highly intangible and difficult for the layperson or typical client to understand and assess, in terms of quality and value. As such services are often costly, the degree of risk to the consumer is also high. Credence will play a key part in provider selection. Effective management of marketing mix variables can help reduce uncertainty and enhance customer confidence. Physical evidence, in the form of an efficient, smart office environment and qualifications or awards on display, can help create the right image. Informative communications programmes can enable potential customers to make better informed choices about service providers, leading to greater satisfaction levels in the longer term.
- Similarly, professional organisations need to inform the market about their offerings simply to communicate their availability to the public who may not be well informed.
- The 'people' element in the service provision is a critical factor; such services are dependent wholly on the skills and competence of individual professionals (or small teams) so there needs to be a clear focus on people

through internal marketing, staff development and customer care programmes, for example. The provider/client interface is at the heart of this type of service and the traditional notion of a 'good bedside manner' for the medical profession reflects this. Customer retention will almost certainly be contingent upon a strong rapport and feeling of confidence and trust between the client and the provider.

- The image of the organisation will also be dependent on the activities of those individual professionals practising within it. Effective marketing programmes can play a pivotal role in creating an integrated focus which can lead to greater efficiency and higher quality.

In reality, however, many professional organisations are passive in the extreme, waiting for clients to come to them and viewing marketing activities as unnecessary or even forbidden. One of the reasons put forward for this response to marketing on the part of professional service providers is that the employment of strict codes of conduct governing many professions, particularly those regulations concerning advertising and promotion, has been equated to anti-marketing.

Some possible barriers preventing professional organisations from successfully undertaking marketing activities stem from the traditional structures and constraints imposed on professionals in the past. They may also arise out of a 'myopic' view of marketing as a set of promotional and selling tools rather than a strategic, organising and integrative function within the organisation. The view that good work will inevitably lead to successful practices, or that revenue fluctuations are normal and not a great deal can be done about them, are examples of the ideas or misconceptions which can prevent organisations from taking marketing on board. The management structure of many professional organisations can also lead to possible constraints, being based around the professional partnership and not necessarily organised by function or role.

A survey of fifteen large and medium-sized regional UK law practices revealed that only one firm had any identified business mission statement – that of survival during the recession. Negligible effort appears to be targeted at business development or planning by such firms. This lack of planning appears to be due to two main factors:

- poor knowledge about marketing
- time constraints imposed on the busy professionals who actually carry out the activities associated with provision of the service.

Another reason for the virtual rejection of marketing has arisen from the historical strength of the professions in the marketplace. There is, in effect, zero substitutability for a professional service by and large; a customer requiring legal assistance is forced to go to a law firm and someone who is critically ill needs medical help. This is different to other types of service with relatively high substitutability such as travel (by sea, land or air, for example) or entertainment (an evening at the cinema/pub/restaurant/bowling alley/theatre).

What has happened, however, is that there has been a dramatic proliferation in the number of professional practitioners and service organisations in the latter half of this century. This is due to a number of factors including the growth of business activity generally, demographic changes and particularly the post-war increase in population size and the more widespread accessibility of higher education and training. The number of practitioners competing in the market has grown considerably and the degree of provider substitutability has grown likewise. The effect of this has been increased competition and the effects of economic recession have led to further intense competitive pressure. This situation would appear to underline the need for effective marketing within professional service provision to ensure survival, profitability and growth.

2. THE IMPACT OF DE-REGULATION

Traditionally, professional services have been subjected to wide-ranging advertising restrictions. Most professions have had detailed codes including dentists, opticians, the law society and the stock exchange which are reinforced by disciplinary committees. The need for such fierce constraints on advertising has been attributed to the following reasons:

- Advertising could easily mislead as professional service provision is based mainly on trust and takes the form of specialised knowledge and expertise on matters about which the layperson, or typical client, knows little.
- Advertising might have an adverse effect on professionalism as it might de-value 'professional honour'.
- Service quality levels might deteriorate as advertising might lead to unscrupulous practitioners profiting from price cutting and dealing with volumes of clients in an unsatisfactory manner.
- Advertising can lead to harmful effects on industry structure due to unfair competitive practices such as excessive price cutting.

Arguments can be put forward to undermine each of the above 'reasons', however:

- It could be as easy for providers of consumer goods and services to attempt to undertake misleading or unscrupulous advertising practices as it might be, in theory, for professionals. Indeed, advertising standards and codes of practice exist specifically to ensure that advertising is not harmful.
- Service quality might actually improve if advertising allowed prospective customers to shop around for professional services and make comparisons.
- The industry might benefit from increased customer attention stimulated by advertising.

Pressure for a relaxation of these regulations was brought to bear from various sources including The Director General of Fair Trading in the UK. The UK Monopolies and Mergers Commission and the United States Supreme Court generally agreed to move for disallowing professional bans to advertising (with monitoring to safeguard against abuse or unfair practices). The result was 'de-regulation' or, at least, a major relaxation of the rules concerning the use of many form of advertising and promotional activity in the UK in 1984. This followed a similar move in the USA in 1977 which was found to have led to benefits for both service providers and consumers in the case of the legal profession, for example, with lower fees and more new clients.

A growth in the use of advertising has been seen in certain professional sectors since de-regulation. Examples include opticians' services which now advertise widely on television and use many forms of sales promotion and frequent local press advertisements offering specialist legal and other services. The situation may have changed with regard to the implementation of advertising and external communications, however, but it is the adoption of improved internal communications and a marketing perspective which is important for professional services.

Developing a customer and market focus within the organisation and breaking down the barriers to marketing strategy development and implementation is the real task.

3. MANAGEMENT AND MARKETING CULTURE

Marketing is not only concerned with the development and implementation of successful programmes and strategies. For professional services marketing to be successful, there needs to be a marketing orientation throughout the organisation which fosters the marketing concept and demonstrates a marketing approach to all internal and external activities. The marketing concept must be embraced throughout the organisation and given strong managerial support.

Marketing can be described by means of all the practical aspects within a marketing programme: product development and management, advertising, promotion, strategic planning, market analysis and segmentation, for example. A marketing orientation goes beyond this, however. It is based around a philosophy which places the customer first, and it recognises that every action taken by the organisation or its employees ultimately impacts on that customer relationship.

The role of management in developing a positive marketing culture, therefore, is critical. Chapters 4 and 6 look at the role of marketing within the organisation and the marketing management task. The emphasis in professional services marketing needs to focus on relationships and the people element of the marketing mix. This is important due to the characteristics of the professional service exchange process and the service delivery/client interface. Customer care programmes, staff development and empowerment are all important issues in building and retaining client satisfaction and repeat business.

Relationship marketing is discussed more fully in Chapter 9, but some of the essential ideas are highly relevant here:

Relationships with customers Relationship marketing is about building relationships with customers, rather than creating exchange processes. Customer contact should be maintained after the service exchange has been completed and the focus is on retaining customers.

Referral markets The level of business arising from referrals is extremely high in professional services. 'Word of mouth' recommendation can be a key factor in the service provider selection process. In professional services marketing, referrals may be informal, as in the case of recommendations from friends and family, for example, or formal such as an estate agent recommending a particular firm of solicitors or a surveyor recommending a firm of architects.

Internal markets Internal marketing is an important part of relationship marketing. It is explored in more detail in a separate chapter (Chapter 8) because it is so significant in terms of services marketing. Internal marketing addresses the internal market and develops appropriate strategies and programmes to satisfy both organisational and customer objectives.

Effective implementation of marketing programmes requires coordinating the efforts of all employees. Their co-operation is essential in realising strategies designed to increase service efficiency and effectiveness and to enhance levels of customer care. The marketing planning process provides a structured framework for marketing activities to achieve organisational objectives but the key task for managers lies in implementation.

The role of management in developing a marketing orientation and culture can be explored by looking at examples of marketing in practice within professional organisations. The following case examples highlight many of the important issues identified within this chapter and illustrate both the practical and more philosophical aspects of developing a positive organisational culture with a customer and market focus.

A professional service organisation which has adopted a proactive approach towards business development and marketing is a regional UK firm of accountants, Latham Crossley and Davis. Rated the fastest-growing UK accountancy firm by the *Financial Times* league table of the top thirty firms in 1994 at a time when half of the accountancy firms reviewed were reporting a drop in fee income levels, the firm has a marketing team headed by a partner who is a marketing specialist, not an accountant. The firm has focused on internal marketing and relationship marketing to produce a powerful organisational culture. They have provided staff with training, technology and development opportunities to develop their potential and, as a result, believe that they will '*strive to exceed our clients' expectations.*'

Latham Crossley and Davis are also one of the first professional service organisations to have won recognition for its staff development and training programmes when they were presented with the Investors in People Award as part of a national programme run by the UK Training and Enterprise Councils. Key factors which have contributed to their success in this area and which they continuously develop can be summarised as follows:

Improving communications within the company

Progressive internal initiatives to create a culture where everyone feels their contribution counts
Empowerment of individual members of staff
Encouraging teamworking and supportive management

In addition, the firm produce newsletters for internal and external audiences, they operate active PR, from ensuring publicity coverage in the media to sponsoring schools cricket, and they emphasise throughout publicity and corporate literature that client care is the key to their growth and their service to clients. They have also achieved corporate growth through product development, extending the range of services available beyond standard accountancy to include strategic planning for marketing, budgeting and taxation, training in subjects ranging from customer care to financial management, pensions and investment advice.

Another leading accountancy firm, Ernst and Young, was included in the 1994 *Financial Times* review, being ranked fourth largest accountancy firm in the UK and showing a higher rate of growth than three others in the top five. They exhibit a strong customer and marketing orientation in their corporate literature, stating that they employ quality people who share in core values and also that they will achieve organisational objectives by helping their clients to achieve their own objectives. Both firms discussed emphasise their business partnership role with their clients – a key foundation for relationship marketing.

4. DEVELOPING MARKETING PROGRAMMES

The aims of marketing are as follows:

To understand and anticipate customer needs
To provide benefits and satisfactions to meet those needs
To ensure consistent quality and satisfaction
To retain existing customers and attract new ones
To achieve organisational objectives

Each of these aims can clearly be applied to professional services. Professional service providers can achieve each of these aims by applying marketing tools and concepts as follows:

Understanding/Anticipating customer's needs This is at the core of the marketing concept. Marketing research provides tools for understanding customers and markets in a structured and organised way. Environmental analysis and monitoring examines and predicts trends and influences which will impact on the organisation's activities.
Provision of benefits/satisfactions Variations on the product/service offering design can be developed to meet the needs and wants of clients in target segments in which the firm wishes to operate, supported by marketing mix(es) tailored to each segment.
Setting consistent quality standards Internal and external research can be carried out to assess and measure customer expectations and both customer and

employee understanding and perception of service quality. Internal marketing can be used to ensure consistent high standards of service delivery, together with benchmarks where appropriate. Even in highly specialised professional services where the service itself is highly unique and cannot be standardised, attention can be given to quality in routine transactions and processes such as:

- the length of time taken to reply to routine correspondence
- invoicing procedures
- the professional quality of reports and documentation
- keeping within specified time periods and general customer care.

Customer retention/attracting new customers   Relationship marketing focuses on building relationships and provides a framework for higher customer retention, enhanced customer and employee satisfaction levels and improved corporate image. This can be reinforced through the marketing mix; especially through the use of promotions and communications (both internal and external), people and physical evidence, as the examples shown earlier illustrate.

Attainment of organisational objectives   A fundamental feature of a properly structured and implemented marketing programme is the role of marketing planning. The marketing planning process coordinates and directs the organisation's marketing effort. It contributes to overall organisation objectives by setting down action programmes to meet agreed marketing objectives. Planning can help focus management thinking in terms of the business mission and strategic objectives setting by addressing the questions:

Where are we now? (analysis stage)
Where do we want to be? (planning stage)
How do we get there? (implementation stage)
How successful are we? (monitoring stage)

The marketing audit can also be a very useful planning tool to check out current practice and evaluate systems and procedures. It usually consists of several audits which are likely to be made up various components as follows:

Marketing environment
Marketing strategy
Marketing organisation
Marketing systems
Marketing productivity
Marketing function

The marketing audit can perform a number of functions:

- To analyse the organisation's overall marketing effectiveness
- To create awareness and involvement in marketing throughout the organisation
- In organisations where there has been little or no previous formal marketing activity, a marketing audit can be used to highlight what activity should be undertaken and to what extent a marketing orientation exists. This can be especially applicable to professional service organisations.

The marketing audit and the planning process are both covered in more depth in Chapter 7.

5. THE PROFESSIONAL SERVICES MARKETING MIX

The importance of selecting and balancing the right marketing mix elements has been stressed in relation to professional services marketing. Creating and fine-tuning the marketing mix is a task for management which will produce unique outcomes for every organisation and their individual activities within target markets. Some key issues which do have particular relevance for professional service organisations are raised here:

The service package (product)

The service offering needs to be looked at carefully to ensure it meets customer needs as closely as possible. The range of services offered may require extending or updating in response to new developments within the market. Some large accountancy firms now receive only a small proportion of their income from audit and accounting work as the revenue from their other specialist services has grown as these have developed. Anderson, including Anderson Consulting, is one such example, earning less than twenty per cent of revenue from audit and accountancy in 1994 with the remainder coming from other specialist services.

Pricing policy

It is well recognised that price represents other factors than simply costs and is often used by prospective clients as a guide to quality. For this reason, as well as profitability concerns, pricing or fee setting should be regarded as a strategic element of the overall marketing programme rather than a basic costing exercise. Many professional fees are charged at hourly rates although other alternatives include fixed fees for fairly standard jobs (for example, house conveyancing or health screening checks offered at set fees) and tendering or quotation schemes for contracts. The competitive situation should also be considered in relation to pricing with regard to possible provider substitution.

Promotional programmes

Promotional objectives need to be clearly defined before a strategic promotional programme can be designed. Many professional service providers may have more than one promotional objective and will use a variety of messages and media to communicate with target audiences. Advertising can increase aware-ness of the organisation and its services. Cosmetic surgery clinics advertise widely, using a mixture of informative details of the various services provided together with visual images of the possible results to attract customers.

Newsletters or house magazines can be a useful tool for communicating with existing customers and other publics. Sponsorship, PR and publicity can be used to attract attention and inform target audiences about changes and innovations within the organisation. A higher profile and enhanced corporate identity will not only make the organisation more attractive to customers but also to potential recruits – an important issue in areas of highly qualified and skilled expertise.

Distribution

Location decisions are important in professional services marketing as many clients use convenience as a key factor in provider selection, effectively walking in off the street to make an appointment for an eye test or for legal advice. Location may be less important for highly complex or specialist services where the service provider may actually visit the client to perform the service in any case, thus making accessibility and availability more important than physical location. Some services, such as accounting audits or building surveying, have to be carried out at the client's premises. Professional service organisations seldom have channels as such, usually dealing directly with clients and being more likely to open branch offices and subsidiary operations when moving into new market areas.

People aspects of successful service delivery

The importance of the people element of the marketing mix has been highlighted throughout this chapter. Professional service delivery quality depends on the person delivering the service. Internal marketing and staff development pro- grammes can help to optimise staff performance through allowing individuals to fulfil their potential and to understand more fully their role in the organisation and their contribution to success.

Process design

There are many aspects of the process design which can play an important role in creating and delivering a quality service, even in highly customised specialist services. Administration quality, customer care, appointments systems, methods of communication, office opening hours and operating efficiency in terms of delegation or teamworking are all examples of aspects of the service delivery process which may be improved or revised. Primary nursing, where a nurse takes responsibility for a patient from the time they arrive in the hospital until they leave, is an example of a process change with apparent benefits for both parties. Efficient appointment systems at the doctor or the dentist with queuing systems so that it is clear whose turn is next can help improve satisfaction levels and help the service to operate more smoothly. In long drawn-out legal cases, brief regular updates can be sent to clients to let them know the case is still progressing or being monitored.

Physical evidence

As stated very early in this chapter, credence plays an important role in customer assessments of professional service quality. Customers will base their judgement on the physical evidence available to them. Professional qualifications and affiliations will be listed on company literature and stationery and certificates displayed. Awards such as the Investors in People award won by Latham Crossley and Davis can be well publicised to help build the organisation's image. The firm's premises and working environment should reflect the professionalism and expertise of the service provider and also the prices charged. Staff may wear uniforms or other workwear such as white coats, as is very common in the medical professions, or they may adhere to certain dress codes in business.

6. SUMMARY

Traditionally, little marketing activity has taken place within many professional organisations. This may be due to the virtual ban on any form of advertising or promotion activity imposed by regulatory bodies within the professions in the past. Some relaxation of the rules has taken place since the early 1980s which has led to some organisations adopting a marketing approach.

Professional services encompass a wide range of activities but they are associated with certain features:

High expertise
Qualifications required
Membership of society or governing body
Confidentiality
High barriers to entry

Many of the characteristics of professional services strengthen the argument in support of the adoption of marketing, for example:

Highly intangible services
Dependence on people in the service delivery process
Image and reputation are key factors in gaining and retaining clients
Proliferation in the number of practitioners; increased competition
Low service substitutability but high provider substitutability

Many reasons have been put forward for the banning of advertising and promotional activity by professional organisations, mainly concerned with possibly misleading advertisements and the undermining of professional integrity. Eventually professional bans on advertising were removed when pressure was brought to bear from the UK Monopolies and Mergers Commission as they represented a potential restrictive trade practice.

Management must play a key role in developing a marketing orientation within the organisation. Staff development and empowerment and customer care schemes are two possible ways of developing and fostering a customer orientation. Relationship marketing has particular relevance for professional services. Professional organisations can design and develop effective marketing programmes to enable them to satisfy the needs of both internal and external customers.

The marketing audit can be especially helpful for professional organisations which have done little marketing previously. The marketing mix should be designed to take account of the special characteristics of professional services marketing and fine tuned to the client's needs.

Progress test 22

1. Give examples of professional services which operate in each of the following market sectors:
   consumer
   industrial
   business-to-business

2. What are the main characteristics shared by professional services in different fields?

3. Identify possible barriers preventing professional service organisations from adopting marketing?

4. Explain what is meant by substitutability and its relevance to professional services.

5. How has de-regulation affected professional services marketing?

6. Why is relationship marketing particularly appropriate in professional services marketing?

7. Outline the various functions which the marketing audit can perform.

Discussion

1. Prepare a presentation to convince traditionalists in the professions that marketing is not only desirable but essential for survival.

2. Consider the promotional actvities undertaken by professional organisations and look out for examples in the press and on local and national broadcast media. To what extent do you agree with the reasons put forward for banning all such activity? Can you identify any potentially harmful or unfair practices arising from such activity?

23

THE INTERNATIONALISATION OF SERVICES

INTRODUCTION

As the service economy continues to grow both in size and importance, the scale of services marketing internationally can be seen to be increasing dramatically. This increase is inevitable; if service organisations are to grow and survive in today's global marketplace, they have to develop their international operations. Obviously, trends in international trade will affect all service organisations to a lesser or greater degree, and some locally-based service providers may never become involved with international marketing, as such. However, in all sectors of service industries, there are organisations which do operate internationally.

This is true of commercial service organisations and others, such as charities and voluntary bodies. Some services are intrinsically international in nature; shipping, offshore banking and airlines, for example. Other services have entered international markets to exploit existing or new opportunities.

Many charities carry out fundraising activities in westernised, developed economies to aid their relief programmes in developing countries. Universities in the UK undertake extensive recruitment programmes in overseas student markets. Advertising agencies may have expanded into foreign markets to meet the needs of their clients, active in those markets. Even voluntary organisations such as the Scouts and the Church maintain links with overseas counterparts, and engage in various types of international activity.

This chapter examines the importance of international marketing in the services sector, and considers some of the opportunities – and risks – involved. Market entry modes are explored and specific considerations for international services are considered.

1. THE GROWTH IN INTERNATIONAL MARKETS

There are many reasons for the rapid growth in world trade during the latter half of this century. Central to all of these is technological development which has led to advances such as:

* Affordable air travel

- International transportation
- State of the art international telecommunications
- Rising living standards

These factors have all contributed to the powerful expansion in world trade. The importance of invisible exports (earnings from services, as opposed to physical goods exported overseas) to the UK balance of trade should not be underestimated, and the USA economy similarly depends on exports of services to a large extent.

Services represent more than a quarter of all world trade. Even this may be underestimating the total figure by a long way because various sources differ in actual figures as there are problems involved in measuring services because they cross national boundaries. An advertising agency, for example, might carry out work for a domestic client at home and overseas within one project. Similarly, an international chain of hotels might bill an executive at his or her company in the UK, or locally at his destination. There are other difficulties in assessing the true picture of services in international trade, some of which are listed here:

Changing markets Services tend to be centred in some of the fastest growing, most dynamic market sectors, such as telecommunications, finance and travel.

Differences between products and services in international trade The barriers to international trade which apply to exporting physical goods are not the same as for services – but barriers do exist. The inseparability and intangible nature of services mean that different approaches to, for example, modes of market entry exist. Also, as mentioned previously, some services are intrinsically international in nature.

The service economy Within national economies, the significance of services may differ, and the level of activity may be increasing at different rates. For example, a country such as the Gambia may have little in terms of invisible exports such as finance, shipping and professional services, yet may rely heavily on its relatively new tourism industry.

Many service industries are centred around people and knowledge; technical expertise, for instance, in professional services, construction, software services and consultancy. In countries where there is a lack of such specialist knowledge, particularly in emerging economies such as those from the former eastern bloc, there are substantial market opportunities.

Additionally, services are frequently labour-intensive (think of hotels or fast food) and organisations can seek attractive opportunities in markets where labour is far less expensive than in, say, the USA or the UK. Manufacturing companies have moved into overseas operations for this very reason, with parts and sub-assembly manufacture sometimes taking place in many foreign markets. It is easy to see how service organisations are in many ways geared up to take advantage of international marketing opportunities.

It may be less risky, however, for manufacturing organisations to enter foreign markets as they can start by exporting actual product – perhaps through an agent or distributor – and may not need to undertake any investment overseas at all.

In this way, they can 'test the waters' and assess the success of the export operation before investing further, say by setting up an overseas sales office. The inseparable nature of services, however, means generally that the service provider must be physically in the overseas market in order to effect the service provision.

This is most critical where services are highly intangible. Services such as consultancy may require the relevant expertise to be imported – in the shape of the physical presence of the consultant. Advertising agencies may have no alternative but to establish local offices in overseas markets and employ local specialists in order to overcome language or legal difficulties, for example. More tangible services, such as cash and travellers cheque services, may simply require the appointment of agents from banks and similar institutions with established networks in the overseas market.

Having considered some of the key differences impacting on international trade in services, it is also important to reflect on the similarities. Many of the risks involved in international marketing are the same for producers of physical goods and service providers. Often, service providers enter markets which have already been exploited by manufacturers exporting products; they may even be parts of the same multi-national corporation. Lessons can be learned by both sides.

Many of the techniques and strategies developed in international marketing can be adopted by service providers as well as producers of physical goods. This chapter explores some of the key developments in international marketing in relation to services marketing, and looks at those aspects of services marketing which require special attention in the international context.

2. GLOBALIZATION

A common perception nowadays is that markets around the world are increasingly becoming similar. Easier travel and communications worldwide have led to the term the 'global village' as countries become much closer in practical terms. This closeness not only refers to the geographical distances becoming less significant in business and social life, but also the growing sense of shared tastes and fashions among people around the world. Whilst cultural differences continue to exist, many aspects of modern life lead to shared expectations and consumer needs.

Traditional methods of doing household chores have frequently been replaced with modern domestic equipment, such as washing machines, leading to widespread demand both for domestic appliances (consumer durables) and household products such as soap powder. Many consumer goods, from disposable babies' nappies to designer perfume brands, are on sale in markets all around the world. Satellite television has entered homes in many countries, bringing westernised programmes and films into many cultures, spreading westernised ideas of lifestyle and fashion.

This notion of globalisation has arisen out of these changes. International marketing has traditionally been concerned with undertaking marketing in a number of distinct geographical regions and adapting the marketing mix to each region. Global marketing focuses on the idea that there are customer markets traversing geographic regions who share the same needs for products and services. The aim of global marketing, therefore, is to target groups of customers, wherever their location, with standardised, global mixes.

Debate exists as to whether it is possible to achieve true globalisation effectively, without some fine-tuning of the marketing mix to suit local requirements. Certainly, however, so-called global products and brands do exist, such as Coca-cola. In the services sector, Macdonald fast food restaurants do offer slightly different menus in particular countries to reflect differing tastes. The overall mix, though, remains largely unchanged with restaurants, staff uniforms, promotion and the famous logo remaining instantly recognisable. Hilton hotels maintain the same corporate image throughout their international locations and focus on the sameness – levels of service, decor, facilities and so on – in their promotion.

On balance it may be that the ideal approach is to aim for powerful global branding, but to be prepared to make fine adjustments to create distinct marketing mixes for different regions. Some very strong cultural influences such as fundamentalist religion, for example, lay down strict codes of moral and social conduct which must be taken into account in planning advertising and other aspects of the mix.

3. OPPORTUNITIES OVERSEAS

There are a number of reasons why service organisations may seek to expand internationally. These include:

Following customers Organisations such as advertising agencies may be forced to extend their operations internationally to service existing clients who have themselves entered foreign markets.

The nature of the service Some services require international operations due to their intrinsic international characteristics. Examples include airlines, shipping, tour operators and services for travellers such as car rental, financial services providing travellers' cheques and credit facilities, and international hotel chains.

Market expansion Service providers such as financial institutions or fast food restaurants faced with increasing competitive pressure or saturation in home markets may seek new markets overseas.

Potential market opportunities Organisations can simply seek growth through newly identified areas of unsatisfied demand overseas which may have developed out of some of the effects of globalisation discussed earlier.

An organisation embarking on international marketing activities for whatever motive must undertake a detailed analysis of the market(s) it seeks to enter. This is not unlike the type of analysis which would be undertaken within the domestic market when assessing a potentially attractive new sector of the market, for example. However, the task becomes far more difficult when undertaking market research in foreign markets for various reasons:

Availability of data   Government data on income, wealth and population may not be easily available or accessible. When it is available, it may not be reliable, or it may be collected and presented in different formats to that which we are used to.

Limitations of formal market research   Quantitative assessments of market size, structure and so on will not reveal underlying cultural or language difficulties which may be effective trade barriers. Local knowledge might prove essential, but difficult and costly to obtain.

Multiplicity   Entering one or more overseas markets will mean duplicating the market research and environmental analysis effort in each case, with added costs incurred in translation and so forth. The sheer scale of this undertaking might be prohibitive for organisations with relatively limited resources.

However, whilst it is important to appreciate the difficulties involved the key task is to identify what needs to be looked at when assessing international marketing opportunities. A systematic evaluation must include the following:

Detailed environmental analysis, especially;
Political/legal factors
Socio/cultural factors
Economic factors, and the level of economic development

The competitive domain
External competition; other organisations from outside the market, operating within it
Internal, or domestic, competitors

Consumption uses and trends relating to the service
Levels of demand
Forecasts of future demand
Potential market size and growth

Marketing mix issues
Factors influencing price
Modifications required to the service product
Promotion methods – available advertising media
Distribution channels – use of, e.g., local agents or establishment of direct network

Specific market characteristics
Accessibility and barriers to trade
Legal requirements
Regulatory practices

There are many sources of information available to organisations wishing to develop international marketing opportunities. This type of secondary data should always be looked at first in undertaking any analysis as it is far less costly then obtaining primary, first-hand information. This is especially true in international marketing situations.

4. FOLLOWING CUSTOMERS

As mentioned previously, many service organisations seek to enter international markets in order to service existing clients who have expanded their own activities. An important example of this is advertising agencies, and it is worth including some information to illustrate this example here.

The importance of international trade and its phenomenal growth has already been commented on. With increased sales of all kinds of products and services around the globe, there are similar increases in advertising – and opportunities for advertising agencies. The advertising industry itself is growing rapidly and assuming increased importance in many countries. There are various reasons for this but the global influences on lifestyle and consumer tastes, mentioned earlier, have played a critical role, coupled with economic advances worldwide and the emergence of new economies and consumer markets.

The reason why advertising agencies went international was to follow their clients. Most of the international agencies established today originated in the USA, including J. Walter Thompson and McCann Erickson. They have now been joined, however, by agencies such as Saatchi and Saatchi originally from the UK and Dentsu from Japan. These were the agencies who worked for major companies, promoting major brands in cigarettes and soft drinks, for example. The client companies wanted the agencies to serve them in the new market areas they were entering. As a result of mergers between these large agencies with agencies from other parts of the world, they have become truly international.

Companies will tend to choose agencies with established overseas operations for a number of reasons:

- *Ease of communication*
- *Centralised control*
- *Creative effort also centralised* – ideal when developing global branding and advertising strategies
- *Avoidance of duplication* – some companies were dealing with twenty or more different overseas agencies, before appointing one with offices in all its markets

Other types of services, especially in the accounting and legal professions, have established international bases for similar reasons. As with all reasons for international expansion, the organisation must consider carefully the market potential and the risks involved. As well as existing customer business which will be taken on in new markets under these circumstances, there may be excellent opportunities for attracting local business too. These issues will be extremely important in making market entry decisions (which markets to enter) and selecting appropriate entry modes (how to serve the chosen markets), discussed in the next section.

5. FOREIGN MARKET ENTRY DECISIONS

One of the most crucial steps a firm or organisation ever takes is the decision to introduce a product or service to a foreign market. Having made the decision to venture into world markets, the next crucial step is determining the foreign market entry strategy. Whether to 'go it alone' or enter into some form of co-operative venture is often a key issue. The choice open to most firms covers a whole range of options, including many degrees of co-operation, both formal and informal. In general, the greater the degree of dependence on the actual provider (the agent, for example) as opposed to setting up direct service provision by establishing overseas branches, the greater the risk of loss of control for the parent company. The advantages and disadvantages of each type of method need to be carefully evaluated against all other factors. The following list outlines the most common methods of foreign market entry available to organisations generally, and details the level of co-operation involved.

Market entry method level of co-operation (low to high)
Wholly owned subsidiary: 'go it alone approach' may be sales only, or production facilities too.
Exporting: may be restricted to complying with delivery or packaging requirements, for example.
Trading company: may need to undertake product adaption or special delivery requirements.
Piggy-back: must develop relationship with the piggy-back partner.
Agent (no title): must develop relationship and marketing support.
Distributor (title)/Franchise operation: support not only for marketing but servicing and sales training and so on.
Licensing: may include management contract and local training.
Industrial co-operation: very close liaison required between participants.
Joint venture: may be contractual or joint equity; in either case a high degree of mutual co-operation required.

As the above illustrates, most market entry options require some level of co-operation, and will involve a partner of some kind in the overseas market. Some options are more suitable for service organisations than others; obviously exporting may not be a viable proposition for a service. Additionally, different strategies may be more appropriate for entry into different markets. Similarly, a particular strategy may not always be appropriate for one market, especially as the organisation develops its activities in various markets, or market conditions become more favourable.

Generally speaking, the selection of a particular entry method will depend on factors both internal and external to the organisation.

Internal factors include:

- Company objectives: volume and rate of international expansion sought,
- Company resources: assets and available capital for investment, expertise and personnel
- The service offered: the degree of intangibility and inseparability, the importance of branding
- Level of international experience.

External factors include:

- Competition.
- Market coverage required and number of markets.
- Costs related to entering attractive markets.
- Political and legal restraints: for example, some countries may prohibit the establishment of wholly owned foreign subsidiaries, so alternative options must be sought.
- Personnel: availability of suitably qualified personnel locally.
- Risk factors associated with different entry methods – the higher the level of investment required, the greater the risk.

Typical market entry methods adopted by service providers include:

Wholly owned subsidiaries
Setting up local outlets, either from scratch or by acquiring existing outlets staffed initially by personnel from the parent company, but recruiting and training local staff, and buying in local expertise where required.

Agents, licensing agreements and franchises
All involve the provision of marketing support, frequently with training and other expertise. Many services are 'exported' in this way, from local banks providing credit and cash facilities on behalf of major credit card companies, to fast food franchises and car rental.

Joint ventures and co-operative arrangements
Service providers may enter markets in co-operation with organisations already operating in that market, on either a permanent basis, or with a view to later developing full ownership.

As stated previously, the most likely scenario is that more than one option will be viable, and organisations will almost certainly select a combination of market entry strategies in order to serve each market most effectively.

6. SPECIFIC CONSIDERATIONS FOR INTERNATIONAL SERVICES

As stated previously, some services are intrinsically international in nature, such as shipping, airlines and offshore banking. They have to start from an international perspective in developing their strategy. If this is the case, they may not be able to start off slowly and utilise the benefit of a learning curve in becoming established internationally. It is likely that any organisation setting up in these business sectors would need to buy in the appropriate expertise and experience.

These services share common characteristics with all other types of service offering, however:

Intangibility
Inseparability
Heterogeneity
Perishability

These special characteristics of services have a significant impact on services marketing internationally, and some important aspects for consideration are as follows:

Intangibility The problems associated with the intangible nature of service products have been covered in earlier chapters, but evidence of the steps international service providers take to tangibilise their offering is widespread. Shipping and airlines utilise the same livery, for example, throughout their operations and focus on a uniformity of levels of customer care in promotion. They create an international corporate image which is linked to ideas of quality and efficiency.

Inseparability The inseparable nature of services means that the service provider and the customer interact at the point of exchange. This means that, ideally, the service provider should be physically present wherever the service is offered. This is not very practical, however, so service providers need to find ways of ensuring that quality and customer satisfaction is maintained, such as:

- Careful training and screening of agents acting on the service provider's behalf, to ensure uniform high standards and levels of customer care.
- Provision of remote service by telephone, for example, so that customers of, for example, travel insurance organisations or major credit cards can always get personal service over the telephone, perhaps by a single, toll-free number which can be dialled from anywhere in the world.

Heterogeneity The heterogeneous nature of services – the idea that each service act is unique, because once it is completed it will never occur again in exactly the same way – can cause problems in terms of variable quality of the service offered. Again, service providers use careful screening and training for all agents and staff at remote locations to ensure uniform standards are achieved. In international marketing, this aspect is frequently used to promote services, and reassure customers that, wherever they are in the world, they can expect the same level of service always.

Perishability The fact that services are perishable means that, unlike physical goods, they cannot be stored or transported easily across national boundaries. They must be made available wherever required. Thus airlines and hotels need to focus on the demand levels in the markets they serve, and ensure that adequate provision is made to meet that demand, at the right time and in the right place. This applies to all services, and is a key part of the services marketing management task, in domestic and international markets.

There are different types of international activity which might be undertaken by service organisations. Essentially these fall into the following key areas:

Service provision in one country for incoming customers from elsewhere (for example, tourism or education)
In this case, the main service takes place at the domestic point of contact but many aspects of the mix are undertaken in the target overseas markets. This is especially true of advertising and promotion designed to attract customers to the service. Even pricing policies may have to be formulated with the overseas market customers in mind, rather than prevailing factors in the domestic market. Tourism in some countries – China is an example – has only really taken off since hotels of an acceptable standard to western guests have been built. This aspect of the 'product' element of the service mix is often one which must be adjusted to the needs and tastes of the target market.

Services offered through networks of international agents
Examples of this are found in the banking and financial sectors, and car rentals markets. Often the need for local convenience will be the key influence in determining the vast number and widespread location of outlets. The benefits of using agents in these circumstances will far outweigh the possible problems arising from the potential loss of control for the parent company.

Service provision offered as a 'satellite' service from the domestic market
This occurs frequently in specialised fields where the service provider does not set up formal trading links within the overseas market, but simply provides the service in the foreign market for the duration of the project or contract. Examples of this are consultancy or project management in civil engineering or environmental management.

Service provision through wholly or co-operatively owned outlets in the overseas market
Here the outlets may be subsidiaries of the parent company, or set up by a franchise or other arrangement. The service is created and delivered in the foreign market and may be staffed by ex-patriots from the parent company, or local personnel, or a mixture of both. Many service providers invest in overseas operations in this way, such as fast food restaurants, international hotel chains and advertising agencies. Even some hairdressers have international chains. In general, whatever the set up, such organisations will operate under a recognisable corporate umbrella, and this will be evident in uniformity of aspects of the marketing mix and strong global branding.

7. SUMMARY

The scale of international services marketing has grown in line with the development of the service economy throughout the world. Some services are intrinsically international in nature, such as offshore banking, shipping and airlines, while others are based in more than one country due to the functions involved in the service promotion, creation and delivery. Tourism, for example, targets customers in one country to encourage them to purchase a service which will be delivered in another country. Charities base their marketing operations in the westernised world in order to raise funds for their activities in developing nations.

Several factors have led to the growth in international markets including easy and affordable international travel, transportation and communications. Services are estimated to represent more than a quarter of all world trade but even this figure may be underestimated as it is difficult to assess the true value of services in international trade. Service organisations might want to expand internationally for a number of reasons:

Following customers
The nature of the service
Market expansion
Potential market opportunities

Difficulties can arise, however, out of operating in more than one country, usually in relation to the complexities associated with information gathering and analysis for market research and environmental monitoring, coupled with potential problems related to cultural differences and trade barriers, for example. Foreign market entry strategies must be carefully evaluated for advantages and disadvantages. More than one type of market entry method may be chosen if the organisation is operating in more than one market or if the market situation within a particular country changes over time.

There are some specific considerations for services marketers engaging in international marketing stemming from the special characteristics of services: *intangibility, inseparability, heterogeneity and perishability.* Service organisations can undertake different kinds of international activity, for example:

- Service provision in one country for incoming visitors from elsewhere
- Services offered through networks of international agents
- Service provision offered as a 'satellite' service from the domestic market
- Service provision through wholly or co-operatively owned outlets in the overseas market.

Progress test 23

1. What are the reasons for the growth in world trade? Why is it difficult to assess the true value of services in the balance of trade?

2. Why might it be less risky for manufacturers to enter foreign markets than for service organisations?

3. Explain what is meant by the notion of globalisation, outlining the possible implications for international services marketing.

4. Give some of the reasons why service organisations might want to expand internationally, using examples.

5. How do organisations assess international marketing opportunities? What factors must be considered?

6. Why have many types of service organisation entered international markets due to their customers' activities?

7. Detail the various market entry methods which are generally available and comment on those which are most suitable for service organisations.

8. What will the selection of a particular entry method depend on?

Discussion

1. In what ways might the Single European Market influence the development of international services marketing? What opportunities/threats does it present?

2. Using any service organisation as an example (commercial, public sector, not-for-profit or charity) analyse the likely opportunities in an overseas market and select the most appropriate market entry method. Give reasons to justify your decision.

24

THE IMPORTANCE OF AFTER-SALES SERVICE; CONSUMER/INDUSTRIAL MARKETS

INTRODUCTION

Historically, after-sales service was regarded in most manufacturing companies as a necessary evil – as a supporting but relatively minor function in the overall structure of the organisation. This also applies in some degree to the channels – in the case of industrial products, it will usually be the manufacturer who provides service, whilst for many consumer and other types of goods it is the responsibility of the retailer, dealer or agent.

While it was realised that it was important to provide a 'reasonable' level of after-sales service, the role and function of service was generally viewed purely as a cost centre. It may well have been the last area for development and investment in many organisations.

Changes came about as a result of increasing consumer pressure and more intense competition. As consumers grew more sophisticated, they became less willing to accept poor quality goods and services. Consumer protection legislation forced firms to take responsibility for after-sales service, but, at the same time, organisations started to realise that by offering guarantees and service warranties they could enhance their competitive position.

This applies not only to providers of actual 'goods' but to service providers as well. If insurance organisations failed to deal with queries and claims promptly their customers might switch insurers. If a tour operator promises trouble-free travel and then problems arise (even if they are the fault of an airline or hotel), the tour operator must take steps to rectify the problems immediately. Bad publicity resulting from poor after-sales service can be the fastest way of losing custom.

1. A SERVICE-ORIENTATED APPROACH

Some companies anticipated this, and invested in after-sales service consistently. They were able to establish a leading competitive position based on their reputation for fair and unparalleled service.

Marks and Spencer, the leading high street retailer in the UK, was providing instant money-back guarantees long before its competitors followed suit.

In the market for photocopying equipment, which is notorious for breaking down, Xerox, a leading manufacturer, advertises the fact that wherever their customers are located, throughout the whole of the USA, they are never more than three hours away from a service engineer.

In the last few years there has been increasing corporate awareness of the strategic importance and value of service both as a profit centre and as a marketing tool. As this awareness has become established, there has been a considerable increase in the resources being made available to maximise its value to the overall profitability, directly and indirectly, of the company.

It would be hard to imagine buying a car, a washing machine, or any other major purchase without some form of guarantee that long-term service will be available promptly. After-sales service has been part of the augmented product for so long now that it is no longer a special feature – consumers demand it.

2. THE PRODUCT CONCEPT AND AFTER-SALES SERVICE

The product concept describes all products as being made up in more than one stage, or level:

Level 3: The augmented product
Level 2: The physical, or expected, product
Level 1: The core product

The *core* product relates to the product's function in terms of the consumer need which it will satisfy. A washing machine will provide clean clothes, or aid family hygiene.

The *physical,* or expected, product describes the actual shape, form and features provided by the product. In considering washing machines, attention would be paid to such aspects as variety of washing cycles available, colour options, size, ease of use and so on.

The *augmented* product relates to the (often intangible) features which providers of goods and services endeavour to incorporate into their products to make them stand out from the competition. In the case of washing machines, an automatic drain feature might have been part of the augmented product twenty years ago. If it was perceived as an 'extra' by the potential customer it could help to differentiate the firm's offering from the competition.

Of course, automatic draining is taken for granted now, and has become part of the physical product. The consumer expects and demands it as a feature.

Similarly, firms have built intangible qualities into the augmented product, which are now taken for granted. One year guarantees have been superseded by three and five year guarantees.

Company name and image plays a more important role as mass advertising can be used to reinforce images of quality, strength and durability. Brand image is one of the most important intangible features which can influence consumer buying decisions.

3. AFTER-SALES SERVICE AND BRAND CORPORATE IMAGE

After-sales service plays a crucial role in ensuring the long-term credibility of company and brand image. When Perrier, the leading brand of bottled mineral water, suffered a contamination scare, it was not solely their brand image which helped them to rebuild their market share very quickly, it was the superbly efficient way in which they handled the incident, recalling the product and arranging instant refunds. Their after-sales service in the face of an extreme crisis (and in a potentially health-damaging situation) was seen to be concerned, responsible and anxious to rectify the situation.

The brand lived up to its image as the leader on quality and satisfaction. It is even suggested that the contamination crisis actually improved the firm's standing in the consumers' eyes.

4. THE IMPACT OF SERVICE PROBLEMS ON BUYER BEHAVIOUR

With growing interest in the area of quality and customer satisfaction, there has been an increase in research into the impact of service problems on buyer behaviour. The sort of findings which are beginning to emerge illustrate clearly the importance of post-purchase customer satisfaction levels. The figures given show the range of information coming from various sources and illustrate the extent of the problem, even though actual sources differ and have been generalised here. Reports reveal evidence that the following factors and influences need to be considered:

- The average business never hears from the vast majority of its dissatisfied customers.
- For every complaint received, the average company has up to 26 customers with problems, 6 of which are defined as serious by the client.
- Of those who register a complaint, over half will do business again with the organisation to whom they are complaining if the complaint is rectified.
- If the complaint is rectified quickly and professionally then 95% will do business again with that vendor. In this event problems are, in this context, opportunities to demonstrate what a good company the vendor really is.

- The average customer who has had a problem with an organisation will tell another 9 or 10, and 13% of people with problems will tell over 20 others about it. Bad news travels wide, far and quickly.
- People who have complained and have had their complaint resolved quickly and professionally will tell 5 others on average.

It is, therefore, easy to see that customer satisfaction in the product and in the service represents a critical factor in the purchase decision. This implies that the service arm of any manufacturer can play an important role in the future marketing success of not only its own operations but those of all its channels of distribution.

Customers' perceptions of a company's image may owe more to the efficiency (or otherwise) of the service department than to the quality of the actual product. For this reason the measurement of customer satisfaction is a subject which currently attracts a great deal of interest, and which is be explored further in Chapter 10.

5. CUSTOMER SATISFACTION AND ITS ROLE IN THE BUYING PROCESS

Manufacturers, retailers and all types of marketing organisations are now involved in massive campaigns to improve their quality of service and its profitability by ensuring customer satisfaction. Looking after the customer is at least as important as looking after his equipment, and this is borne out in surveys made both in the United States and in the United Kingdom. *This is equally important in business-to-business and industrial markets as it is in consumer markets.*

A large number of independent market studies have clearly shown that customers place considerable value on the quality and responsiveness of the service organisation, as well as the reliability and availability of the equipment itself, in making the decision to purchase from one supplier versus another. In over 50 separate product studies carried out by just one research group in a wide variety of markets, it was found that issues of service are significantly more important than the product price and product features in the final purchase decision.

In essence, models of the buying decision process show that the typical purchaser will screen out all non-responsive suppliers (i.e. those whose price and features/capabilities do not meet needs). The remaining acceptable suppliers are then usually chosen on the basis of service responsiveness and quality. In a study of over 3,000 users of data processing, office automation and telecommunications equipment, the key importance of service and service-related issues in the decision to buy was measured. In this particular study of the information technology market, users were asked to place a weighting, on a scale of 1 – 9 (with 9 being most important), as to the factors utilised to influence the buy decision. The results can be briefly summarised as follows:

- The highest rating factor was reliability of the equipment followed by

service response time and capability of service organisation, all weighed higher than 8.
- Four further factors relating to service (e.g. speed of parts delivery) were weighted between 7 and 8.
- The actual cost of the equipment was given an importance rating of only 6.5, slightly higher than the cost of service at 6.4.
- Only delivery times and instruction/training were weighted lower than this.

Clearly, as this study related to the type of products where technical service support would be seen as essential – telecommunications and computer equipment – the results are perhaps not too surprising. However, for many consumer purchase decisions these factors rate highly in importance in exactly the same way.

Cars, domestic appliances and home electronics are good examples. The more 'technical' a product in the consumer's perception, the greater the importance attached to after-sales service. It may be the level of service provided which has helped to maintain the strength of the television and VCR rental market in the UK, even though equipment prices have dropped dramatically in real terms, and consumer credit is far more widely available.

6. SERVICE VALUE AND MARKET SHARE

In substance, the quality, image and responsiveness of the service organisation supporting the manufacturer or supplier of goods and services can significantly influence the decision to buy and thus gain market share. Many major suppliers of computers, cars, and goods and services for industrial and consumer markets place great emphasis on the quality, performance and responsiveness of their service operations. They actively highlight service performance and responsiveness in sales, advertising and marketing efforts.

In many cases, not only are such organisations able to gain and control market share, but they are also able to charge a premium price for the products being sold. This has come about as a result of a high degree of emphasis on service as a strategy aimed at both market perception and actual service delivery.

Experience in a number of markets, including data processing, office automation, telecommunications, medical electronics, and health care, for example, indicates quite clearly that the market will actually pay a premium price of up to 20% over its competitors in order to deal with a supplier with a high service image of quality and responsiveness. Thus, the primary value of service with respect to influencing market share lies in its vital importance to the customer in the supplier selection decision, and the customer's willingness to pay a premium price even though product features of a variety of suppliers are essentially the same.

In recessionary times, organisations face increasing competitive pressure in what is often a buyer's market. Standardised products and services combine with aggressive advertising and pricing to reduce the opportunities available for differentiation in the marketplace. Increasingly the only differentiation between suppliers relates to the quality of service provided and the standard of customer care.

7. CUSTOMER CARE PROGRAMMES

Service organisations are particularly dependent on levels of customer care, as the 'people' element in the marketing mix reflects. Customer care can play an equally important role, however, in manufacturing, production and other organisations providing goods and services. For customer care programmes to be successful they need to span the entire organisation. Training will not work if it is carried out on a piecemeal basis and should be supported all the way from top management.

Superficial attempts to develop customer care levels will undoubtedly lead to failure. Research among customers of computing and database services highlighted that only three of the top six suppliers scored consistently high marks across a range of service criteria even though all six claimed to have carried out customer care training. The size of the organisation is no guarantee of customer care quality – frequently, smaller companies demonstrate a more conscientious approach to individual customers.

Customer care training may initially be a very lengthy process as the ball starts rolling through all sectors of the organisation and costs will grow, too, as further investment is required to update and maintain the initiative in the future. Other activities are likely to arise as a direct result of customer care programmes such as the publication of internal newsletters, the establishment of incentive schemes and new ways of conducting staff appraisals; for example Rank Xerox has introduced a scheme whereby future pay rises for managers throughout Europe will be based on the results of a survey of customers.

Customer care programmes will typically be comprised of six main stages, as follows:

Objectives setting Define the programme objectives
Current situation analysis Conduct a customer service audit – internally and externally
Strategy development Develop a strategy for raising levels of customer service from the current to the desired standard
Functional planning Define training needs and other requirements (problem-solving sessions or teambuilding for example) to execute the strategy
Implementation Implement training and other initiatives through workshops, seminars. Promote the programme both internally and externally. Develop internal marketing programmes.
Monitoring Test results through customer and employee surveys, evaluate the training methods. Improve and update the programme on a continuous basis.

Evaluating customer care programmes can be extremely difficult, in terms of their overall value to the company or their impact on profitability. Methods include using customer and employee satisfaction surveys and monitoring customer complaints. More tangible evidence of the value of customer care programmes may be seen in the balance sheet; British Airways went from a loss-making situation to turn in a healthy profit following its 'putting people first' campaign. The campaign itself was a substantial investment which involved training over 36,500 personnel at a reported cost of over £23 million.

8. SUMMARY

After-sales service and customer care represent key means of differentiating a service or product offering from the competition. Many aspects of service and service delivery are not solely the domain of service organisations but are of equal importance to manufacturing and other types of organisations. After-sales service can play a key role in ensuring the long-term credibility of company and brand image through the quality of routine installation, maintenance and repair services as well as the the organisation's response to crisis situations such as contamination scares and product recalls.

Research has been carried out into the effect of service problems on buyer behaviour and this supports the view that service in its various forms can be the key to brand loyalty and repeat purchase. Current trends towards relationship marketing and customer retention reinforce this through the idea of 'zero defections'.

Customer satisfaction studies illustrate that after-sales service quality, response times and similar factors were ranked more highly in industrial buying decisions than price and equipment specification. Organisations in all market sectors must continuously build and maintain service quality to remain competitive. One way of developing and improving service quality is through customer care programmes. These should be implemented throughout the whole organisation, emphasising further the need for organisations to develop a customer and marketing orientation which is integrated and flexible.

Progress test 24

1. Why has after-sales service become viewed as more important in recent years?

2. How can companies use after-sales service to gain competitive advantage?

3. Briefly describe the product concept and try to describe the different product levels in respect of:
   (a) A Hi-fi system
   (b) A car.

4. Explain the link between brand image and after-sales service.

5. To what extent are customers willing:
   (a) to tell suppliers if they experience problems with any purchases?
   (b) to tell other people?

6. Outline the role of after-sales service and perceived service quality in customer buying decision processes.

7. In what ways does service have an impact on market share and price?

8. What are the main steps in designing and implementing effective customer care programmes?

Discussion

1. Give examples of any organisations you know of which have made outstanding levels of customer service part of their overall image. What tactics and methods have they used?

2. Describe any negative experience you have had with goods or services and discuss how your attitude may have been affected by it.

APPENDIX 1

Useful Sources of Information

The Chartered Institute of Marketing
Moor Hall
Cookham
Maidenhead
Berkshire

The Institute of Practitioners in Advertising
44 Belgrave Square
London SW1X 8QS

Industrial Society
3, Carlton House Terrace
London SW1 5DQ

The Institute of Personnel and Development
IPD House
35 Camp Road
Wimbledon
London SW19 4UX

The Association of Chambers of Commerce
4, Westwood House,
Westwood Business Park
Coventry CV4 8HS

DTI Export Publications
PO Box 55
Stratford on Avon
Warwicks CV37 9GE

The Chartered Institute of Bankers
Emmanuel House
4/9 Burgate Lane
Canterbury
Kent CT1 2XJ

APPENDIX 2

Bibliography

Services Marketing, Lovelock, C.H., 1991, Prentice Hall International

Managing Services Marketing, Bateson, J.E.G., 1991, The Dryden Press, USA

The Essence of Services Marketing, Payne, A., 1993 Prentice Hall International

Principles of Services Marketing, Palmer, A., 1994, McGraw-Hill

The Marketing of Services, Cowell, D., 1991, Butterworth Heinemann

Marketing Services, Berry., L., and Parasuraman, A., 1991, The Free Press, Macmillan Inc.

Retailing of Financial Services, McGoldrick, P.J. and Greenland, S.J., 1994, McGraw-Hill

Marketing in the Service Industries, Foxall, G. (Ed.), 1984, Frank Cass and Co., UK

Leisure and Recreational Management, Torkildsen, G., 1987, E. and F.N. Spon UK

Tourism Marketing and Management Handbook, Witt, S.F. and Moutinho, L.(Eds.), 1987, Prentice Hall International

Marketing, Dibb, Simkin, Pride and Ferrell, 1991, European Edition, Houghton Mifflin

Marketing Management, Kotler, P., 1991, Prentice Hall International

INDEX